2. THE WET PROCESSES

Hotel and Catering Training Board/Macmillan Education

Mastercraft Series

Foodcraft 1: The Dry Processes
Foodcraft 2: The Wet Processes

Servicecraft: Food and Beverage Service
Servicecraft: Table Service Workbook
Servicecraft: Counter Service Workbook

Barcraft: Bar and Alcoholic Beverage Service

Housecraft: Accommodation Operations
Housecraft: Operations Workbook

Customercraft: Keeping the Customers Satisfied

Guestcraft: Front of House Operations

Core Books
Mastercraft 1: Working in the Hotel and
Catering Industry
Mastercraft 2: Health, Hygiene and Safety in the
Hotel and Catering Industry

FOODCRAFT

2. THE WET PROCESSES

Series editor: Roy Hayter, Hotel and Catering Training Board

MACMILLAN

First published 1988

Published by
MACMILLAN EDUCATION LTD
Houndmills, Basingstoke, Hampshire RG21 2XS and London
Companies and representatives throughout the world

Produced by Edition, 2a Roman Way, London N7 8XG
Edited by Jill Hollis
Designed by Ian Cameron

Printed in Great Britain by
Scotprint Ltd, Musselburgh

ISBN 0 333 457870

CONTENTS

The wet processes

The publishers and the Hotel and Catering Training Board gratefully acknowledge the contribution made to the text by the following people:

Robert Wright at the South East London Technical College (Introduction), Brian Beesley, Michael Coyle, Helen Eustace, Brenda Waller and Keith Waller at Blackpool and Fylde College (Boiling, Poaching and Steaming), Robert Wood at Norwich City College (Stewing and Braising), Yvonne Johns at Macclesfield College (Microwave), Harry Cracknell and Gianfranco Nobis at Dorset Institute of Higher Education (Cook Chill and Cook Freeze), Daniel R. Stevenson (Practical examples).

The publishers and the Hotel and Catering Training Board are also deeply grateful to the following people for their advice and support: Patricia Scobie for advising on nutritional information in the text; James Jones for advising on food science; Clive Finch, Daniel R. Stevenson and Ivor Hixon for general advice. They would also like to thank the staff of the library of the Hotel, Catering and Institutional Management Association.

The Hotel and Catering Training Board and Macmillan Education would like to thank the following sincerely for their assistance with illustrations:

Barclays Bank, London
Clarkes Restaurant, Kensington, London
Clifton Inns, London
E. Coaney & Co., Birmingham
Cranks Wholefoods, London
Dorset Institute of Higher Education, Poole
Frame Hill School, Camberley, Surrey
Gatwick Hilton International, Sussex
Harrods, London
M.E.L. Philips, Crawley, Surrey
Merrychef Ltd, Guildford, Surrey
Muskaan Ltd, Letchworth, Herts
Olivers Winebar, Mayfair, London
Oxford Polytechnic, Oxford
Royal Lancaster Hotel, Bayswater, London
Safeway Naturally, Safeway, Wood Green, London
Sheraton Park Tower, Knightsbridge, London
South East London Technical College
Travellers Tavern, Victoria, London
White House Restaurant and the Wine Press, London

The Hotel and Catering Training Board and the publishers wish to acknowledge the following illustration sources:

Cover
Transmedia

Introduction
Compass Services (UK), Richard Kirby, David Spears, Chris Browning, Ian Cameron, Keith Turnbull

The Customer
Caterer & Hotelkeeper, Rank Hotels, V.S. Photo Library (Boiling), V.S. Photo Library, Chris Browning (Poaching), Caterer & Hotelkeeper, Fiona Pragoff, Courage Ltd, Keith Turnbull, Ministry of Defence (Stewing), Alexia Cross, Royal Lancaster Hotel, White House Restaurant and the Wine Press — braised beef and stuffed pepper prepared Ian Brown, Head Chef (Braising), J.G. Mason, Barnabys Picture Library, Caterer & Hotelkeeper, V.S. Photo Library (Steaming), Keith Turnbull, Transmedia, Caterer and Hotelkeeper (Microwave), British Rail, British Caledonian Photo Library, Keith Turnbull (Cook Chill), Keith Turnbull, RHM Retail Ltd, Compass Services (UK) Ltd (Cook Freeze)

Insight
David Spears and Richard Kirby briefed by Roy Hayter, Chris Browning, Keith Turnbull (Cook Freeze and Cook Chill), Mike Trier, Ron Hayward & Associates

Food Selection
Chris Browning assisted by David Spears and Richard Kirby, food items chosen and prepared by Daniel R. Stevenson and David Simmons of Oxford Polytechnic assisted by Roy Hayter, Claire Myers and Sarah Vacher

Terms & Equipment
Chris Browning and David Spears assisted and briefed by Gill Verstage, Garland Catering Equipment (Steaming), Stangard/Browns Hotel (Boiling), British Gas North Thames Employee Services Division Food Production Centre, Bromley-by-Bow (Cook Chill), Hobart (Cook Chill), British Rail (Cook Chill)

Method
Chris Browning, David Spears, Keith Turnbull

Practical Examples
Chris Browning assisted by David Spears and Richard Kirby; demonstrator: Daniel R. Stevenson, assisted by David Simmons, Roy Hayter, Claire Myers and Sarah Vacher

Problems, Tips & Tasks
Chris Browning, David Spears, Keith Turnbull, Ian Cameron

Artwork for Insight, Method, Terms & Equipment and Practical Examples sections
Photographic reference: Ian Cameron; demonstrator: Roy Hayter; visualiser: Mike Trier; illustrators: John Woodcock and Ron Hayward & Associates.

The Foodcraft approach

The successful preparation of food, whether it will form an elaborate meal or a simple snack, depends on a thorough understanding of whichever cookery process is being used. The cooking processes in which 'dry' heat plays a primary role are covered in Foodcraft 1: baking, roasting, grilling, shallow frying and deep frying. Cold preparations and vacuum cooking (also known as sous-vide) are also covered in Foodcraft 1.

Foodcraft 2 covers the 'wet' processes where water, steam, or a liquid such as stock play a primary role: boiling, poaching, stewing, braising and steaming. Microwave cooking, cook chill and cook freeze are also covered in Foodcraft 2.

The structure

For each process the same stages are covered:

The Customer looks at the needs and expectations of the people who will be eating the food and the variety of situations in which it might be served.

Insight investigates what happens to the food in the particular process, covering all stages from purchase to service.

Food Selection examines the foods that can successfully be cooked by the process and how their quality can be judged.

Terms & Equipment covers the terms associated with the cooking process and the main items of equipment which are likely to be used.

Method gives the steps that need to be followed in preparing a dish by the particular process, with guidance notes. The information on these pages will help readers gain the relevant Caterbase module indicated by the Caterbase symbol in the text.

Practical Examples demonstrates the process by providing specific recipes. Basic methods of preparation (e.g. filleting fish) are explained alongside the recipes where necessary. The number of servings have been varied to encourage adaptation of recipes and alternative ingredients are suggested where appropriate.

Problems, Tips & Tasks reviews some of the difficulties that can arise, with indications of what may have gone wrong and hints on how to avoid the problems. Tips are given and so are **Test yourself** questions to help the reader check understanding of the text and to prepare for City and Guilds 706 examinations.

How the book is planned

Each stage is covered in a double page spread (or more than one if the information is extensive), thus providing easy-to-use, self-contained learning blocks. Additional features include general information on nutrition, health, hygiene and safety, dealt with in boxes throughout the text. Many spreads also have a practical activity in a **To do** box. Other points which are relevant to the use of all processes, such as information on working methods, hygiene, safe practices, nutrition and digestion, costing and purchasing, basic equipment, herbs, spices and seasonings and the making of stocks and sauces, are covered in the introduction to each book. A glossary and index are also provided.

Certification

The Foodcraft books and videos form part of the Hotel and Catering Training Board's Mastercraft programme. They are intended to provide support for readers seeking certification in practical food preparation skills under the Caterbase scheme, but are also useful study aids for qualifications administered by City and Guilds and SCOTVEC in the theoretical understanding and knowledge of cookery as well as the joint certification (recognised by the National Council for Vocational Qualifications) which incorporates both practical and theoretical requirements.

The Foodcraft videos

References are given on a number of pages to the Foodcraft videos. Healthy eating is the subject of Video 8, *Catering for Health*. Other videos include demonstration recipes which illustrate the application of a cooking process to a particular commodity.

Video 1 *The Professional Kitchen* – knife skills, making white and brown stocks, kitchen design, equipment, hygiene and safe working practices, uniforms, food storage.

Video 2 *Meat* – stewing, grilling, boiling.

Video 3 *Fish* – poaching, cold preparations, deep frying.

Video 4 *Poultry and Game* – shallow frying, braising, roasting.

Video 5 *Vegetables* – boiling, shallow frying, steaming, roasting, braising.

Video 6 *Cakes*, **Video 7** *Pastries*, **Video 9** *Eggs with dairy products* and **Video 10** *Flour and yeast* all cover baking.

Video 11 *Desserts* – cold preparations, steaming.

1 INTRODUCTION

The need for organising your work

The Foodcraft books are about preparing and cooking food and the skills and knowledge needed to do this well. But perhaps the greatest skill of all is being able to organise working methods so that no matter how many tasks have to be done, they all come together at one crucial service time. It is not much good preparing delicious, nutritious food if it is not ready when it is needed or the wrong quantity has been produced.

To help you organise your work, the Method pages in this book outline the basic steps for each of the cookery processes described which should help you to judge how much time to allow for the work you need to do.

There are also certain general tasks you will need to do and points to consider whichever process you are using.

Before you start

The first step is to think through the dish(es) you will be preparing and cooking. In most catering situations the menu or list of dishes that will be offered to the customers decides what has to be done. In kitchens that have to cater for large numbers the work is usually divided between a number of chefs, often with one person preparing one dish, another a second. When there are a lot of dishes on the menu, the work is often divided into types of preparation and cooking activity, and the layout of the kitchen may be organised around this principle, for example, one chef's responsibility might be to do salads and cold preparation work in a cool area of the kitchen, while another might do sauces and soups, another the vegetables, another the roasts, another the pastries, and so on. This is sometimes called the *partie system* and is the traditional way to organise work in a kitchen.

In most kitchens, the simpler tasks will be done by less experienced chefs, trainees or staff specifically employed to undertake them. Always make quite sure you know which parts of the preparation are your responsibility.

Points to consider in advance

1. How many servings you need to prepare.

You may be told how many portions are needed or you (or your supervisor) may have to make an estimate, for example if customers have a choice between dishes, or when the exact number of customers is not known.

2. The time when the dish should be ready for service.

This may be a precise service time, for example when a soufflé is served as one of the courses in a banquet, or an exact time may not be known, as in the case of a cold sweet that might be kept in the refrigerator for several hours or even a day before service.

The food may have to be cooked in small quantities at several times over the service period, so that it does not lose flavour, or spoil through being held too long, as, for example, for a self-service hot food counter.

If you have to prepare a number of dishes, you will need to work out timings so that they are all ready at the same time. Think through the recipe in case there is some stage you need to allow a specific time for, like chopping vegetables. Remember, as well, that some jobs have to be done in a certain sequence.

3. The method of preparation or cooking to be used.

If this means finding and following a recipe, read the recipe through so you are sure you understand what is involved.

4. Any special service requirements.

These will be necessary if, for example, the food is for a banquet, or if it has to be taken some distance before it is served (as it might be in a hospital), or if cooking is to be completed at the table as part of the presentation, as with crêpes suzette (which are flambéed).

5. Any adjustments to the recipe.

Quantities will have to be increased if you are preparing more servings than the recipe allowed for, or decreased if you are doing fewer. Do this very carefully. If the recipe is based on metric measurements with imperial equivalents (as in the Foodcraft books), but you are using imperial, change the metric quantities first and then convert back to imperial. This is very important when the ratio of one ingredient to another has to be very precise (as in most cake and bread recipes). If you are in doubt about how to do this, ask your supervisor or tutor for help.

Some job titles

Executive chef – chef in overall charge in large kitchen.

Head chef or *head cook* – chef in charge of a small kitchen.

Sous chef – chef who is second-in-command.

Commis chef – junior chef, working as assistant or apprentice.

Chef tournant or *relief chef* – chef who fills in temporarily for an absent chef of section.

If the executive chef is absent, the sous chef will take charge. When the chef in charge of a section, for example, the pastry chef (chef pâtissier), sauce chef (chef saucier) or larder chef (chef garde-manger), is absent, the work will be done either by a relief chef or by commis chefs in that section under the supervision of the executive or sous chef.

---

6. Collecting the equipment.

Whatever equipment is needed should be collected in advance so that once you start, your work is not held up or interrupted. If you are going to need large pieces of equipment that other staff might also want to use, for example, a mixer, deep fryer or steamer, check in advance that the equipment will be available.

The priority will be given to anyone who has to use equipment at a specific or critical time, for example, a deep fryer immediately before service, or a proving oven when the bread dough has been mixed.

7. Collecting the ingredients.

Sometimes you may have to make sure that ingredients have been obtained, either by placing an order with a supplier, or by going to the kitchen stores and collecting them. In some establishments this may involve completing a written order (sometimes called a requisition) and getting it signed by the head chef or a supervisor.

If a particular ingredient is not available, it may be possible to substitute another, for example, by using tinned rather than fresh pineapple in a fruit salad. But some ingredients, such as apples for baked apple, cannot be substituted and an alternative dish would have to be chosen and the menu changed.

8. Organising equipment and ingredients.

Having collected what you need to prepare and cook the dish or meal, it is important to organise your equipment and ingredients in a logical and hygienic way so that you have space to work in and can see what you are doing. Make sure you have space for the chopping board (if you are using one), and room to keep cooked and raw ingredients separate. It is also important that you can work smoothly from the unprepared food to the prepared, working from left to right (or right to left). Well-organised work goes faster and is less tiring than doing things in a disorganised way.

INTRODUCTION

Using the right equipment for the job is essential if food is to be prepared and cooked to a high standard. In the Foodcraft books, each section covers a particular cooking process and the equipment associated with it is described in the Terms & Equipment pages, for example, frying pans are dealt with in Shallow Frying, steamers in Steaming.

Knowing what equipment to use and how to look after it is an extremely important part of the chef's job. Work will only run smoothly if equipment is kept clean, in working order and in the right place.

Cleanliness is very important indeed. Many pieces of equipment, especially those with small holes or spaces that are difficult to clean, such as sieves, graters, mincers and mandolins, make excellent breeding grounds for bacteria and need to be washed and checked carefully.

As soon as possible after use, all dirt, grease or other matter should be removed from equipment with hot water and detergent or some other cleaning agent. It should then be sterilised in scalding water or with a bactericidal cleaning agent, and finally stored in its proper place. Pots and pans, for example, are usually stored after cleaning in a pot rack specially constructed for the purpose (which must also be kept clean). Hand tools such as knives, spoons and ladles should be kept in a box, cupboard or drawer or, if they are used frequently, may be kept hanging on a rack. Chopping boards need special attention (*see* box).

▶▶▶ TO DO

Make a list of the equipment in the kitchen where you work or visit a local catering equipment supplier. Select the ten items that you are least familiar with and note what sort of preparation processes each is used for, how it should be cleaned and any special precautions that should be taken.

Not all kitchens are as spacious as this one. Sometimes the building, particularly if it is a conversion, simply does not allow enough space. But whatever the size of the kitchen, and especially if it is a bit cramped, the chefs who work in it have a responsibility to help keep it clean and to organise their work in a systematic way. This means collecting the ingredients and equipment needed, but otherwise keeping the workspace clear and uncluttered, and tidying up after completing each job.

Chopping boards

Chopping boards need to be used with great care because of the risk of cross-contamination. This is what happens if food-poisoning bacteria in raw food are transferred to cooked food. So separate boards should always be used for the preparation of raw and cooked food, especially meat.

Wooden chopping boards are easily cut and then absorb liquid (and bacteria) which can contaminate food next time a board is used. They are also very difficult to clean properly, so should not be used. Special boards are available made of hard, durable plastic, which is easily cleaned and resistant to scratching.

Butcher's blocks are the exception. As they are always used for cutting raw meat, there is no problem of cross-contamination. Secondly, butchers need a wooden block for cutting, because a plastic board would tend to slip around when large carcases are being handled or meat chopped. Butcher's blocks should be cleaned daily, using a wire brush, detergent and chemical sterilant or salt.

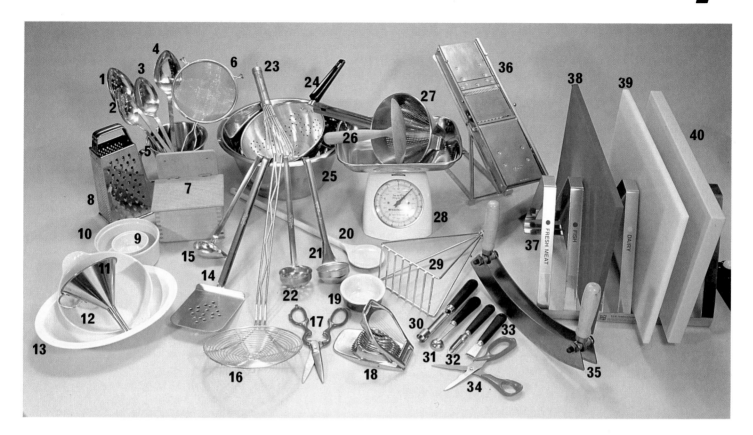

Professional kitchens use a wide range of small items of equipment, ranging from spoons and slices for handling and serving food to ovenproof china containers made for cooking specific dishes: 1) and 2) Perforated spoons for draining food. 3) and 4) Metal spoons for portioning or serving. 5) Measuring jug – essential for accuracy. 6) Sieve, with many uses including removing lumps in flours or liquids, draining liquids off foods and puréeing soups and sauces. 7) Salt box – useful in a busy kitchen, where a small dispenser might easily get knocked over. 8) Grater with different sizes of serrated holes, the larger ones for hard vegetables like raw carrots, the smaller for finer jobs like grating lemon zest. 9) Ramekin made of ovenproof china, used for cooking and serving individual dishes like individual soufflés and crème brulée. 10) Soufflé dish, made from ovenproof china (various sizes are available). 11) Funnel – for pouring liquids into jars and other containers with small openings. 12) *Sur le plat* dish – for cooking *oeufs sur le plat* (eggs baked in the oven). 13) Oval pie dish – for cooking and serving sweet and savoury pies. 14) Fish slice – for handling small solid or semi-solid food items (not just fish). 15) Sauce ladle, with a lip for accurate pouring. 16) Spider – for scooping food out of a deep-fat fryer or vegetables out of boiling water (as long as they are not so tender that they could be damaged by the thin wire). 17) Poultry secateurs for cutting through (tender) bones/joints. 18) Egg slicer, shaped to hold an egg and fitted with fine wires that will cleanly cut through hard-boiled egg to produce undamaged, whole slices. 19) Cocotte dish used for *oeuf en cocotte* (an egg dish that is baked in the oven). 20) Large spoon made of heat-resistant, durable, plastic; this is better than a wooden spoon which might absorb and transfer food flavours and bacteria. Best for stirring food in aluminium saucepans (metal spoons can cause discoloration). 21) Ladle – for handling liquids, testing pouring consistency, skimming impurities and fats off surfaces of liquids. 22) Perforated ladle for handling small foods or finely cut items which need to be lifted clear of the cooking liquid. 23) Balloon whisk for beating air into liquids such as cream and egg whites, or for thoroughly blending two or more liquids. 24) Colander for draining foods, e.g. vegetables that have been boiled or salad vegetables after washing. 25) This type of stainless steel bowl is available in a wide range of sizes and is useful for mixing and storing food. 26) Wooden mushroom – for pounding purées, crushing brittle foods and forcing semi-liquids through sieves (a liquidiser is easier!). 27) Conical strainer – for removing solids/lumps from liquids. 28) Small measuring/weighing scales. Scales are essential in any recipe where the success of the dish depends on accurate weighing of ingredients. 29) Masher for puréeing cooked potatoes, turnips, apples. 30) Corer for removing the centre (including the pips) from apples and similar fruit. 31) Round scoop (also known as a parisienne cutter) for cutting balls out of melons, potatoes, carrots and similar items. Scoops of this kind come in different sizes and can also be oval in shape. 32) Peeler – for removing skin from vegetables and hard fruit like pears. 33) Zester – for removing the thin outer skin (not the pith) of lemons and other citrus fruits. 34) Kitchen scissors for general purpose use. 35) Chopper with double blades (some have three or four blades) for chopping parsley (using a rocking action). 36) Mandolin for slicing (one blade produces a plain cut, the other a serrated cut). 37) Chopping board holder, colour-coded and labelled to indicate where particular boards should be kept, and what they should be used for. 38), 39) and 40) Colour-coded boards, blue for raw fish, white for dairy products and the thicker, turnip-coloured board for chopping vegetables. Red boards (not shown) are for raw meats.

1 INTRODUCTION

Using knives

One of the most important skills that a chef has to learn is the care and use of knives. It is essential to know exactly which knife to use for which job: dicing, shredding, boning, etc. Once you have understood the basic movements involved in particular uses of knives, it is a matter of practising until you have got to the kind of standard needed in any professional kitchen. Speed and accuracy are very important and can only be achieved by:

— selecting the correct knife for the job

— making sure it is clean and sharp

— taking care that only the tools and equipment needed are laid out and the rest of the work area is uncluttered

— working methodically, for example, keeping unprepared and prepared food quite separate.

Always keep knives in a safe place when they are not in use, and take special care *not* to leave them:

— lying around blade upwards. The blade should always lie flat against the work surface.

— near the edge of a table or chopping board where they could easily be knocked off

— hidden in washing-up water

— hidden in a pile of partly prepared food.

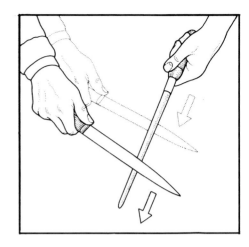

To sharpen a knife using a steel, hold the steel steady in one hand, pointing away from the body and upwards at a slight angle. Then, holding the knife with the sharp edge of the blade pointing away from you, sweep it along the steel, starting from the base of the steel and the end of the blade nearest the knife handle, and moving the blade diagonally across the steel until you reach the tip. Repeat, using alternate sides of the steel, until the blade feels sharp.

Some chefs like to move the knife blade towards the body. Others prefer to use a knife-sharpening machine or special block made of carborundum stone.

To test that the blade is sharp, run your thumb crosswise over the blade. If it is sharp, you will feel a distinctive rasping sensation. Take great care not to run your thumb in the same direction as the blade because you will then cut yourself.

Choosing knives

The most hygienic knives have waterproof handles that can be sterilised. The handle is made of two pieces riveted together through the metal that forms the knife blade. In less expensive knives, the blade is attached to the end of the handle and may snap off with heavy use.

Knife blades are made either of carbon steel or stainless steel. Stainless steel knives do not rust or stain and they will not colour foods, unlike carbon steel which can stain certain foods such as onions and hard-boiled eggs. But stainless steel is more difficult to keep sharp.

The safest way of carrying knives around the kitchen is in the special case, wallet or box that most chefs have to keep them in. If it is necessary to walk a short distance with a knife, hold it close to one side of the body, pointing downwards, with the blunt edge facing in the direction you are walking.

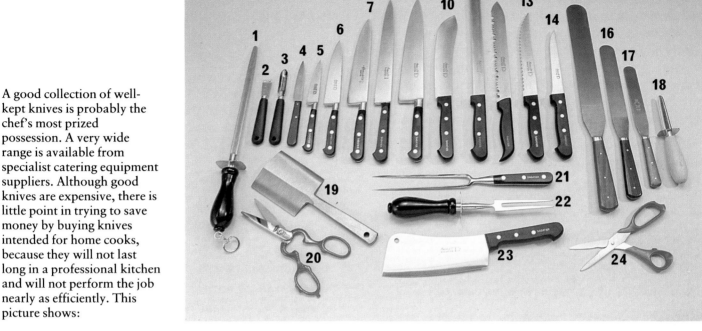

A good collection of well-kept knives is probably the chef's most prized possession. A very wide range is available from specialist catering equipment suppliers. Although good knives are expensive, there is little point in trying to save money by buying knives intended for home cooks, because they will not last long in a professional kitchen and will not perform the job nearly as efficiently. This picture shows:

1) Steel to sharpen knives – note the safety guard near the handle. 2) Zester for removing the fine outer skin from oranges, lemons, limes, etc. 3) Peeler for peeling potatoes and other vegetables and fruit with a firm but thin skin. The sharp point is used for cutting out eyes from potatoes and small blemishes from other vegetables. 4) Paring knife, with a thin, sharp and slightly flexible blade, useful for hand-held work, for example cutting an apple into segments, and for trimming sinew off meat. 5), 6) and 7) Cook's knives (sometimes called French cook's knives or professional cook's knives) of varying sizes. With firm blades and sharp points their uses include slicing, shredding or chopping vegetables, trimming and cutting meat. 8) Filleting knife with a thin, very flexible blade that makes it ideal for drawing closely along the backbone of a fish. 9) Large (and heavy) cook's knife used for chopping large items and also for tasks like chopping parsley when a rocking motion is used (the end of the knife is held down on the board with the outstretched palm of one hand, while the other hand moves the knife in a rapid up-and-down motion, moving backwards and forwards over the pile of parsley). The wide blade is also useful for crushing garlic cloves. 10) Butcher's steak knife, an example of a knife developed for a very specific use. The firm blade with its curved end makes it useful for slicing raw meat quickly. 11) Carving knife. The long, thin, flexible blade makes it possible to slice meat thinly. Some carving knives have a serrated blade (like a bread knife, *see* 13). 12) Deep-freeze knife with a serrated blade specially developed to cut through frozen meat. This knife is strictly for use when frozen meat has to be used at short notice and there is no time for defrosting to take place, but it is not a particularly practical tool in a catering kitchen. 13) Bread knife, with a long thin blade and a serrated cutting edge. 14) Boning knife which, when held like a dagger, can cut close to the bone in meat joints. Because it has a strong, firm blade it will not bend or break under the considerable force that may have to be used. But this means that great care

must be taken, because if the knife slips it could cause serious injury. 15), 16) and 17) Palette knives of varying lengths and widths to shape smooth mixtures, or lift firm foods such as a chicken suprême. The blade is flexible, has a rounded end instead of point and is not sharp. 18) Oyster knife. Used to force open the shell of a fresh oyster, it has a short firm blade and a safety guard. 19) Cutlet bat for flattening pieces of raw meat, for example, escalopes, minute steaks, chicken suprêmes. 20) Poultry secateurs for cutting through poultry bones (some chefs prefer to use a knife to do this). 21) Cook's fork: a particularly dangerous item with its long, sharp points. It is used for lifting roasted meats, although this needs to be done with great care to avoid piercing the meat, which would allow the juices to escape. In the case of a chicken or duck, for example, you should insert the fork into the chest cavity and then lift. 22) Carving fork with a guard to protect the fingers from slipping into the way of the carving knife and short prongs to hold the meat firmly in place. Wherever possible, avoid piercing hot joints repeatedly with a fork. Some joints can be safely held by the bone, when the meat has been scraped off the bone before cooking, e.g. leg of lamb. 23) Cleaver or chopper, found mainly in the butchery section of kitchens and used for chopping through large bones. The back of the chopper blade is used for cracking bones. 24) Kitchen scissors for cutting the fins and tails of fish (some chefs prefer to use a cook's knife for this job) and for more general tasks like cutting the string or the paper for a steamed pudding.

▶▶▶ TO DO

Choose three recipes from the Practical Examples sections of this book and list the most suitable knives and small equipment you would need to collect before you started work.

Purchasing

Each catering establishment obtains its food in a slightly different way. Larger ones, for example, may buy whole carcases of meat, direct from the market or wholesale butcher and employ their own butcher(s) to prepare the meat as required. Others will buy in pre-prepared food, ready for cooking, which will exactly match requirements as to quality, size and weight that have been set out in a purchase specification in advance.

How far in advance of use the food is ordered will depend on many factors, including:

– how long it will keep

– what storage facilities are available

– whether larger quantities will bring a price advantage

– any delivery restrictions

– what number of people have to be catered for

– when the food is required on the menu plan.

Costing and stock control

While preparing food is the most important job a catering unit does, in the end the establishment will not be able to work properly unless accurate records are kept of what is used in relation to the number of meals served and how much it has cost.

This control over the use of both food and non-food items (such as fuel and cleaning materials) is important whether the establishment is a commercial one like a restaurant, which needs to make a profit, or a non-commercial one like a college or school dining room operation, which has to operate within a specific budget laid down by the authorities.

Working out how much it costs to buy the food for meals involves keeping careful stock records and details of how much items have cost. The calculation is usually done weekly by adding together the costs of purchases made on a day-to-day basis, and the cost of issues from stores and freezers of products bought in bulk, and subtracting the value of the stocks remaining at the end of the week. Minor fluctuations from the norm would usually be acceptable, but major differences would be examined carefully because if the establishment is spending too much on producing too few meals it could get into financial difficulties and in the end have to close.

Storage

This information will help you gain the Caterbase qualification in *Storing of Goods*.

Flours, herbs, seasonings, dried fruits, pasta, rices, bottled and tinned foods and other items that do not require refrigerated conditions are usually kept in a 'dry store'. This may be only a small cupboard, or a large room with special shelving (as shown in the photograph below) and a desk area for the storesperson to process and file the different paperwork involved in whatever control system is being used.

A dry store room or cupboard should:
– have good ventilation
– not be below 15°C (60°F) or above 21°C (70°F)
– be dry
– be secure from insects or vermin
– be open only to authorised staff
– be organised so that both incoming and outgoing orders can be easily checked, weighed or counted.

Food items should be:
– stored away from the floor (on shelves or in bins)
– kept in secure packages, boxes or containers
– clearly labelled
– stored so that the oldest items are used first (first in, first out)
– stacked safely with no danger of tins rolling off shelves or piles collapsing
– stored on the lower levels if they are particularly heavy to make handling easier
– stacked so that stock counting is quick and straightforward (no part-filled boxes, no hidden items, all like-items together).

Food costing example

1. During a week, a total worked out from invoices and/or delivery notes for fresh foods bought daily, e.g. meat, fish, vegetables, fruit, comes to £300.

2. The cost of items issued from stores comes to £25. This is worked out by looking at the records of what stock was issued to the kitchen and calculating its value at the purchase prices.

3. There was also £90 worth of frozen goods used. This can be worked out from the records kept of what was issued from the frozen food stores, then its value is calculated at current prices. If no issue records are kept, and the frozen goods are simply used as and when they are required, then the calculation would be done from stock and purchase records. In this example the value of the stock at the beginning of the week was £650. Purchases of frozen foods during the week came to a further £400. The value of the stock at the end of the week was found to be £960, so £90 of goods had been used:

opening stock	£650
plus purchases	£400
minus closing stock	£960
	£90

4. The value of the food in the kitchen at the end of the week is £15. This is calculated by counting/weighing the food left in cupboards and refrigerators and multiplying this by the unit cost which will be on the invoices. For example: 2 kg of stewing beef at a purchase price of £1.50 per kg = £3 stock value.

5. From this information the cost of the food used can be worked out:

fresh food purchases	£300
plus issues from stores	£25
plus issues from freezers	£90
	£415
less closing stock value	£15
cost of food used	£400

To be useful this information has to be related to the number of meals served (in an establishment like a canteen where no money changes hands) or the income from sale of meals in a commercial establishment. Alternatively, or in addition, the information can be related to the budget for the week. The formula for this is:

$$\frac{\text{food cost} \times 100}{\text{food sales}}$$

If sales of food in the restaurant (excluding sales of wines and cigars, value added tax, service charge, etc.) amount to £800, then the percentage food cost is:

$$\frac{400 \times 100}{800} = 50\%$$

Other non-food costs should also be taken into account in order to help keep a check on profitability. In the example these include:

wage costs (plus related costs such as the employer's contribution to national insurance)	£295
electricity, gas and telephone	£15
rent	£50
cleaning materials	£10
	£370

This means the restaurant has made more than it has spent, in other words, it has made a profit:

sales	£800
less food cost	£400
	£400
less other costs (as above)	£370
profit	£30

This profit of £30 is called the net profit. To work out what percentage of sales it makes, you need to do the following calculation:

$$\frac{30 \times 100}{800} = 3.75\%$$

Low profits can result from many factors, but the most common cause is that the restaurant is using too much food to prepare the number of meals served. This might be the result of:

– over-estimating how much food needed to be prepared and having to throw away large quantities of uneaten meals

– incorrect storage of food so that it spoiled before it could be used

– poor control of the issue of foods

– not following recipe quantities accurately

– preparing over-size portions.

Another obvious reason could be that the restaurant needed to serve more meals to cover the costs of paying staff and still make a profit. In other words, the sales revenue was not high enough.

▸▸▸ TO DO

Using the figures given in this box, work out

1. the cost of food used

2. the cost of food as a percentage of sales

3. non-food costs

4. profit or loss

5. profit or loss as a percentage of sales

fresh food purchases	£350
issues from stores	£35
issues from freezers	£120
closing stock value	£20
sales of food	£1,200
wage costs	£295
electricity, gas and telephone	£20
rent	£50
cleaning materials	£15

How can food be dangerous?

Food can be dangerous to eat for a variety of reasons:

– It may contain natural poisons, for example, potatoes that have turned green or undercooked kidney beans.

– Certain metals may have got into it during growth or processing, such as lead or copper.

– Pesticides or weed-killers may be present on it.

– Parasites may be in it, for example, the Trichinosis worm which is sometimes found in pork.

But by far the most common type of food contamination is bacteria. There are many ways in which the growth of bacteria can make food unsafe to eat if it is not handled properly and if safe practices are not followed. So it is extremely important for anyone in catering to understand what causes food to spoil and become harmful, especially because some of the most dangerous bacteria do not change the appearance of food at all and can only be seen under a microscope.

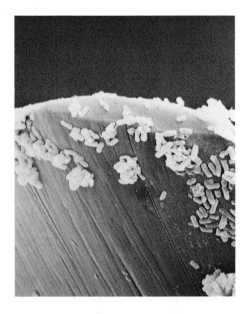

This knife blade looked clean, but under the microscope the bacteria still clinging to its surface are all too obvious.

Useful, harmless and dangerous bacteria

Some bacteria are not only harmless, they are actually useful and are necessary in the manufacture of cheese and yogurt, for example.

Other bacteria help digestion and live in the intestines where they produce nutrients and fight off harmful bacteria.

There are also types of bacteria that are not particularly dangerous, but which spoil the appearance of food – giving it, say, a slimy, sticky surface – and make it smell bad. These are so obvious that the food is very unlikely to be eaten.

But certain kinds of bacteria are very dangerous and can cause illness or even death. These are called pathogenic bacteria. Unfortunately they cannot be seen (without a microscope) and they cannot be smelt or tasted. They can contaminate food at almost any point in its handling, including harvesting, butchery, storage, preparation, cooking and service, so the only way to make sure that food is safe is for strict practices to be followed at every stage.

To multiply to dangerous numbers, bacteria need:

– food (especially those containing a reasonable amount of protein, e.g. meat and meat products, poultry, fish, eggs, milk and milk products)

– moisture (they tend not to develop on dried or salted foods)

– time (under ideal conditions it is possible for some bacteria to double in numbers every 10 to 20 minutes

– warm conditions – between 10° and 63°C (50°-145°F). Above 63°C, bacteria will die. The higher the temperature the faster bacteria will be destroyed.

Most bacteria also need oxygen and therefore air, but one particularly dangerous kind which causes botulism grows only if there is no air (for example, in a tin).

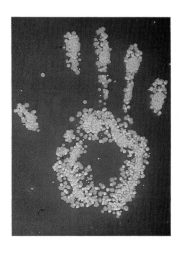

This photograph was taken only a few hours after an apparently clean hand was placed on the glass plate, and shows how much bacteria was transferred from the hand.

Food poisoning bacteria and symptoms

Salmonella (over 40 different types)

Occurs in the intestines of many animals (and humans), flies, cockroaches, rodents and pets. Raw meat, poultry, fish and meat products such as sausages are often contaminated when they arrive in the kitchen.

Symptoms appear 6 to 72 hours (usually 8 to 48 hours) after eating, and include abdominal pains, nausea, vomiting and diarrhoea. These can last for 7 days or more and very old, very young or sick people can die of *Salmonella* poisoning.

Staphylococcus (various strains)

Occurs in infected cuts, sores, boils and inflamed throat conditions and on normal healthy skin, especially on the face and hands. Poor personal hygiene – unwashed hands, leaving cuts or boils uncovered and coughing or sneezing over food – can transfer it to food. *Staphyloccus* is destroyed by normal cooking, but if it has been allowed to multiply on food it produces a heat-resistant toxin that cannot be destroyed even by thorough re-heating or recooking. This is why great care must be taken with partly prepared dishes. Milk and egg products are easily contaminated with *Staphylococcus*.

Symptoms appear 1 to 6 hours after eating, and include nausea, diarrhoea and vomiting.

Clostridium perfringens (welchii)

Occurs in the intestines of animals (and some humans). When conditions are unfavourable for the growth of this bacteria, it forms spores and these are found on raw poultry, meat and in the soil (therefore on vegetables). Normal cooking methods will kill the bacteria but not the spores, and in certain conditions, for example, a large pan of food cooking slowly, the spores can reactivate and start growing again.

Symptoms appear 8 to 22 hours after eating. They include abdominal pain, headaches, diarrhoea and (rarely) vomiting.

Clostridium botulinum

Occurs (rarely) in inadequately processed canned foods. Discard any damaged or bulging cans.

Symptoms appear 12 to 36 hours after eating. Botulism is usually fatal. Unfortunately the first symptoms are similar to those caused by other food-poisoning bacteria and by the time the second stage has been reached (difficulty in swallowing and breathing, and double vision) it is probably too late to save the patient.

Bacillus cereus

Occurs in rice, cereals and vegetables. Long moist storage at warm temperatures will allow the spores to reactivate and the bacteria can then multiply.

Symptoms appear either 1 to 6 hours after eating and include nausea, vomiting and some diarrhoea, or 6 to 16 hours after eating and include acute diarrhoea and occasional vomiting.

Campylobacter

Occurs in undercooked poultry, sometimes as a result of it not being defrosted thoroughly. Milk which has not been properly treated before sale is another source.

Symptoms appear 1 to 10 days after eating, and include abdominal cramps, followed by foul-smelling, bloody faeces.

Destroying bacteria

Most harmful bacteria are killed at temperatures above 70°-75°C (158°-167°F), so:

– make sure that meat (especially poultry) reaches this temperature even at the centre during cooking

– thaw frozen foods thoroughly before cooking, so that the centre heats properly

– sterilise equipment after use by thorough washing and rinsing at above 75°C (167°F). Some chemicals will kill bacteria and are safe to use in food handling.

Controlling pests
Rats, mice, flies, cockroaches and other pests carry all sorts of bacteria and should never get near food, so storage and food-handling areas need to be properly protected:

– block any holes or cracks in walls and cupboards

– check that screens on windows and doors are in place

– cover waste bins

– keep all areas clean, and make sure that no food particles are left anywhere, even in corners that are difficult to reach

– store food away from floors, either covered or in pest-proof containers.

Hygiene checklist

Strict personal hygiene is the first important way of stopping bacteria getting to food:

– keep yourself clean and tidy

– keep fingernails clean, trimmed, and free of varnish

– store outdoor clothing and footwear in a proper storage area, well away from food-handling areas

– wash your hands regularly: when coming on duty, after leaving the kitchen, handling raw food, going to the toilet and especially after meal or rest breaks when you have been eating, drinking or smoking

– if you sneeze or cough, hold a disposable paper tissue over your nose and mouth and then wash your hands

– cover cuts or abrasions with a blue waterproof plaster

– do not lick your fingers or touch your nose or mouth

– never smoke or spit in food handling areas

– do not sit on work tables

– report any illness or infection.

Cross contamination, which is the transfer of food-poisoning bacteria from raw food to cooked food (especially if they are high in protein) can happen extremely easily, for example, if the same knife is used first to portion raw chicken and then to slice roast beef, so if you are working with raw food:

– never allow utensils (including chopping boards) that have been in contact with raw food to be used for cooked food unless they have been properly washed

– keep raw foods well separated from cooked foods, for example, raw meat and poultry should be stored in a different refrigerator from cooked food.

The temperature of the food is also a very important factor in preventing the growth of bacteria:

– keep food at temperatures which are too low for rapid growth of bacteria, that is, below 10°C (50°F), or too high, above 63°C (145°F)

– if the food has to be in the critical temperature zone, this should be for as short a time as possible, so serve food immediately after it has been cooked. If it has to be chilled, because it is to be served cold, for example, the cooling process should happen as fast as possible (within 1½ hours) and the food refrigerated to prevent growth.

– if food is reheated, this should be done quickly (to prevent spore reactivation) and thoroughly to a high temperature.

Hygiene regulations

Obviously it would not be in the interests of any commercial catering establishment to sell or serve contaminated food. But there is legislation to protect the public from poor hygiene practices. It is an offence to sell or to offer for sale any food which is likely to make people ill or is not fit for human consumption. In England and Wales most of this legislation is in the Food Hygiene (General) Regulations (1970), the Food Act (1984) and the Food Labelling Regulations (1984). In Scotland the equivalent legislation is in the Food & Drugs (Scotland) Act (1956), the Control of Food Premises (Scotland) Act (1977), the Food Hygiene (Scotland) Regulations (1959/78) and the Food Labelling (Scotland) Regulations (1984). The people who enforce these regulations, in other words, who may check up that proper practices are being followed, are environmental health officers (EHOs) who work for local authorities. They have powers to examine, seize and remove food and other samples, and can even make recommendations for establishments to be closed down, if they feel there are really serious problems that cannot be solved.

Moulds are small fungi. There are thousands of types of mould and certain kinds are used by the food industry: for example, in brewing and bread-making (yeasts are fungi) and in cheese-making.

Very few moulds are actually poisonous, but they do spoil food. When moulds develop, the surface of the food becomes soft and moist, and the starches, sugar and proteins in the food are broken down and produce waste products. All this makes the food look unpleasant and taste musty.

Moulds are more likely to develop in moist conditions than in dry, which is why storage spaces should be dry and airy.

Safety at work

Most accidents in kitchens happen when people are for some reason not doing their work in the safest possible way. This may be because they do not know about the safe practices they are supposed to follow, or because they forget them or simply because they are being careless.

Working safely is so important that there are various rules and regulations which lay down exactly what the obligations are of everyone at a workplace.

The Health and Safety at Work Act (1974), sometimes referred to as HASAWA, states that everyone at work, whether employer or employee, trainee or contractor brought in to do some of the work, has a duty to look after the health and safety of colleagues as well as customers, visitors and members of the general public and anyone else affected by his/her work.

It is the responsibility of employees and trainees to be aware of all the rules and regulations regarding safety in their workplace and to obey them. On the other hand, it is the employer's responsibility to ensure that the rules and regulations are brought to the attention of their staff and to check that they are obeying them. In other words, everyone is responsible for making sure that work is safe.

An offence under the HASAWA is a criminal offence and can result in an unlimited fine and/or a prison sentence of up to two years. Anyone can be prosecuted.

Safe working checklist
- Be alert.
- Know emergency procedures. Wear the correct protective clothing and footwear.
- Take care that you do not create hazardous situations.
- If you see a hazard that can be easily put right or removed do so without delay.
- If you see a hazard that will put you in danger and you don't know what to do about it, report it immediately to someone who can get it put right.
- Use correct lifting/carrying methods.
- Follow safety instructions for chemicals and cleaning agents.
- Always follow instructions exactly when operating equipment, and leave it in a safe condition after use.
- Do not use or clean dangerous machinery without suitable training and/or supervision.
- Keep knives and cutting implements sharp, make sure you select the correct type and size of knife for the task and always cut away from the body.

Clothing

Chefs' uniforms need to be comfortable and cool so are made of pure cotton or a cotton/polyester mixture. Nylon, if something very hot touches it, will melt (rather than simply scorching as cotton would) and then stick to the skin of the wearer. Long sleeves protect the arms from contact with hot surfaces and accidental splashes; the double-breasted jacket protects the chest from heat.

White shows up dirt or stains quickly, encouraging a regular change of uniforms (a freshly cleaned uniform should be worn every day).

The chef's hat reduces the chance of loose hairs falling into food or catching in moving machinery such as mixers.

Shoes must have non-slip soles, be comfortable (as chefs spend many hours on their feet) and give protection against spills and dropped equipment.

No jewellery should be worn, although a wedding ring is permissible.

First aid

The Health and Safety (First Aid) Regulations (1981) require employers to make adequate first aid provision at the workplace. This means that specific members of staff have to be appointed either as qualified first aiders, or as people who can take charge if there is an accident and no first aider is available. Properly stocked and distinctly marked first aid boxes must be provided (they are normally green with a white cross).

Employees must make sure that they know:
- who their first aider is
- where the nearest first aid box is.

Safe use of machinery

There is separate legislation covering the safe use of machinery. The Factories Act (1961) states that no-one under 18 years of age may work certain machines except in special cases. The Offices, Shops and Railway Premises Act (1963) makes it illegal for anyone to work certain machines unless they have been properly instructed and trained or are in the process of training and are being supervised at the machine. Power-driven machines (and some manual ones) for mincing, mixing, slicing, chopping, sawing and packing, which are specified in the Prescribed Dangerous Machines Order (1964), have notices above them reminding their operators of instructions for use.

Reporting accidents

Under the Reporting of Injuries, Diseases and Dangerous Occurrences Regulations (1985), often referred to as RIDDOR, all accidents must be reported. Employers keep an accident book or special forms, so that all the relevant information about how a dangerous occurrence came about and what exactly happened can be accurately recorded.

Anyone who witnesses an accident may need to describe what has happened, so it is important to learn to make a mental note of the circumstances surrounding any accident, and to write them down in the book or on a form as soon as possible.

Reportable diseases

There are two kinds of reportable disease. The first kind is developed as a direct result of the kind of work a person is doing, and, under the requirements of RIDDOR, it must be reported. Diseases of this sort associated with kitchen work include cataracts which sometimes develop when a person is exposed to radiant heat a great deal, and occupational asthma which may happen as a result of handling something that produced a great deal of dust (e.g. flour, wheat or maize).

The other kind of reportable disease is one that must be reported because it could be passed on from the person who has it to others. Under the Food Hygiene (General) Regulations (1970) in England and Wales, and the Food Hygiene (Scotland) Regulations (1959/78), no-one with, for example, typhoid, paratyphoid, *Salmonella* infections, dysentery or any staphylococcal infection (e.g. septic cuts, boils or throat infections) should handle food and if someone working anywhere in the catering business is discovered to be suffering from any of these diseases, they have to be reported to the local medical officer of health.

AIDS is not covered by existing legislation but employers and work colleagues should be aware of the risk of spreading AIDS through infected blood. A booklet, *AIDS: What Everybody Needs to Know*, is available from Dept. A, P.O. Box 100, Milton Keynes MK1 1TX.

Fire

The Fire Precautions Act (1971) is the main piece of legislation controlling fire safety. It imposes standards for fire prevention and for suitable and adequate means of escape and protection if a fire does break out. All but the smallest catering establishments have to apply for and obtain a fire certificate from their local fire brigade or fire authority. When they have this certificate, they have to give staff proper training about what to do in the event of fire and hold regular fire drills.

The enforcing authorities

In most hotel and catering operations, environmental health officers or EHOs (who work for the local authority) are responsible for enforcing HASAWA and RIDDOR.

In factory canteens, sports and leisure clubs, theatres and cinemas, health and safety inspectors, employed by a national organisation set up by the government called the Health and Safety Executive (HSE), are responsible for enforcing HASAWA and RIDDOR.

Whether it is an environmental health officer or an official from the Health and Safety Executive who does the checking, he or she has powers to:

– comment on and ask for improvements

– serve an improvement notice which gives a set time to improve specific faults

– serve a prohibition notice closing the premises where the circumstances are so dangerous that they must be stopped immediately

– examine, seize and remove food and other samples.

Fire prevention checklist
Find out where the fire-fighting appliances are in your work area, what type of fire they can be used on (indicated on the label) and how they work (also indicated on the label). Make sure you know the fire drill at your workplace, which will include all or some of the following instructions:

– raise the alarm and call for help

– evacuate the building

– close windows and doors

– carry out any special responsibilities (like taking a register of names to the assembly point).

If it is safe to do so:

– switch off power supplies

– attack the blaze with suitable extinguishers (so long as there is no immediate personal risk).

▶▶▶ TO DO

Draw a rough plan of your workplace or college kitchen. Indicate on it the location of all fire-fighting appliances, fire exits, and the switches that control power supplies.

What to do if an accident happens

In general

Stay calm and act quickly.

Call whoever is appointed to deal with accidents at once (normally a first aider) or your supervisor.

Make sure that the injured person is in no further danger, for example, if an accident has happened with a slicing machine, turn it off at the mains immediately.

Reassure the injured person and help him or her to feel more comfortable, but make sure that the person is not moved more than absolutely necessary. Don't allow people to crowd around the injured person because this may increase his or her distress.

Electric shock

In the case of an electric shock, turn off the power immediately at the mains switch or plug. Do not touch the injured person until you have done so (otherwise there is a danger that you could get a shock).

Cuts

If bleeding is slight, it can be controlled by pressure on the area, using a bandage or adhesive waterproof dressing (normally blue ones are used in kitchens, so that the position of the injury is clearly visible and extra care can be taken that it does not come into contact with food).

If bleeding is severe, then direct pressure should be applied over the bleeding points and the injured person helped to lie down with the injured part raised slightly and supported. The sides of a large wound should be pressed together. As soon as a dressing is available it should be applied over the wound. If the bleeding continues before help arrives, further layers of dressing may be necessary, bandaged more firmly.

Dirty wounds should be cleaned before dressing, if possible, either under running water or by wiping carefully with swabs or clean cotton wool.

Burns and scalds

– Reduce the pain and the spread of the heat by running cold water over the burn or immersing it in cold water, for at least ten minutes or until the pain stops.

– Remove any jewellery or tight clothing or footwear in the area of the burn (before swelling makes this impossible).

– Burnt clothing should be left on if it is dry (it will have been sterilised by the heat). Wet clothing should be carefully removed.

– Never apply any lotions, oils or ointments to a burn.

– Be careful not to infect burnt areas, for example, by breathing over them or touching them.

– If clothing catches fire, put out the flames with water or smother them with a rug or blanket (but never use any synthetic material that will melt, e.g. nylon).

Lifting safely
If you have to pick up a heavy weight of any sort, like a large bag of flour or a box, be careful not to strain your back. Keeping your back straight, bend your knees until you are as close to the object as possible. Then grasp the object firmly against your chest with both hands, and straighten into a standing position using your leg muscles rather than taking the strain with your back.

🮢 INTRODUCTION

The human body needs a variety of foods so that it can grow and function properly. Particular chemicals – called nutrients – in foods do particular jobs. There are six groups of essential nutrients:

Carbohydrates are a source of energy and are found, for example, in potatoes, bread, pasta, grains (rice, wheat, etc.), fruit and honey.

Proteins are important for growth and present in a wide range of animal and vegetable foods, especially meat and dairy products.

Fats (lipids) are a concentrated source of energy and are found in dairy products, margarine, cooking oils and nuts, among other foods.

Vitamins and *minerals*, present in all natural foods, help control body functions, and maintain health.

Water, although people do not always think of it as a nutrient, is essential for life. About 70% of our bodyweight is made up of water, but in a reasonable diet it is quite easy to get this, because most food has a high water content.

All these nutrients should be eaten daily if possible. Some, like carbohydrates and proteins, are needed in gram quantities, and others, like vitamins and minerals, are needed only in tiny amounts measured in milligrams (mg.) or even micrograms (μ g.). (There are 1,000 milligrams and 1,000,000 micrograms to every 1 gram.)

Too little or too much of a particular nutrient will result in serious health problems, for example, if children do not get enough Vitamin D over long periods, they suffer from rickets, which means that their bones become soft and bendy. Eating too much fat can make a person seriously overweight (obese) and may cause heart disease. Too many sweet products can also lead to obesity and to tooth decay.

> Cellulose and pectin cannot be digested by humans and so they pass straight through the digestive system, but they are necessary because they provide fibre – or bulk – which is one of the things that helps the whole system work properly and prevents disease.

Carbohydrates

Carbohydrates are a group of nutrients that include starches and sugars. Listed below are some of them, with the foods they are commonly found in. They all supply energy, except for pectin and cellulose (*see* box).

Sucrose is found in sugar cane and sugar beet and refined to make table sugar, brown sugar, sugar syrup, etc. Processed foods – whether they taste sweet or savoury – often contain sucrose, and chocolate, cakes and biscuits, especially, contain a lot of it.

Lactose is the particular type of sugar found in milk and is not normally used in cooking in its pure form. Milk contains about 4% lactose.

Maltose is the main sugar that occurs in malt (which is made by allowing barley to germinate). It is also produced by the body when starch is being digested.

Although maltose is not used in its pure form in cooking, it is extremely important in bread-making because the yeast makes the maltose in the flour ferment and this produces the carbon dioxide that makes bread rise.

Glucose and *fructose* both occur naturally in many sweet fruits and in honey.

Starch is found in potatoes, pulses (e.g. peas and kidney beans), cereals and cereal products (e.g. rice, flour, bread and pasta).

Cellulose is the substance that makes up plant cell walls and is found, for example, in pulses, brown rice, wholemeal flour and bread, fruit and vegetables.

Pectin is also found in plant cell walls, especially in ripe fruit, and is used for setting jams.

Protein

The human body is made up of many different cells: brain cells, blood cells, muscle cells, skin cells, etc. Protein is needed for any cell to be formed so it is very important that children eat enough of it while they are growing. Even when the body has stopped growing, protein is essential so that old cells can be replaced.

Adults need between 60 to 80 grams (about 3 oz) of protein per day. All natural foods contain some protein, but it is particularly concentrated in meat, fish, cheese, eggs, nuts and pulses (especially soya beans). It is best for the protein in a person's diet to come from a variety of sources, because some protein-rich foods – meat and cheese, for example – also contain a great deal of saturated fat.

▶▶▶ TO DO

Many people have got used to a diet which has a lot of fat or a lot of sugar in it. So chefs have to use all their skill and inventiveness to produce meals which are both tempting and healthy.

Keep a record of what you have eaten over a period of 5 days. What changes might be made to cut down the fat and sugar and increase the starch (and fibre) and yet still result in a pleasant diet?

Importance of a balanced diet

Everyone needs to eat a balanced diet so that they stay healthy. This means eating a fairly wide range of foods so that all the nutrients are obtained in the correct amounts. Energy is supplied by fats and oils, sugars, starch and protein. Experts have discovered that many people in developed countries get too much of their energy from saturated fats and sugar, which can lead to coronary heart disease – the cause of well over a quarter of deaths in Britain. In general, more starch should be eaten instead of the fat and sugar, which would also increase the amount of fibre eaten.

Fats and oils

The only difference between fats and oils is that fats are solid at room temperature whereas oils are liquid. Some oils are specially processed so that they are solid, e.g. margarines. Fats are the most concentrated source of energy.

The fat content of some foods, like meat, meat products and cheese, can vary quite considerably, but the table below shows which kinds of food tend to be high or low in fat:

High fat	Low fat
most cheeses	fruit
cream	vegetables
lard and dripping	bread
egg yolk	egg white
butter	white fish
margarine	low-fat yogurt
most meat products	milk (especially skimmed and semi-skimmed)
most cuts of meat	cottage cheese
all oils	poultry
oily fish	grains, e.g. rice
nuts	pulses, e.g. peas, haricot beans

There is now a lot of evidence that eating too much fat leads to health problems. This is partly because it can make people overweight, which is always unhealthy, and partly because certain types of fat – called saturated fats – can increase the level of cholesterol in the blood, and a high cholesterol level can lead to heart disease. The other two sorts of fat are polyunsaturated and monounsaturated. Monounsaturated fats are much less likely to cause problems, and polyunsaturated fats are thought to be the most healthy alternative. The table below shows which foods contain which kinds of fat.

Hidden fat

Quite often, people eat fat without realising they are doing so. Some of the sources of this hidden fat are:

cheddar cheese	34% fat
double cream	48% fat
flaky pastry	40% fat
mayonnaise	about 79% fat
raw pork sausage	about 32% fat

In most cases this is saturated fat – the most unhealthy kind.

Food containing mainly saturated fat	Food containing mainly polyunsaturated fat	Food containing mainly monounsaturated fat
milk	fish	poultry
butter	nuts	groundnut oil
cream	game	olive oil
most cheeses	wild fowl	
meat and meat products	most soft margarine	
lard and dripping	corn oil	
hard margarines	sunflower oil	
palm and coconut oils	safflower oil	
egg yolk	soya oil	

⫽ INTRODUCTION

Vitamins

Vitamins are substances of various sorts that the body cannot make for itself, but which it needs in small amounts so that it can function properly. For example, vitamin deficiencies can lead to tiredness or an inability to fight off infections and to stunted growth in children.

Vitamins A and D are fat-soluble (not water-soluble) and are not destroyed by cooking, but water-soluble vitamins (Vitamin C and the B vitamins) are easily destroyed or lost into the cooking water. Vitamin C vanishes the most easily: vegetables that have wilted or have been stored for any length of time in a refrigerator will already have lost a lot of their Vitamin C, and peeled or sliced fruit and vegetables start losing it as soon as they are exposed to the air.

Serious vitamin deficiency diseases are very unusual in Britain because for most people a wide range of food is easily available, but it is still possible to go short of a vitamin. If a person eats no fresh fruit or vegetables, for example, they will not get enough Vitamin C.

The table below shows the common sources of vitamins, what the body uses them for and what eventually happens if they are left out of the diet completely.

VITAMIN	FOOD SOURCE	FUNCTION	DEFICIENCY DISEASE
Vitamin A or retinol	Cheese, milk, cream, butter, margarine, eggs and liver. Also apricots and spinach. Carrots contain carotene which is converted to Vitamin A in the liver.	Necessary for vision in dim light and for the protective mucous membranes, e.g. in the nose and throat, to work properly.	Night blindness and eventually flaky skin.
Vitamin B1 or thiamine	Found in a variety of foods, but good sources are wheat germ, unroasted peanuts, roast pork, oat meal, bacon and eggs, kidney and liver.	Controls the release of energy from glucose in the diet.	Beri-beri and nervous disorders.
Vitamin B2 (contains riboflavin)	Liver, kidneys, cheese, milk, eggs and yeast extracts.	Riboflavin is needed for proper functioning of muscles so it is especially important for athletes or people doing hard physical work.	Stunted growth in children. In adults: sore tongue, itching eyes.
Niacin	Liver, kidneys, sardines.	Necessary for healthy skin.	Pellagra (inflammation of the skin).
Vitamin C or ascorbic acid	Blackcurrants, strawberries, blackberries, green peppers, cabbage, cauliflower, potatoes, Brussels sprouts, oranges and lemons.	Necessary for healthy connective tissue.	Scurvy (the breakdown of connective tissue). First symptoms are easy bruising, bleeding, spongy gums.
Vitamin D	Oily fish, fish oils, margarine and eggs. It also forms in the body when the skin is exposed to sunlight.	Helps calcium to be absorbed properly, which keeps teeth and bones healthy.	Rickets.

Minerals

There are about twenty different minerals needed by the body so that it can work efficiently. Like vitamins, they are needed only in quite small amounts and they help with a number of different functions in the body. If a person does not have enough of these minerals over long periods, then he or she will become ill. The most common deficiency disease in Britain is anaemia – a lack of iron. A great many people, particularly women, suffer from this form of anaemia; the main symptoms are tiredness and listlessness. Pregnant women are often advised to take iron tablets. Vitamin C helps the body to take in iron from food.

It is possible to have too much of a mineral. The most common example of this is sodium – common salt. High sodium intakes can lead to high blood pressure and the risk of coronary heart disease. Many people have got used to eating very salty food – in Britain the average intake is about ten times higher than it should be, partly because so much salt is used in processed food.

Iron
Occurs in red meat and offal, bread, shellfish and some vegetables.
Essential for the production of haemoglobin, the oxygen-carrying part of blood.

Calcium
Occurs in milk and milk products, small fish (if the bones are eaten), bread and some cereals.
Essential for healthy bones and teeth.

Phosphorus
Occurs in a wide range of foods.
Essential for healthy bones and teeth.

Sodium
Occurs in salt, bacon, ham, soy sauce and some processed foods.
Essential for nerve and muscle action. Regulates body fluids.

Digestion

It has been calculated that an average well-fed person eats something like 35 tons of food in a lifetime. All this food has to be digested so that it can be turned into a form that can be absorbed and used by the body.

The process starts in the mouth, where the food is broken into small pieces as it is chewed and is also lubricated by saliva (so that it can be swallowed easily). After it has been swallowed, the food passes down through the oesophagus into the stomach. Here it is smothered in digestive juices containing acid and a few of the digestive enzymes needed to break down food so that it can be absorbed. Muscular action mixes everything together and liquifies it.

Next the liquified food is passed in small amounts through a valve into the small intestine. This is where the majority of the digestive enzymes that break down proteins, fats and carbohydrates do their work. Fats are a special case because they have to be broken down into small droplets before the enzymes can work. This is done by bile which is made in the liver, stored in the gall bladder and added to food in the small intestine.

The small intestine is where most nutrients are absorbed into the bloodstream. Vitamin and mineral molecules are small enough to pass through the intestinal wall without being acted on by enzymes. As the small intestine is 5 metres (5½ yards) long, all the useful parts of food will have had a good chance to be absorbed by the time it passes into the large intestine. At this point, what is left is mainly water and indigestible material.

In the large intestine the water is squeezed out to leave waste, called faeces, which is collected in the rectum and passes out through the anus. In a low-fibre diet, the faeces tend to be very hard and difficult to move, sometimes causing constipation. Some experts also think that low-fibre diets make it more likely that a person will develop varicose veins, appendicitis, haemorrhoids, diverticulitis or cancer of the colon. If the fibre intake is high, these problems are less likely to occur.

Energy
The energy value of food is measured in *calories* (cal.). As this is a tiny unit, energy value is more often measured in *kilocalories* (kcal.). A more modern unit called a *Joule* (J.) is sometimes used for energy calculations and equals 4.2 calories.

Children and adolescents need different amounts of energy at different times, depending on how much they are growing at a particular time and how physically active they are. Once the body is fully formed – at about 18 years – energy needs even out a bit.

There are two main uses of energy:
1. The basic functions which the body must be able to do or it will die, like breathing, making new cells, heart beating.
2. Physical activity like walking, running, sport, etc., which varies enormously from person to person.

In a healthy adult of the right weight, energy input from food and drink should balance energy output. If energy input is greater than output, that is, if too much food and drink is taken, the excess will be stored as adipose tissue (fat), and once this has formed, it is very difficult to get rid of.

⫽ INTRODUCTION

Under the heading, Food Selection, each module in this book contains information about the food items or commodities that are most suited to that particular process and, if appropriate, advice on buying and preparation, for example, which cuts of meat can be boiled, stewed or steamed. But there are general commodities that can be used for flavouring in virtually any process and some of these are dealt with here.

Herbs and spices

Herbs and spices are used to add flavour to food during cooking. They may also be used in marinades so that the food absorbs the flavour before it is cooked. There are many dishes that traditionally use a particular herb or spice, for example, tarragon with chicken, rosemary with lamb or paprika with Hungarian Goulash. But a chef with a thorough knowledge of herbs and spices can develop original combinations of flavours to create really individual effects.

With herbs, e.g. parsley, sage, thyme, it is almost always the leaves of the plant that are used. They should preferably be used fresh, but all herbs can be obtained in dried form and it is sometimes more practical to use them dried. Traditionally, the herbs that are used in a particular country's cooking grow in that country.

Spices, on the other hand, have traditionally been imported and, for the British, at least, they are associated with distant, exotic countries. Most spices are aromatic seeds, though a few are aromatic roots, or even bark, and they are usually imported in a dried state, sometimes whole (e.g. cloves and nutmegs) and sometimes already ground.

Seasonings and condiments

Salt is perhaps the most commonly used seasoning. But only a small quantity of salt is actually necessary to provide the sodium and chlorine essential for the body. Some people prefer to eat as little salt as possible, either because they do not like the taste or for health reasons – a high salt intake can contribute to high blood pressure.

Salt is added during manufacturing to many processed food products, such as bread, cereals, hams, sausages, soups, tinned meats and vegetables, partly for flavour but mainly to extend the storage life of the particular food. For the various types of salt, *see* box.

Pepper is made by grinding peppercorns, the dried berries of a tropical shrub. When they are fresh and unripe, peppercorns are green and these are usually bought canned, bottled, or freeze-dried. Black peppercorns are dried in their skins, and are stronger and more

pungent than white peppercorns, which have the skins removed before drying. Both can be used whole, crushed or milled.

Mustard comes from the seeds of the mustard plant. It is grown in many countries including Britain, and can be bought in a wide variety of forms from highly refined powder to made-up liquid mustard containing some whole seeds. It can be used in the preparation of food in the kitchen or as a condiment on the table.

Vinegar comes in many varieties and is made by fermenting alcohol, including malt, wine, cider, sherry and rice wine. Some vinegars are now chemically produced.

Vinegar has a variety of uses: as part of a marinade to flavour and help tenderise meat, to add a certain flavour to sauces, as a preservative (e.g. pickled onions) or as part of a salad dressing, in particular, vinaigrette.

Concentrated stock preparations, in the form of cubes, powders or liquids, are used in some kitchens as a convenient alternative to making real stock. They are mainly chicken or beef-flavoured (and usually also contain salt and monosodium glutamate) but it is possible to obtain vegetable stock cubes (useful in vegetarian cooking) and fish stock cubes. The important thing to remember is that although they are a useful short cut, most stock preparations do not have the subtlety of flavour or nutritional value of real stocks.

Monosodium glutamate, sometimes called taste powder or gourmet powder, has almost no taste itself, but is used to bring out the flavour of food in Chinese and Japanese cooking and in some processed foods, canned goods and stock preparations. Some people are careful to avoid eating or using it though, because it has been discovered to have unfortunate side effects if eaten in large quantities – parts of the nervous system can be upset.

There is also a huge range of *bottled sauces* used for flavouring, often known by the names of particular manufacturers. A few have come to be associated with specific dishes, for example, Worcestershire sauce in steak and kidney pudding, soy sauce (made from soya beans) in Chinese-style stir-fried dishes. Most hot sauces, used in highly spiced dishes, are based on chilli peppers.

Herbs: 1) Sage 2) Flat-leaved parsley
3) Curly-leaved parsley 4) Coriander
5) Dill 6) Chervil 7) Thyme 8) Chives
9) Marjoram 10) Basil 11) Mint
12) Tarragon 13) Rosemary 14) Bay leaf.

▸▸▸ TO DO

Make a list of the dried herbs and spices available in your workplace. (If a large number is used, select 10 of the more unusual ones.) Against each item, note which dishes it can be used for (if necessary asking your colleagues and supervisor for help). Then find out as much as you can about the origin of the item and what other uses it can be put to, and keep the list as a reference for future use.

Spices: 1) White mustard 2) Black mustard 3) Black peppercorns 4) White peppercorns 5) Green peppercorns (dried) 6) Allspice 7) Juniper berries 8) Chillies (dried) 9) Fenugreek seed 10) Coriander seed 11) Poppy seed 12) Sesame seed 13) Dill seed 14) Fennel seed 15) Cumin 16) Caraway seed 17) Cloves 18) Cardamoms 19) Star anise 20) Mace 21) Nutmeg 22) Cinnamon 23) Cassia 24) Asafoetida.

Types of salt

Sea salt, produced by evaporating sea water, is considered by some chefs to be the best type of salt. It does not have the bitter aftertaste that kitchen or table salt often has and still contains its natural iodine (a mineral that is very important to the growth and activity of every organ in the human body).

Rock salt comes from deposits in rock that were formed as a result of ancient seas drying out. A small amount of it is mined and thought by many to have an even better flavour than sea salt. It is so hard that it has to be milled or ground before use, whereas coarse sea salt can be sprinkled directly on to food, e.g. bread, to create a crunchy, attractive surface. Most salt (kitchen or table) is pumped out of rock salt deposits as brine (salt dissolved in water) and then evaporated and crushed. Table salt is coated with an additive so it will not absorb moisture from the air and will flow properly.

✳ NUTRITION

Too much salt in food can cause high blood pressure which can in turn lead to heart failure. So use as little salt as possible in cooking. Customers who like the taste of salt in their food can always add their own.

– Weigh the amount used: ½ g per portion is a reasonable average.

– Use fresh foods (wherever possible) in preference to pre-prepared or convenience foods which have had salt added during their manufacture. Alternatively, use products which state on the label that no salt has been added.

1 INTRODUCTION

The information in this section will help you gain Caterbase certification in the module, *Preparing Stocks*.

Meat, poultry and game stocks (white and brown)
Fonds blancs/bruns

INGREDIENTS	MAKES 5 litres (10 pints)	
2 kg	raw bones	5 lb
	(beef, lamb, veal, chicken, game)	
200 g	onions	½ lb
200 g	carrots	½ lb
50 g	celery	2 oz
50 g	leeks	2 oz
5 l	cold water	10 pt
	sprig of thyme, bay leaf and parsley stalks	

1. Break up or saw into smaller pieces any large bones that will not fit easily into the saucepan or stockpot. Remove any fat and any marrow in the centre of beef bones.

2. *For white stocks:*
a) Cover the bones with cold water. Bring to the boil, simmer for a few minutes, pour off the cooking water and wash off the bones in cold running water.
b) Place the blanched bones, the vegetables (prepared but left whole) and the herbs into the stockpot.

For brown stocks:
a) Put the bones in a roasting tray and place in a hot oven – 220°C (430°F).
b) Roughly chop the prepared vegetables. Then after the bones have been in the oven for 15 to 20 minutes and have turned a light brown colour, put the chopped vegetables in the oven with them.
c) When the bones have turned a darker brown and the vegetables have also browned (another 10 to 15 minutes), remove them from the oven, and, using a fish slice, transfer the bones and vegetables to the stockpot, carefully allowing any fat to drain off them as they are lifted off the roasting tray.
d) Pour off the fat from the roasting tray into a bowl or jug so that it can be thrown away when it has cooled. Then put a little cold water into the tray and bring it to the boil on top of the stove, scraping the bottom and sides of the pan so that the residue left by the bones and vegetables is dissolved in the water. Add this to the stockpot with the herbs.

3. Add the water and bring to the boil.

4. Skim off any surface fat and impurities that rise to the surface. Slowly simmer beef, veal, lamb and mutton stocks for 6 to 8 hours, and poultry and feathered game stocks for 3 hours.

5. During cooking, skim off any impurities that rise to the surface regularly.

6. When the stock is ready, strain it off into a clean container. If it is not going to be used immediately, chill it quickly, then cover with a lid and place in the refrigerator or cold room.

🍴 CHEF'S TIPS

As an alternative to being browned in the oven, the vegetables (and the bones if they are small and easy to handle) can be browned by shallow frying in a little hot fat.

If additions are made to the stockpot during the course of a day (as often happens in busy kitchens), the water level can be topped up again without any loss of strength in the finished stock. It is important not to keep the same stock simmering day after day, as the original ingredients will be overcooked, add nothing to the flavour and may even turn the stock sour.

Preparing vegetables for stocks and sauces
Onions: peel, trim off the root and wash.
Carrots: wash, trim off the root end. If the carrot has a tough skin, peel it, otherwise just scrape off any blemishes.
Celery: wash, trim off the root end, separate the stalks, discarding any that are old or damaged. Wash again.
Leeks: wash, remove any discoloured or damaged leaves. Trim off the root end, cut in half lengthwise and wash again if there is dirt trapped between the leaves. Keep the leaves together as much as possible to make chopping easier.

Fish stock

INGREDIENTS		MAKES 5 litres (10 pints)
2 kg	white fish bones	5 lb
	(haddock, whiting, sole, turbot)	
250 g	onions	10 oz
50 ml	lemon juice (1 large lemon)	2 fl oz
5 l	cold water	10 pt
5	peppercorns (optional)	5
2	bay leaves	2
	parsley stalks	

Above: the ingredients for a white stock. Because marrow has a high fat content, it has been removed from the centre of the raw bones. The vegetables (carrot, leek, onion, celery) are left whole. In the background are some bones which have been blanched and are now ready for adding to the stock. Parsley stalks, bay leaf and whole peppercorns are also added to the stock, but never salt, which should be added in the final stages of the preparation of dishes in which stock has been used when the liquid content has been reduced.

Below: brown stocks use the same herbs and vegetables as white stocks. But for a brown stock the bones and roughly chopped vegetables are browned before being added to the water. In the background of this picture are the browned ingredients.

The tin-lined copper stockpots shown in both pictures have a tap at the base which makes it very easy to drain off the stock once it has been cooked.

1. Slice the onions finely and place them in the stockpot or saucepan with the other ingredients.

2. Add the water, bring it to the boil and skim off any impurities that rise to the surface.

3. Simmer for approximately 20 minutes, and skim as required during cooking.

4. When it is ready, strain the stock into a clean container and use it immediately or chill until required.

✚ HYGIENE

To cool stock quickly, stand the saucepan or basin in a sink and run cold water around it. This is important because if the stock is held warm (rather than boiling) for too long it may turn sour and there is a danger of bacteria multiplying. Many sinks have a special device that will keep the water level below the rim of the cooling stock. Alternatively, rest the stockpot on a triangular wooden stand so that cool air can circulate under it. Never cover the stockpot with a lid during cooling as this could also slow down the cooling process.

Making fish stock is an excellent way of using up what is left over when fish has been filleted. The only other ingredients required are: onions (finely sliced), lemon juice, a few herbs (parsley stalks, bay leaves and black peppercorns) and water.

Butter is also shown in the photograph (on the tray with the plaice carcases), because traditionally the fish bones and onions are sweated in butter before the water is added to enrich the flavour of the stock. This stage would be left out for a low-fat meal. You would also leave out the fat if the stock was going to be used to make fish aspic (*see* Boiling/Practical Examples 4), because the fat would prevent the aspic clarifying properly.

Basic brown sauce
Sauce espagnole

INGREDIENTS		MAKES 1 litre (2 pints)
90 g	*dripping*	3¾ oz
125 g	*flour*	5 oz
100 g	*onions*	4 oz
100 g	*carrots*	4 oz
50 g	*celery*	2 oz
50 g	*leek*	2 oz
50 g	*tomato purée*	2 oz
1½ l	*brown stock*	3 pt

sprig of thyme, ½ bay leaf and parsley stalks

1. Roughly chop the prepared vegetables.

2. Melt 75g (3 oz) of the fat in a saucepan then mix in the flour (this mixture is called a roux).

3. Cook the roux (stirring continuously to avoid burning) until it has turned a good even brown colour.

4. Heat up the stock.

5. Allow the roux to cool slightly, then mix in the tomato purée. (The cooling is important because otherwise the roux may spit as the purée is added.)

6. Mix in the hot stock, a little at a time, stirring it smooth and bring it to the boil.

7. When all the stock has been added and the mixture simmered for a few minutes, skim off any fat or impurities that rise to the surface. Add the herbs.

8. Shallow fry the vegetables in the remaining dripping until they are lightly browned.

9. Add the vegetables to the simmering sauce and continue cooking for about 4 hours. During cooking, skim frequently and top up with additional stock if the sauce is reducing too much and becoming too thick (when it may start to burn at the bottom).

10. Strain the brown sauce into a clean saucepan or bowl and use it immediately or chill until required.

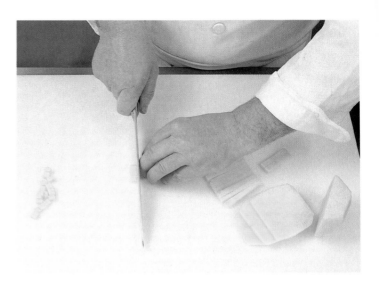

Two of the most common causes of accidents in kitchens are bad knife techniques and untidy working practices. This photograph shows the correct way of dicing vegetables, a practice which involves using the fingers of one hand as a guide for the knife blade and so can be dangerous. The knife should be held firmly with the thumb on one side of the handle the forefinger crooked on the other and the remaining fingers curling around the handle. With the other hand the lengths of turnip are being held firmly, with the knuckles acting as a guide to the chopping/slicing motion. To avoid any risk of injury, the thumb and finger nails are tucked well away.

The four steps involved in dicing vegetables are being followed methodically. The turnip has been peeled, its ends are trimmed off so that it will rest firmly on the board. Slices have then been cut and then the slices cut into strips. Finally the strips are cut into dice.

Demi-glace

INGREDIENTS		MAKES 1 litre (2 pints)
1 l	*basic brown sauce*	2 pt
1 l	*brown stock*	2 pt

1. Bring the brown sauce to the boil.

2. Add the brown stock (which may be hot or cold) and return the liquid to the boil, simmering until the sauce has reduced by half.

3. Skim off any fats or impurities that rise to the surface during cooking and stir occasionally.

4. Strain into a clean saucepan or bowl and use immediately or chill until required.

Jus lié

INGREDIENTS		MAKES ½ litre (1 pint)
125 g	small veal bones	5 oz
10 g	dripping or white fat	½ oz
50 g	onion	2 oz
50 g	carrot	2 oz
25 g	celery	1 oz
25 g	leek	1 oz
¾ l	brown veal stock	1½ pt
10 g	tomato purée	½ oz
	sprig of thyme, ¼ bay leaf and parsley stalks	
2	black peppercorns (optional)	2
	Thickening	
10 g	arrowroot	½ oz
25 ml	cold water	1 fl oz

1. Trim off any fat from the bones and chop the bones into small pieces.

2. Roughly chop the prepared vegetables.

3. Melt the dripping in a saucepan, add the bones and fry them until they are a good brown colour on all sides.

4. Add the vegetables and continue frying until they are lightly browned.

5. Drain off as much fat as possible then add the stock, tomato purée and peppercorns.

6. Bring to the boil, skim off surface fat or impurities that rise to the surface and simmer for 3 hours. Skim as necessary during cooking. You should end up with about ½ litre (1 pint) of liquid.

7. Mix the arrowroot and the cold water thoroughly together and stir the mixture into the simmering stock.

8. Reboil and simmer for 2 to 3 minutes.

9. Strain the jus lié into a clean saucepan or bowl and use it immediately or chill until required.

♟ CHEF'S TIP

If the liquid is allowed to boil vigorously instead of simmering during step 6, it will reduce too much. If this has happened add some more brown stock so that there is about ½ litre (1 pint).

Use of stocks

Good stocks form the basis of good soups and a huge range of savoury sauces to accompany, for example, grilled or shallow fried meats, poached fish and egg dishes, boiled meats, rice and pasta, baked savoury dishes, braised and stewed meats and vegetables and to make roast gravies.

They can also be heavily reduced until they form a thick, very flavourful liquid (when they are known as a glaze) and used in this way as a sauce (so avoiding the need to thicken with fat or even flour). If stored chilled in this concentrated form they can be kept for several days and used instead of commercially produced flavourings such as stock cubes.

When stocks are being made for a specific purpose they can be given a more individual flavour, for example, by adding fresh tarragon and chervil, garlic, tomato purée, juniper berries and sage (to game stock) and wine (but red wine should be used only in dark-coloured stocks).

Good use can be made of clean vegetable trimmings by adding them to stockpots, particularly the stalks of mushrooms, the skins and seeds of tomatoes, the trimmings of celery, leeks, carrots and onions.

Certain strong-flavoured vegetables such as cabbage, Brussels sprouts, swedes, turnips and cauliflower should not be added to stocks unless their flavour is specifically required. If they are used, they should not be left to simmer in the stock for more than about 30 minutes, otherwise they will produce off-flavours which will ruin the stock. Starchy vegetables such as potatoes should never be added to stock as they will thicken and cloud the liquid.

Stocks containing meat and therefore some fat, should never be boiled vigorously because the fat will break up into such tiny globules that it will be almost impossible to remove effectively. Once as much fat as possible has been skimmed off the top of a stock, any that remains can be soaked up by floating a piece of clean kitchen paper on the top for a few seconds and then removing it. Also when stocks are chilled, any remaining fat will solidify on the surface, and can be easily removed before reheating.

A vegetable stock can be made very simply and quickly, with water and a good collection of different vegetables – any of those mentioned above and in the ingredients listed for stocks on the previous spread. If they are available, celeriac, asparagus, sweetcorn and watercress can also be added. If you have only a small selection of fresh vegetables, a good vegetable extract can be added, preferably one with a low salt/sodium content (for health reasons). For vegetable stocks it is important to chop all the vegetables up small so their flavour can be extracted quickly – 20 to 30 minutes for the simmering stage will avoid the dangers of any vegetables developing off-flavours.

2 BOILING

Boiled foods can be very attractive and often form the basis of healthy, appetising and nutritious meals: for example, boiled shoulder of lamb stuffed with bacon served in a hotel restaurant, shellfish salad eaten in a bistro, savoury rice and pasta dishes for the children's ward of a hospital, even cockles and mussels bought from a street stall.

Unfortunately many customers may have bad memories of boiled food. Images of over-cooked stodgy rice and limp, colourless cabbage have to be overcome. These disappointing examples of boiled food are the result not of any shortcoming in the method itself, but of lack of care, understanding or skill on the part of the chef.

There are many dishes that use the technique of boiling to produce their distinctive tastes, flavours and textures and they range from soups and sauces, rices and pasta, meats and shellfish, potatoes and vegetables, to puddings, jams and jellies as well as the sauces to accompany fried, grilled, baked or steamed dishes.

Many traditional British dishes were boiled and the excellent flavours of some of these old recipes are now being appreciated because of a revival of interest in old-fashioned British cookery. Improved standards of presentation mean that the simplest of dishes can be served in the smartest restaurants. Some of the items that you may see on the menus are: Country Broths, Boiled Leg of Mutton and Caper Sauce, Tripe and Onions, and Haggis.

One of the benefits of serving boiled food is the health aspect. Some people are concerned about eating fatty foods, and boiled items can offer a healthy and wholesome alternative to fried dishes.

✱ NUTRITION

Boiling, poaching and steaming are popular cooking methods with people who want to eat a healthy diet because no fat is added, and some foods cooked by this method are high in dietary fibre, e.g. pulses and whole wheat spaghetti.

▶▶▶ TO DO

Boiled dishes can appear in any course in a meal. Look at the menus in your workplace (or a local restaurant) and see if you can identify a first course, a main course and a sweet which use boiling as the main cooking process. Are they popular dishes? If so, why?

What happens

Boiling is cooking in liquid at boiling point, that is when it is bubbling and giving off steam. Heat is transferred from the gas burner or electric element by conduction through the bottom of the cooking container to the liquid. Convection currents form in the hot liquid, dispersing the heat throughout it.

The liquid used is water, stock, milk or a combination based on these with herbs and flavourings.

The movement of the liquid ranges from a rapid and vigorous bubbling action to a gentle simmering, when small bubbles rise to the surface or break up before they reach the surface. The temperature of the liquid when it is bubbling vigorously is the same as when it is simmering very gently. It will not get any higher, no matter how much heat there is, unless the pressure above the liquid's surface is increased, as in a pressure cooker (*see* Steaming/The Customer). This makes boiling a straightforward method of cooking with a single, accurate standard temperature control that means there is no need to use thermometers or thermostats.

Starting temperature of the liquid

Some foods are placed into cold liquid, which is then brought to the boil. Others are lowered into boiling or very hot liquid.

Starting with a cold liquid

The cooking process is started in cold liquid when it is important to remove excess salt, for example, from cured or pickled meat, or to remove undesirable substances like blood and fat from poor-quality meat.

For extremely salty food, such as the bacon joint in the photograph, the food may be brought to the boil in a large pan of water to dissolve out the salt. This water is then discarded and the process may be repeated once or twice more to reduce the salt content.

Impurities that rise to the surface during the heating process should be skimmed off (if the liquid is not to be replaced). Otherwise they will spread throughout the liquid making it cloudy and unpleasantly flavoured.

See: Videos 2 and 5

Boiling point can be affected by:
pressure
The boiling point of pure water is 100°C (212°F) at sea level. Atmospheric pressure affects boiling point; the lower the pressure the lower the boiling point will be, and the longer the cooking time required. So on a mountain top, where the air pressure is low, cooking a potato takes a little longer. On the other hand a pressure cooker, in which high pressures can be created, cooks food at a much higher temperature and the cooking time can be reduced to a third of the time it would take in a normal saucepan.

adding substances to the liquid
A small amount of salt added to cooking water raises the boiling point a little above 100°C. Sugar, which is present in large quantities in some recipes (e.g. caramel), causes boiling to occur at very high temperatures.

▶▶▶ TO DO

Using two saucepans, one containing cold water, the second with boiling water, cook two equal quantities of a green vegetable of your choice. Time how long it takes to cook each sample, from adding to the water to reaching boiling point, and from this stage to being cooked. Compare the colour of the finished products. Which do you think looks more appetising and why?

Starting with a boiling liquid

Placing foods directly into boiling or very hot liquid reduces their cooking time. This is most important for tender or delicate items, such as the broccoli in the picture, as it helps to stop the texture of the food getting damaged. For the same reason, the liquid should not be allowed to bubble too vigorously either.

A short cooking time also minimises the loss of Vitamin C from vegetables. Enzymes released when the vegetable is chopped or shredded attack the Vitamin C and destroy it. These enzymes are most active at warm temperatures: in one minute they can destroy up to 20 per cent of the Vitamin C content of vegetables put into warm water. Luckily when the temperature reaches boiling point, the destructive work of the enzymes is stopped. So the sooner boiling point is reached, the lower the loss of Vitamin C.

Which method to use

Potatoes or root vegetables, like carrots and parsnips, do not lose colour when they are over-boiled, and are often cooked by being put into cold water which is then brought to the boil. This method has the advantage that it is easier and safer to handle pots of cold water than pots of boiling water. The disadvantage is that the long time the water takes to reach boiling point will give the enzymes a good opportunity to destroy the Vitamin C in potatoes.

The amount of liquid movement allowed during boiling depends on the type of food being cooked. Prolonged, rapid boiling would cause these potatoes to break up, and not make them cook any more quickly. However, when a glazed effect is required, for example, with carrots, turnips or button onions, the speed of cooking is usually increased in the final stages in order to evaporate off the remaining water, leaving the butter and sugar used in the recipe to coat the vegetables.

Most of the goodness from these spring greens has been lost in the cooking liquid as a result of prolonged boiling in a large amount of water. If sodium bicarbonate had been added to improve the colour (a bad practice that you may come across), most of the Vitamin C would have been destroyed and the greens would have become very mushy.

Advantages of boiling

The general advantages of boiling are:

– the cooking liquid is in contact with the whole of the food's surface and so can transfer its heat energy to the food quickly and efficiently

– there is no drying out or browning

– the food's flavour can be added to by replacing the water with stock or milk, or by adding, for example, salt, spices, herbs, lemon, vinegar or wine to the water, where this will be a benefit

– flavour can be extracted from meats, fish and vegetables for the making of stocks, sauces and soups.

♦♦♦ TO DO

Blanch a cabbage leaf by plunging it into boiling water for about a minute, then stop the cooking process by putting the leaf into cold water. Take a second raw cabbage leaf of the same size. Try folding both the raw and blanched leaves and compare the results.

Boiling also has special advantages for particular types of food.

Vegetables can be cooked quickly so that they are tender but not flabby, and as long as the cooking time is kept short, only a small amount of Vitamin C will be lost. Green vegetables will keep their colour, and some white vegetables which might otherwise discolour (e.g. artichoke bottoms) should stay white if a little flour, salt and lemon juice is added to the water.

In jam-making, fruit has to be boiled to extract the pectin – which is what makes the jam set (although some fruits are low in pectin and have to have it added).

Meat that is tough can be made more tender by boiling (the collagen in the connective tissue is converted to gelatin).

Most meats that have been pickled or salted will need to be boiled to remove impurities and most of the salt or pickling compounds.

Shellfish can be tenderised by being cooked in a court-bouillon with vinegar.

✳ NUTRITION

If a pan is covered with a lid during cooking, less water needs to be used and the vegetables are partly cooked in steam. This helps to reduce loss of Vitamin C. The lid should be lifted from time to time during cooking to allow any volatile acids (such as those created during the cooking of cauliflower, broccoli or Brussels sprouts) to escape.

Green vegetables are an important source of Vitamin C in the average diet – provided that they are carefully prepared and cooked, as are potatoes especially when eaten in fairly large quantities. A serious deficiency in Vitamin C results in (among other things) a lack of connective tissue in the body. This leads to scurvy, a disease which makes teeth fall out and joints swell, and wounds take a long time to heal.

Carrots and spinach are important sources of carotene, which is converted by the body to retinol (Vitamin A). A deficiency in Vitamin A leads to difficulty in seeing in dim light and a severe deficiency can cause complete blindness. Vitamin A is also necessary for healthy skin.

Carotene does not dissolve in water and is stable at most cooking temperatures. Light and air do lead to some loss and prolonged storage of vegetables should be avoided.

△ SAFETY

Boiling is a good way of making foods safe to eat where there is a risk of food poisoning, as with meat, for example, because the high temperature kills most bacteria. But it is important to remember that some of the tiny, invisible and tough dormant spores that bacteria produce can even survive lengthy boiling. So boiled foods which are not going to be used straight away must be cooled rapidly and then stored at temperatures between 0° and 3°C (32°-37°F) so that any spores do not have a chance to germinate and grow.

Blanching — boiling as a method of pre-cooking

This information will help you with the Caterbase module, *Blanching*.

To shorten the pre-service cooking time of vegetables and to avoid holding them for a long time in a bain-marie or on a hotplate, some small catering establishments pre-cook vegetables by placing them for a very short time in a small amount of boiling water. This stage is known as blanching.

As soon as the vegetables are cooked, either they are plunged into cold water, or cold water is run into the saucepan through a sieve (this breaks up the water jet and prevents the vegetables, particularly if they are small like peas, from washing over the edge of the pan). This stage is known as refreshing.

The vegetables are then refrigerated until required for service when they are reheated, either by being plunged into boiling water or by microwaving.

The blanching/refreshing/reheating sequence is not good for the flavour or vitamin content of the vegetables, but if it is impractical to cook in small batches, or appropriate steaming equipment is not available, it is better to blanch than to hold completely cooked food on a hotplate for a long time.

Blanching is also used to:

— stabilise food before freezing or chilling (the brief boiling destroys the enzymes which cause discoloration and loss of Vitamin C)

— to make crispy vegetables such as cabbage and celery limp so they can be moulded and stuffed for braising

— to partly cook potatoes before roasting

— to make it easier to peel certain vegetables and skin some fruit.

By dropping these tomatoes into boiling water for 10 to 14 seconds, and then stopping the cooking immediately (plunging the tomatoes into cold water), only the skin softens and so it can be easily removed, while the flesh remains firm.

Soups, stocks, consommés, etc.

Boiling is the main process used in the preparation of soups of all types, and in the stocks that are put into them, as well as in the making of gravies and many sauces.

In the cases of stocks and consommés, the boiling process is used to extract the maximum flavour from the raw ingredients, transferring it to the liquid, which is then strained off. With broths and thickened soups, the boiling serves to blend the various flavours, enrich the liquid and cook the added ingredients, such as diced raw vegetables. It may also release the starch from cereals which have been added to thicken the liquid.

In order to produce this consommé, egg whites were mixed with finely chopped vegetables and minced meat. Cold stock was added and then heated. As the egg whites have set they have in effect collected together the vegetable and meat debris and any impurities in the stock to leave a clear consommé beneath.

31

Vegetables: their classification

The terms vegetable and fruit mean different things to different people. Most of the commodities referred to as vegetables are thought of as savoury. Fruits on the other hand are thought of as being sweet (with a few exceptions like the lemon).

Strictly speaking, tomatoes and aubergines, which are generally referred to as vegetables, are in fact fruits. The same is true of green beans, cucumbers, courgettes, marrow and pumpkin.

But as most people would call all the examples above vegetables, caterers do the same, and classify different types of vegetables according to which part of the plant is eaten:

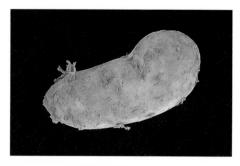

Carrots and turnips are examples of *root vegetables*. The root anchors the plant to the ground, and absorbs and transports moisture and nutrients from the soil up to the rest of the plant.

Potatoes are *tubers*. A tuber is an underground stem, which carries nutrients from the roots to the rest of the plant. It can also store nutrients.

Onions and leeks are *bulbs*. Bulbs are leaf bases swollen with water and carbohydrate stored for the next year's growth, and their many layers would eventually form leaves. A garlic clove is one of many bulblets in a bulb of garlic.

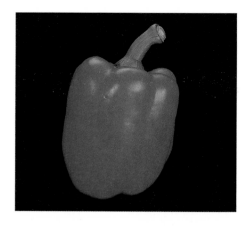

Most edible *leaves* are tender, like spinach, watercress and lettuce. In a process called photosynthesis, they use sunlight to produce food (in the form of sugar) plus oxygen.

Cauliflower and broccoli are examples of *flowers*, in fact of undeveloped flower buds, which would eventually develop male pollen and female ovules, to produce seeds.

The *fruit* is the only part of the plant intended to be eaten – an edible layer surrounding seeds. Animals eat the fruit and the seeds pass straight through the digestive system, and so are scattered far and wide.

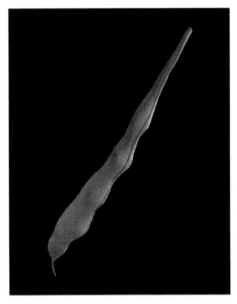

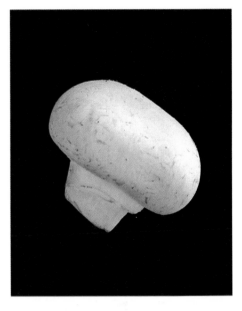

Stems eaten as vegetables include asparagus (stem with bud), celery and fennel.

Seeds eaten as vegetables include haricot beans and garden peas. French beans or mange-tout are seeds which are eaten complete with their seed cases.

Fungi – mushrooms, truffles, morels, etc. – are almost the only vegetable foodstuff that does not derive from a green plant.

Choosing and storing vegetables

It is advisable to use only good quality fresh vegetables. Poorer quality items may be cheaper but any savings will be lost in time wasted on trimming and cleaning. Good quality vegetables are generally clean, compact and crisp with a bright colour, no bruising or damage, and no signs of blight or disease.

Quality is obviously affected by seasonal availability, but modern methods of storage and transportation mean that many types of produce can be supplied from other parts of the world when they are out of season in Britain.

Once delivered to the kitchen, vegetables should be stored in a cool dry place, preferably on racks so that air can circulate freely around each vegetable. Disease and bruising are quickly passed on when vegetables are left packed tightly together in bags, sacks or boxes.

▸▸▸ TO DO

Put two saucepans of water on to boil. When the water has boiled, add a thinly sliced carrot to one and three leaves of thinly sliced cabbage to the other, so that the vegetables are completely covered by the water.

Compare the vegetables after you have cooked both for two minutes. Take the cabbage off the heat, and continue to cook the carrots until they are the same texture as the cabbage and note how long this takes.

Spoilage

The flavour and texture of most vegetables start to deteriorate from the moment they are picked. The cells go on using up food even though the plant has been cut off from food and water. Peas lose up to 40% of their sugar in six hours at room temperature. Broccoli and asparagus go on using sugar to make tough woody fibres.

If the vegetables dry out or wilt, the water loss from the cells will leave concentrated substances that may start to eat away at the cell walls. Damage to the cell walls can mean that enzymes will destroy Vitamin C, develop off-flavours and cause discoloration.

Mould spores quickly spread from mouldy foods to good foods and any damaged vegetable can easily get infected.

If vegetables are sealed off from air, alcohol builds up in them and eventually causes cell damage – this is why apples and pears that have been stored badly often have dry brown spots under the skin.

Low temperatures (e.g. refrigeration) reduce spoilage, but some vegetables and fruits that grow best in hot climates do not respond well to chilling: avocados darken and stay hard, banana skins go black.

Vegetables for boiling

Nearly all vegetables can be boiled successfully. Cooking happens quite fast – fibrous vegetables are softened and, with care, very little colour is lost. Exactly how long the cooking takes depends on the age, quality and size of the vegetable – young, freshly picked vegetables will cook faster than old ones.

For maximum flavour vegetables should be washed, cut and cooked as near to service time as possible. Cutting vegetables into small pieces reduces the cooking time, but as a greater surface area is exposed to the destructive action of the enzymes, it means that Vitamin C is lost. Overcooked vegetables break down quickly, which is useful when making puréed soups, when the vegetables are deliberately boiled for longer than normal to produce a smooth texture. Pulse vegetables such as lentils are particularly good for soup.

▶▶▶ TO DO

If you were in charge of preparing the vegetables for a self-service catering operation serving 100 lunches a day over a 2 hour period, what steps would you take to ensure that the cooked vegetables are at their best and as much of the vitamin content has been preserved as possible when they are served? Discuss your suggestions with your tutor or supervisor.

Roots, tubers, bulbs, etc. 1) Potatoes (old) 2) Celeriac 3) Swede 4) Eddoes 5) Kohlrabi 6) Leeks 7) Carrots 8) Turnips 9) Jerusalem artichokes 10) Salsify 11) Parsnips 12) Onions 13) Shallots 14) Potatoes (new).

Root vegetables, e.g. carrots, are often glazed after being boiled. Butter (or margarine) and sugar are added to the water at the start of cooking and as the water evaporates, they coat the vegetables, giving a glazed or shiny appearance.

Parsnips should be cut in quarters so that the hard inner cores can be removed before cooking. Swedes and turnips need to have the fibrous flesh below the skin removed when they are peeled. Salsify can be blanched after washing to make peeling easier. Like celeriac, it should then be left in cold water with the addition of a little lemon juice to prevent discolouring before cooking. Salsify, celeriac and swede all become glassy or opaque when cooked.

Tubers, e.g. potatoes, yams and sweet potatoes, need to be handled carefully as they break up easily once cooked. There are many varieties of potato, each with a different texture. Some (usually new) are 'waxy' and others (usually old-crop) are 'floury'. Floury potatoes tend to break up when cooked and are best suited to dishes which need puréed potato.

Potatoes should be stored in dark, cool conditions. Light and warmth will make the potato produce alkaloids, which are poisonous and turn the skin green. If the skin has turned green, potatoes should ideally be thrown away, and at the very least heavily peeled. Eyes in the potato or new shoots are also harmful and should be removed. Peeling should usually be thin, because most of the nutrients lie just beneath the skin.

Bulb vegetables hold their shape well, if cooked whole. Whole onions are sometimes used in boiled dishes such as boiled beef and dumplings, but if served separately they are more likely to be braised, when they would normally be blanched first before being finished in the oven. Leeks can be boiled quickly as a vegetable or cut into strips, blanched and used as a garnish. When peeling onions and shallots, take care not to remove the root end as this helps to hold the vegetable together.

Leaves, flowers, fruits, stems and seeds.
1) White cabbage 2) Cauliflower
3) Savoy cabbage 4) Spaghetti marrow
5) Spring greens 6) Butternut squash
7) Broccoli 8) Celery 9) Asparagus
10) Globe artichoke 11) Chayote
12) Fennel 13) Doody (bottle gourd)
14) Runner beans 15) Baby corn
16) Spinach 17) Mange-tout
18) Courgettes 19) French beans.

Leaf vegetables (which include Brussels sprouts and lettuce) tend to be rather delicate and are easily over-cooked. Lettuce, especially, will go limp very fast when cooked, and lose colour and nutritional value.

Flower vegetables are difficult to cook because the stalk tends to be tough and the flower very delicate. If the stalk is tough it should be removed or split. It is a common mistake to cook the stalk until it is edible and end up overcooking the delicate flower.

The leaves of broccoli are a better source of Vitamin A than the buds and so are well worth eating. A cauli-flower stem should have a cone-shaped hollow cut in it to help make cooking even.

Fruits used as vegetables (which include tomatoes, peppers, cucumbers and aubergines) overcook easily although they do not usually lose much colour.

Tomatoes are not usually boiled – they tend to be grilled, baked or served cold. But blanching is often used as a way of loosening the skin before removing it.

Stem vegetables tend to be fibrous. Celery, especially, usually benefits from prolonged cooking, which is why it is often braised after initial blanching.

Asparagus shoots are available, broadly speaking, in three colours: green, white and violet (when the tips are between pink and violet or purple). The straighter the shoot and the more compact the tip the better the quality. They are graded by length of spear and width of the shoot.

Seed vegetables can usually be boiled.

Broad beans should be shelled, but the skin of the bean itself is left on. French beans and runner beans are topped and tailed. The coarse fibres on the outer edges of runner beans are removed and then the beans are usually cut into strips (of about 2 mm).

In their dried form many seeds are known as 'pulses' (*see* next page).

Fungi, which include mushrooms, are not normally boiled, except when used in the preparation of soups.

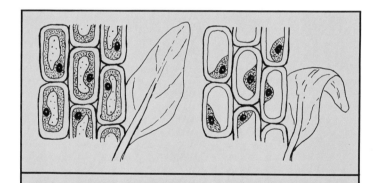

The cell walls of all flowering plants contain a tough substance called cellulose that humans cannot digest. This is partly dissolved during cooking. But the main constituent of plant cells is water, although the amount in the cells can vary. When the cells are full of water, the walls bulge a little, and the pressure of a lot of full cells pressing on each other produces the rigid structure and crisp texture that vegetables and fruit should have when bought and eaten. When the cells lose water, the vegetable becomes limp.

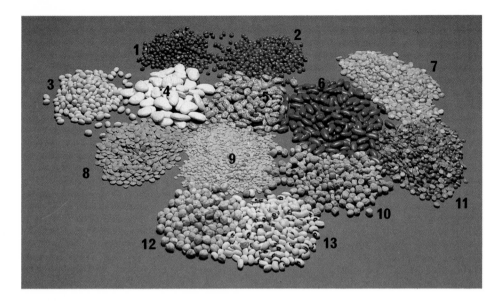

Pulses 1) Mung beans 2) Aduki beans 3) Haricot beans 4) Butter beans 5) Pinto beans 6) Red kidney beans 7) Yellow split peas 8) Green lentils 9) Red split lentils 10) Marrowfat peas 11) Green split peas 12) Chickpeas 13) Blackeye beans.

Pulses

Pulses will cook faster and more easily if they have been soaked – four hours is usually enough but some need soaking overnight, and even then they often need to be cooked for much longer than other types of vegetable. This is because pulses contain poisons and other substances that interfere with digestion. Cooking at high temperatures for a long time makes these potentially dangerous substances harmless. This is the reason for the instruction on packets of pulses (such as red kidney beans) that they should be boiled rapidly for at least 15 minutes in an uncovered saucepan. A tiny amount of bicarbonate of soda can be added to the water to soften the pulses during cooking without too much nutritional loss.

✳ NUTRITION

Pulses are highly nutritious. They are a very good source of fibre, protein, vitamins and minerals and have the added advantage of being low in fat. Their protein content makes them a very good alternative to meat especially when they are used in combination with cereals such as wheat flour. Vegetarians, who do not eat meat, and vegans, who avoid all animal products, are able to rely on pulses as their main source of protein.

△ SAFETY

When using tinned food, check each tin carefully before opening. Look for any holes or signs of rust which might indicate deterioration of the contents. A 'blown' tin, where each end is forced outwards by gas pressure building up inside, is a sure sign of trouble. The gas is created by bacterial growth, and the contents should on no account be used. Any tins in this state should be returned immediately to the supplier.

Convenience vegetables

Many caterers rely on so-called 'convenience' vegetables, that have had most of the cleaning and preparation done before the caterer buys them. They can be frozen, tinned, dried or pre-peeled and trimmed. Pre-peeled potatoes are chemically treated (with Dri-White) to prevent discoloration.

Good quality frozen vegetables have the advantage that they are often frozen only hours after harvesting and so may have a fresher taste and higher vitamin content than so-called 'fresh' vegetables that may have spent days or even weeks in warehouses.

Quality and value for money among tinned vegetables may vary considerably, so it makes sense to sample various brands before ordering large quantities. If you want to compare the value of, say, two tins of peas, drain the contents first.

▶▶▶ TO DO

Under separate headings, list the vegetables that your employer buys fresh, frozen, tinned, trimmed or peeled. Ask why your employer has a preference for each category. Find the price of one type of frozen vegetable and compare it with the price for the same vegetable if bought fresh. Can you explain the difference?

Cereals

Cereals are one of the main sources of starch. They are sometimes boiled whole: barley and rice are used to give body to soups and stews. But on the whole cereals are boiled in their milled state to provide the starch used to thicken and stabilise sauces, soups, gravies and certain sweet dishes.

Most cereals, including grains such as wheat, barley, oats, corn and rice, come from plants in the grass family. These seeds or kernels are an important source of carbohydrate (starch), protein and dietary fibre.

The structure of all cereal grains is more or less the same: the major part, the centre (called the endosperm), stores most of the carbohydrates and protein. Surrounding this, and the small germ or embryo from which the new plant will grow, are a number of layers including the seed coat. These are known as the bran coatings. Grains of oats, barley and rice are also surrounded by a thin but tough protective structure called the husk.

Cereal grains are ground or milled to separate the bran, the germ and the endosperm. The bran is leathery, the germ oily and the endosperm breaks up easily.

In whole-grain flours (brown flours) the germ and bran are put back at the end of the milling process. White flour has a number of nutrients added to it after being milled, because it has lost so much nutritional value in the stripping off of the germ and the bran.

Other sources of starch are potatoes, arrowroot (made from a West Indian plant called maranta), tapioca (made from cassava root) and sago (made from the sago palm).

> **How starches thicken**
> When starch is heated in liquid, the starch granules absorb water and swell.
>
> The temperature needed for this to happen varies. For wheat flour it is about 60°-65°C (140°-148°F). At first the mixture will look as though it is clearing, but soon it becomes more opaque.
>
> After reaching its thickest state (about 93°C for wheat flour), the liquid starts to thin slightly. Prolonged heating, boiling or vigorous stirring shatter the swollen and fragile starch granules into very small fragments, and the result is a thinner liquid.
>
> On cooling the starch molecules move less and less, and the liquid gets progressively thicker. Eventually the mixture will congeal, with water settling into the tiny pockets left between the starch molecules. This is why a sauce which seems to have a perfect consistency when it is first made gets thicker after it has been poured over the slightly cooler food and may even congeal.

Starches for thickening

The type of starch chosen for a particular recipe depends on the qualities that are required in the finished dish.

Wheat flour produces a milky appearance. It has a relatively low thickening power in relation to the amount used and if added directly to the liquid, a noticeable taste of raw flour often remains. Cooking the flour in butter or fat before adding the liquid (that is making a roux) gets rid of this raw flavour.

A second reason for using a roux is that wheat flours are difficult to moisten evenly. The starch granules stick together and form lumps easily. The fat in a roux keeps the starch grains separate.

Tapioca is usually available in the form of tiny balls, and is used for thickening sweet puddings.

Semolina is the coarsest grade of milled wheat. There are also types of semolina made from rice or maize.

Besan flour (produced from chick peas) has a slightly greater thickening power than wheat flour and a higher fibre content. Its yellow appearance and distinctive smell diminish with cooking.

Cornflour (made from maize) thickens more efficiently than wheat flour and gives a sauce a translucent, slightly glossy finish. But it too produces a raw taste, unless pre-cooked.

Arrowroot and *potato starch* have little taste and an even greater thickening power than cornflour. So they are useful for last-minute corrections.

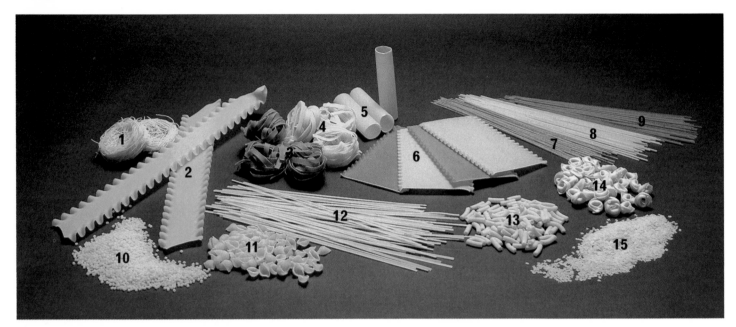

Pasta

This information will help you gain the Caterbase module, *Preparing Farinaceous Products*.

Most types of pasta are made from the same basic recipe, but they come in many different shapes, sizes and even colours. Most pasta is creamy yellow, but there is also green pasta – traditionally made by adding spinach to the mix, and red pasta, coloured with tomato.

Water and flour are the two basic ingredients. Wheat flours are usually used for home-made pastas and commercially-made flat noodles. Durum wheat semolina (made from the larger pieces of endosperm that are sifted out during the milling process) is used for commercially-made pastas. Semolina-based noodles are less brittle than flour-based noodles. Some Italian-style pasta is made with eggs (*all'uovo*).

The high starch content of pasta means that it has to be handled carefully during cooking. It should be placed in rapidly boiling water and then stirred to prevent sticking. Rapid boiling should then continue as the movement of the water will help to prevent the pasta from settling to the bottom of the pan and sticking together. Plenty of water is normally used, which helps to disperse some of the starch.

The pasta should be tested every few minutes to find out when the right texture has been reached and cooking should stop. This is normally before it gets too soft when it is slightly resistant to chewing, a texture sometimes known by the Italian expression – *al dente*.

Once the pasta has been drained it can be tossed with a little oil, which helps prevent the pasta from sticking together. Alternatively oil may be added during the boiling, but most of this will float to the surface and be wasted.

Pasta shapes 1) Vermicelli 2) Lasagne strips 3) Green tagliatelle 4) Tagliatelle 5) Cannelloni 6) Green and white lasagne 7) Whole wheat spaghetti 8) Spaghetti 9) Green spaghetti 10) Pastine 11) Pasta shells 12) Spaghettini 13) Short macaroni 14) Tortellini 15) Alphabet pasta.

▶▶▶ TO DO

Bring 2 litres of water to the boil and add 100 g (4 oz) of dried spaghetti. Keep the pan over the heat for 12 minutes, but do not allow it to boil and do not stir it. Drain the spaghetti into a colander, and allow it to stand for five minutes.

You should now do the same again but this time allow the water to boil rapidly and stir the spaghetti from time to time. When you have drained the spaghetti refresh it with cold water. Compare the appearance and texture of the two batches.

Rice

There are about 2,500 varieties of rice. Most are white or brown or almost transparent. Long grain rice was traditionally used for plain boiled or savoury dishes and short grain rice for milk puddings and sweet dishes, but now that such a huge range of rice is available the distinction between long and short grain and their uses is much less clear.

Indian rice is long grained and tends to be dry, flaky and separates easily when cooked. Other similar long-grained rices are grown in the United States, and all of these are used for savoury dishes. Japanese rice is short-grained and is moist, firm and sticky when cooked because of a high proportion of waxy starch granules. This is better for sweet dishes.

The appearance of rice is greatly affected by the milling process it has been through. If only the hull has been removed the result is brown rice (which contains a great deal of fibre). White rice has had the hull, the bran and most of the germ removed, and sometimes has vitamins added (to replace those lost during processing).

Instant rice (which has been cooked and then dried) is available to caterers. To reconstitute it, water or stock is added and then heated.

Wild rice is only distantly related to common rice. It was first found growing in shallow lakes and marshes in the Great Lakes region of North America and is now cultivated, but it is very expensive, partly because of the special milling process that has to be used. Before hulling, the rice is fermented for one to two weeks to develop the characteristic nutty flavour. The rice is then heated to make the husks easier to remove and to brown the grains, then pounded, then rubbed. The heating gives it a smoky flavour which can be removed by washing the rice before using it. Wild rice is difficult to cook from raw, so it tends to be bought in a partly cooked state.

Some rice is *parboiled* before milling. This process gelatinises the starch in the grain, and has the effect of preserving most of the B vitamins. Milled rice is the principal food for hundreds of thousands of people in the world and before it was known that parboiling could be used in this way a disease called Beri Beri, caused by deficiency of one of the B vitamins, reached epidemic proportions in Asia. The other effect of parboiling is that it stops the enzymes that make the rice taste rancid, so the shelf life of the rice is extended. Final cooking time is the same, or even longer than ordinary rice.

Rice and wild rice 1) Basmati rice
2) Long grain brown rice 3) Wild rice mixed with brown rice 4) Long grain Patna rice 5) Short grain pudding rice 6) Long grain brown rice.

Meat

Boiling is a good way of using cuts of meat that are on the whole unsuitable for faster methods of cookery. Meat can be tough, either because it comes from an old animal or because it comes from a part of the animal where the muscle had to do a lot of work. The lengthy cooking in a moist environment that boiling provides helps to soften tough fibres and connective tissue. So meat which is very flavoursome but would otherwise be too tough to eat is well served by boiling.

Boiling is also suitable for cured meats, whether they are dry salted, salted in brine (sometimes known as pickled) or smoked.

Because the meat is completely immersed in the cooking liquid while it is being boiled its size is unimportant: joints can be as small as 1 kg or as large as 6 kg. What is important is that the joint should be of even shape so that heat penetrates evenly through it during cooking.

Leg of mutton is a good example of the type of meat most suited to boiling, but not easy to buy. It is from an animal over 1 year old and has a much fuller flavour than young lamb.

Silverside and *brisket* are typical examples of the tougher parts of the beef carcase that are often preserved by the salting process. Salted silverside is usually referred to as 'salt beef'. In the picture, left to right, fresh brisket, salted brisket, salted silverside and fresh silverside. A protective layer of fat has been added to the salted brisket.

Thick flank beef, a joint from the hind quarter of beef, is not normally salted and so is boiled from fresh.

Tripe is usually the stomach lining of the ox (although pig and sheep tripe are occasionally used). It is used fresh or pickled and is boiled for several hours in many recipes. It has a rich flavour and contains a great deal of gelatin, but is not easy to digest, even after long cooking.

Tongue can be used fresh or cured. Pickled ox and sheep's tongue should be soaked in cold water for several hours before boiling. Tinned ox tongue has been preserved, cooked and pressed by the manufacturer.

Ox tail. Used for making soup. The boiling process extracts the maximum flavour from the meat and bone.

Beef and *veal bones* play an important part in making stocks (as do the bones and trimmings from poultry, mutton, game and fish). After the meat has been removed, the bones are broken up and any fat or marrow removed before browning (brown stocks) or adding to the liquid (white stocks). For instructions on making stocks, *see* Introduction/Stocks.

Belly of pork and *pig's trotters* are suitable for boiling. The large trotter on the left of the picture has been cut in this way from the front leg of the carcase to improve the presentation of the shoulder joint. At the top of the picture is a roll of pork belly.

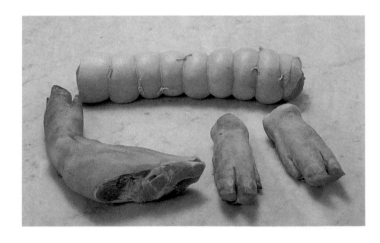

Bacon cuts for boiling 1) Smoked fore hock 2) Smoked gammon 3) Smoked collar 4) Green collar 5) Green gammon 6) Green fore hock.

Bacon. The pigs used for bacon, which is salted meat that is sometimes also smoked, are a different breed from those used for pork, and usually have a much larger carcase. Unsmoked bacon is sometimes referred to as 'green'. Most of a bacon carcase can be boiled although the best cuts (back, streaky and middle) are generally saved for grilling. The most popular bacon joints for boiling are:

Hock and *collar* – tough, full flavoured shoulder and neck cuts. These are often boiled and served with a variety of vegetables. One traditional recipe has cabbage boiled in the cooking liquid after the meat has been removed. Hock bacon is often used to add flavour to pulse soups. The small amount of fat from the bacon also helps improve the texture of the finished soup, which contains no other fat.

Gammon, the hind leg from the bacon carcase, is often cut into steaks and grilled, but it is equally good boiled whole and served, thinly sliced, hot or cold.

Ham is the hind leg, removed from the carcase and cured separately. Boiled ham is one of the most popular forms of cold, cooked meat.

Poultry

Boiling fowls (usually old laying hens) produce tasty boiled dishes, although the flesh can be a bit stringy. Cooking should be started in cold water.

Younger chickens that are boiled very gently are often described (inaccurately) on menus as 'poached'. The cooking liquid is thickened and made into a sauce to accompany the dish.

The chicken carcase and any bones left over after jointing for, say, poached or shallow fried dishes, are excellent for producing chicken stocks.

BOILING

Fish and shellfish

This section will help you with the Caterbase module, *Preparing Shellfish*.

Boiling is generally not the best method of cooking fish. If fish is to be cooked in liquid this should be done at a temperature just below boiling point so that the fish is neither overcooked nor broken up by the bubbling action of the cooking liquid. In other words, it should be poached. Some chefs recommend that poached fish should be cooked in liquid that is just at (rather than just below) boiling point. They may even call this boiling, although the finished dish would almost never be described on the menu as 'boiled'. Shellfish (*see* below) are the exception to all this, and boiling is perhaps the most usual method of cooking them.

One obvious use of boiling in fish cookery is to produce fish stock (*see* Introduction/Stocks), which can then be an ingredient for a sauce or the base for a soup. Unlike beef stock, fish stock needs only a short cooking time.

▶▶ TO DO

Which shellfish can you buy in your locality? Visit a fishmonger and/or local supermarkets and find out what is available. If possible talk to the fishmonger and find out what is most popular and whether there is a demand for more unusual shellfish.

Shellfish are grouped into two categories:

- Crustaceans, e.g. lobsters and crabs, have jointed legs and a tough outer layer covering the whole of the body.

- Molluscs, e.g. mussels and whelks, have soft bodies and usually have a shell into which they can retreat.

Shellfish should be bought live whenever possible. This is the only way to guarantee freshness. Unlike fish, though, shellfish can survive for some time out of water so long as they are kept cool and damp. Crustaceans will show signs of life by obvious movement. The shells of molluscs should be tightly closed or shut rapidly when tapped. If the shells are open or close slowly then it is likely that the creature is dead or dying and the flesh is deteriorating, so they should not be used.

Plunging shellfish into boiling water is considered by most chefs to be the most humane way of killing them.

Buying points

Live shellfish

- All shellfish should sound heavy and full when tapped lightly.

- Crabs and lobsters should have been packed together to keep them moist. Check that there are no claws missing.

- Large lobster claws should be bound with elastic bands to prevent fighting and injury.

- Lobster tails should spring back into place after being uncurled.

Cooked shellfish

- The shells should be intact. If they are cracked, the flavour and texture of the meat may have been damaged by water during cooking.

- Crab and lobster should feel 'heavy' for their size. If they feel light or the shells are soft, they may have cast their shell recently and grown a new one. This rather exhausting process affects their eating quality.

- Poor-quality cooked crab and lobster may contain liquid (this can be tested by shaking them gently) which indicates that the flesh has shrunk inside the shell, a result of overcooking or freezing under poor storage conditions.

Shellfish 1) and 3) Crabs 2) Crawfish (spiny lobster) 4) Mussels 5) King prawns 6) Prawns 7) Scampi (Dublin Bay prawns or langoustines) 8) Lobster. All cooked, except for the mussels.

Cooking shellfish

Crustaceans can be boiled in salted water or in a court-bouillon (*see* next page) in which the acid has a tender-ising effect. The shells help the flesh to keep its shape and protect it from damage, but great care should be taken not to overcook the shellfish or they will become tough.

Boiling is the usual cooking method for crustaceans that are going to be served cold. Pre-cooked shellfish should be stored at 0°-4°C (32°-39°F) for not more than two days. Sometimes the cooked fish is replaced in the shell as an attractive form of presentation.

Boiling is also often used to pre-cook shellfish that are to be cooked by another method, such as grilling or shallow frying.

Mussels and whelks are the only molluscs that are usually boiled. Other molluscs, such as scallops, are more often cooked by different methods such as poaching, grilling or shallow frying.

When shellfish are at their best

	January	February	March	April	May	June	July	August	September	October	November	December
Crustaceans												
Crab				▓	▓	▓	▓	▓	▓	▓		
Crawfish				▓	▓	▓	▓	▓	▓	▓		
Crayfish	▓	▓	▓						▓	▓	▓	▓
Lobster				▓	▓	▓	▓	▓	▓			
Prawns	▓	▓	▓	▓	▓	▓	▓	▓	▓	▓	▓	▓
Scampi				▓	▓	▓	▓	▓	▓			
Shrimps	▓	▓									▓	▓
Molluscs												
Cockles						▓	▓	▓	▓	▓	▓	▓
Mussels	▓	▓	▓						▓	▓	▓	▓
Oysters	▓	▓	▓						▓	▓	▓	▓
Scallops	▓	▓	▓							▓	▓	▓
Squid						▓	▓	▓	▓	▓		
Whelks	▓	▓	▓						▓	▓	▓	▓
Winkles	▓	▓	▓						▓	▓	▓	▓

2 BOILING

Terms

Boiling is cooking in a liquid at its boiling point. The liquid used might be water, stock, milk or a combination of these with added herbs and flavourings.

Simmering is a gentle boiling action, when the surface of the liquid is only just broken by small bubbles.

Blanching is a method of pre-cooking or part-cooking food, particularly vegetables, by plunging them briefly into a small amount of boiling water. It is also a method of removing impurities from poor quality joints.

Refreshing is cooling food after blanching by plunging it into cold water or running cold water over it.

Court-bouillons are cooking liquids that are used to improve flavour and sometimes to tenderise. They include an acid such as lemon juice, wine or vinegar and flavouring ingredients such as onions and carrots, herbs and seasonings. The ingredients and their quantities depend on the type of food being cooked (*see* Poaching/Terms & Equipment).

Blanc is the name of a liquid used to protect the colour and texture of white vegetables and meats when they are being boiled. Lemon juice and flour are added to the cooking water – the flour thickens the water slightly and gives a more gentle cooking movement so reducing the risk of the food breaking up and the lemon juice prevents any discoloration.

Al dente which translates literally from the Italian as 'to the tooth' describes foods (usually pasta, and sometimes vegetables) which have been cooked to a point where they are still firm when bitten into.

Equipment

Saucepans come in a wide variety of shapes and sizes:
– with thick, solid bases to ensure an even spread of heat
– with a wide base and low sides for boiling joints of meat and similar large items (and possibly the vegetables or dumplings that are to be served with the finished dish)
– with a small diameter and tall sides for keeping sauces warm in a larger container of hot water or bain marie
– double saucepans in which one saucepan fits into another larger one that usually contains water in order to provide the gentle heat needed for cooking sauces and delicate items in the top saucepan
– with a wide base and medium height for stews that start with liquid
– with a wide base and very low sides for stews which need a large surface area in relation to their volume. They might, for example, be started with shallow frying and then simmered in stock
– with sloping sides to prevent the food burning on the sides (as in a milk pan)
– with a lip for easy pouring
– with handles on both sides for easy lifting or for dishes that are started on top of the stove and then transferred to the oven
– with a long handle if the pan needs to be held firmly for stirring or shaking, or is light enough to be lifted safely with one hand.

Stockpots are large saucepans (sometimes free-standing with their own heat and water supply) with a tap at the bottom allowing stock to be drained off easily, made of aluminium, stainless steel or tin-lined copper.

Cleaning and maintenance
Saucepans should be washed in hot water and detergent, rinsed in clean hot water and dried thoroughly.
  Steam-jacketed kettles, free-standing stockpots and bratt pans should be turned off and allowed to cool before being washed with a mild detergent solution and well rinsed.
  Thermostats should be checked, counterbalanced lids and tilting mechanisms oiled regularly.

Aluminium is perhaps the most widely used metal for cooking vessels. It is hard-wearing, a good conductor of heat and fairly inexpensive in comparison with other metals. Only the heavier gauges of aluminium are suitable for use in catering establishments.

A disadvantage of aluminium saucepans is their tendency to discolour light-coloured foods. Acids, alkalis and hydrogen sulphide (produced, for example, by over-cooked cabbage and rotten eggs) penetrate the metal surface and cause small amounts of grey or black substances to be formed. Metal spoons should not be used for stirring sauces or soups because they will damage the protective coating of aluminium oxide which develops on the pan's surface.

Copper is a very good conductor, which means that it heats up quickly and evenly. It can be dangerous, however, because cooking liquids can dissolve the copper and produce copper compounds that are poisonous. This is why most copper cooking utensils are lined with tin. Tin lining must be replaced as soon as it begins to wear. Tinned copper saucepans should never be left empty on a hot stove as this will cause the lining to melt. Sugar boilers made of copper are not lined because the tin would melt at the high temperatures reached during use.

Stainless steel saucepans are very expensive and unless they have extra solid bases (some incorporate copper bases) give uneven heating. Stainless steel is a relatively poor conductor of heat, but it is very resistant to damage in cooking and to most cleaning agents.

Above: stockpot. *Top right:* steam-jacketed kettle. *Bottom right:* induction cooker.

Opposite page: 1) Colander 2), 6), 7) Various aluminium pans 3) Bain-marie pan 4) Sugar boiler 5) Tin-lined copper saucepan 8) Milk pan 9) Double boiler 10) Stainless steel pan 11) Wire basket 12) Perforated spoon 13) Skimmer 14) Ladle 15) Wire scoop (pea ladle).

Induction cookers are one of the newer types of equipment used in catering. They are expensive to buy but tend to save on energy costs.

In the cooker there is an electrically generated magnetic field that attracts and repels the base of the cooking utensil placed on the cooker with an alternating current. The overall effect is that the molecules of metal in the utensil are sent into a frenzied activity by the continually changing direction of the magnetic field and so generate heat. This heat is transferred to the liquid and/or food inside the utensil.

The power can be adjusted and this controls the strength of the magnetic field. The stronger the magnetic field, the faster the molecules move and the more heat they generate.

The top of the cooker is made of non-magnetic vitro-ceramic material, strong enough to withstand the weight and heat of the utensils. Because it is non-magnetic it doesn't get hot. This means that the kitchen remains far cooler and more pleasant to work in and cleaning is easier (spills on the top don't burn). As the cooker only works when a pan is resting on it, less energy is used, so operating costs are quite low.

Only ferrous cooking utensils (those made of steel or iron) will heat up on an induction cooker. Other utensils (e.g. copper or stainless steel) are not suitable unless they have an iron base – these are sometimes called ferrous-based vessels. A quick way of checking whether a saucepan is suitable is by seeing if a magnet will stick tightly to it.

Steam-jacketed kettles or boilers provide an alternative to large saucepans or stock pots heated on the top of a range. Steam is forced into a kind of double jacket and its heat passes through the internal surface of the boiler to the food. This equipment has the advantage of providing a source of heat all round the food rather than from the base of the pan only.

It is important to control the temperature of the jacket to prevent too vigorous boiling. Some equipment does this automatically. Mechanical stirrers are available on some steam boilers.

Bratt pans, sometimes called tilting pans or skillets when equipped with a tilting mechanism, are not as good for boiling large quantities of food as steam-jacketed kettles. Their shape and smaller capacity is designed to deal with combined cooking processes, such as shallow frying and stewing, when a large flat bottom is useful. Nevertheless the tilting models do enable large quantities of liquid to be easily handled. Cooking control is provided by the thermostat.

 **BOILING**

Essential points

You will need to know the following steps to qualify for the Caterbase *Boiling/Simmering* module.

1. Prepare the work area, select the equipment you need, making sure it is clean and of the correct type and size.

> If you are cooking vegetables, a minimum amount of water should be used to cut down on vitamin loss, so choose a saucepan of a size and shape that will hold the vegetables easily, but will not need much water to cover them.
>
> Rice or pasta should be in a pan large enough to allow room for stirring during the cooking.
>
> If you are boiling a joint of meat which will need a vegetable garnish or dumplings cooked in the same liquid, make sure you choose a big enough saucepan.
>
> When boiling sugar, choose an unlined copper saucepan. The smooth surface will stop undissolved sugar crystals getting trapped and causing crystallisation.

2. Collect all the ingredients you need, checking that you have the right quantities and that the quality is suitable. Prepare them as appropriate.

> Don't use a blunt knife when preparing vegetables. Not only are you likely to cut yourself by having to press so hard that the knife may easily slip, but the blunt edge will bruise the vegetables more than a clean cut would and cause loss of Vitamin C.
>
> Never soak prepared vegetables in cold water before cooking because water-soluble vitamins will be lost. The exception is potatoes, which will discolour unless they are placed directly into cold water after peeling.
>
> Pulses should be soaked for at least four hours before cooking and salted meats for 24 hours.
>
> Frozen meat should be allowed to thaw completely before boiling. Frozen vegetables, on the other hand, should not be defrosted before cooking.

∗ NUTRITION

Potatoes which are going to be sautéd or used in a potato salad should not be peeled before boiling. Peeling after cooking means that very little flesh will be lost and more nutrients saved.

3. Check that the heat source you are going to use is ready.

> If you are using a solid top heated by gas or electricity then it should be pre-heated (but that does not mean left on for hours before it is required).

△ SAFETY

Be very careful when moving large pans of boiling liquid. If a hot pan is too heavy for you to handle safely on your own, and there are two handles, get another person to take the other handle, or use a ladle to remove some of the contents to another pan.

4. Use sufficient liquid for the item you are boiling.

For green vegetables use less water than will cover the food and put a lid on the pot during cooking. This will mean that some of the food will be partly cooked in steam and that loss of Vitamin C will not be too severe. Check on the vegetables during cooking and toss or turn them over carefully with a spoon.

Use plenty of water when cooking pasta, rice and eggs (so that the water returns to boiling as soon as possible after the food has been added).

For other information relating to points 5-9, *see* tables on next spread.

5. Decide whether the food you are cooking should be put into cold or boiling liquid.

6. Add seasonings, flavourings and thickenings as required.

Consider using spices or herbs as an alternative to salt. High salt intake can cause high blood pressure, a major risk factor for coronary heart disease.

When adding thickenings, stir thoroughly to obtain a smooth result.

▶▶ TO DO

Draw up a list of four dishes which are usually boiled with added salt. Discuss with your colleagues whether the quantity of salt could be reduced without spoiling the flavour, and what herbs or spices could be used in its place.

7. Maintain the temperature at boiling and liquid movement at the right level for the foods being cooked.

8. Skim the liquid if fat or impurities form a scum on the surface.

Skimming a stock or soup regularly will prevent impurities (which would cloud it or spoil the flavour) from being boiled back into the liquid.

Push the scum to one side of the pot using the outside of the ladle. Then move the lip of the ladle just under the surface of the liquid and scoop up the scum. Take care not to remove the good liquid at the same time.

9. Make sure the cooking happens evenly to avoid food burning, sticking or drying out.

This may involve stirring but some foods should not be stirred, or stirred only at specific stages.

10. When the food is cooked, remove it from the heat.

Test to see if the food is thoroughly cooked. Recipe timings should be used only as guidance because they cannot take account of variations in the quality or size of the food. Use the tip of the knife blade, or a cocktail stick (but avoid damaging the food) to determine when the texture has reached the degree of tenderness required. For rice, take a few sample grains out of the water with a perforated spoon and press them between your thumb and forefinger to test the texture (and then discard them).

△ SAFETY

When boiling sugar mixtures, take great care to avoid burning yourself and always have a bowl of cold water next to you to put your hands into immediately if you get splashed.

If the burn is at all serious or if the eyes are affected, go to the nearest hospital casualty department for help. For minor scalds and burns, hold the burnt area under running cold water or wrap ice cubes in a clean cloth and hold them on the burn or scald until the sting has gone out of the area.

Fibre

Dietary fibre is a collection of complex carbohydrates including: celluloses (the fibrous substances that make up plant cell walls), pectins (found in many fruits when they often aid setting of jam or jellies) and the completely indigestible lignin (a woody substance found in some vegetables). None of these can be digested by the body and used to provide energy. But they do provide the valuable service of giving bulk to the waste products of digestion, making it easier for them to be got rid of.

Unrefined wholegrain cereals are high in fibre, so are pulses, fruit and vegetables. There is still a lot of research being done into the benefits of fibre, but in general it is thought that a high fibre diet is better than a low fibre one. A report published in 1983 by the National Advisory Committee on Nutrition Education (NACNE) recommended that fibre intakes should be about 30g per day – a 50% increase on the average UK intake.

▸▸▸ TO DO

Choose one of the recipes from the Practical Examples that follow. Work out how long it would take you to prepare the recipe and what equipment you would need. If possible, calculate the cost of the ingredients.

Foods and how to boil them

ITEM	COOKING LIQUID & SEASONINGS	TEMPERATURE WHEN FOOD ADDED	COMMENTS
Stocks	Water	Cold	No stock should be boiled too vigorously or it will become cloudy Cool stocks quickly after cooking, allowing the air to circulate under the pot, and never covering with a lid
Consommés	Stock	Cold	Do not stir once a crust has started to form, and simmer the liquid gently to keep it clear
Meat	Water or stock	Cold	To test whether the meat is cooked, pierce it with a skewer or trussing needle. Hardly any pressure should be needed if the meat is cooked
Crab and lobster	Water or court-bouillon	Boiling	Lobster, especially, should be boiled rapidly, so that the black and rather unattractive ovary of the female turns red
Vegetables	Water	Boiling	Use as soon as possible after cooking to prevent colour deterioration and reduce vitamin loss
Glazed vegetables	Water, butter and sugar	Cold	Boil to evaporate all cooking liquid and leave a glaze
Rice and pasta	Water	Boiling	Stir occasionally during cooking
Pulses	Water	Boiling	Boil vigorously for the first 15 minutes to get rid of poisonous compounds
Eggs	Water	Boiling	If hard-boiled eggs are to be served cold, cool quickly after boiling
Fruit, jams, jellies, sauces	Water, acid, sugar	Cold	Thicken with natural or commercial pectin depending on fruit
Fruit pulps, purées	Water, lemon juice, sugar	Cold	Stir frequently to prevent burning
Sugar products without fat, e.g. caramel	Water	Cold	Do not stir
Sugar products with fat, e.g. fudge	Depends on recipe	Cold	Stir while cooking to prevent the milk fats and solids burning
Sweet starch mixtures e.g. custard	Milk	Boiling	Stir frequently to cook starch as fast as possible, ensure an even texture, and to prevent burning. Add sugar on completion of cooking (to reduce chance of burning and to minimise thinning effect produced by sugar)
Cornflour and arrowroot sauces	Depends on recipe	Boiling	First mix the cornflour or arrowroot with a little cold liquid and when adding it to boiling liquid, stir constantly

Boiled leg of mutton with caper sauce

INGREDIENTS   SERVES 10 to 15

3½ kg	leg of mutton	7¾ lb
450 g	small onions	1 lb 2 oz
450 g	small carrots	1 lb 2 oz
450 g	swedes or turnips	1 lb 2 oz
450 g	celery	1 lb 2 oz
450 g	small leeks	1 lb 2 oz

bouquet garni
water or cold white stock to cover
seasoning
chopped parsley (optional)

1. Prepare the leg of mutton for boiling.
   a) Cut out the aitch bone (to make carving easier).
   b) Trim the meat from the leg bone just above the knuckle, then saw off the knuckle so that a piece of clean bone about 50 mm (2 in.) in length is left.
   c) Remove any excess fat.
   d) Neatly tie with string to hold the joint in shape.

2. Place the mutton into a saucepan (making sure the saucepan is large enough to hold both the joint and the vegetables that will be added later), cover with the cold water or stock then bring to the boil.

3. Skim to remove any scum and wipe round the sides of the pan above the liquid.

4. Simmer the meat for 1½ hours, skimming as required. Top up with additional liquid as necessary.

Caper sauce

INGREDIENTS   MAKES 500 ml (1 pint)

50 g	butter or margarine	2 oz
50 g	flour	2 oz
500 ml	cooking liquor from mutton	1 pt
50 g	capers	2 oz

salt and white pepper

1. Strain off 500 ml (1 pt) of hot cooking liquor from the mutton.

2. Melt the butter or margarine in a saucepan.

3. Mix in the flour then cook over a low heat for 4-5 minutes. Do not allow to brown.

4. Blend in a little at a time of the hot cooking liquor, stirring smooth with each addition of liquid.

5. Bring to the boil then slowly simmer for about 20 minutes (this will give time for the flavours to develop).

6. Strain if necessary then add the capers.

7. Check seasoning and temperature (the sauce may have cooled down).

5. Meanwhile wash and prepare the vegetables:
   a) Carefully peel the onions, leaving them whole.
   b) Top, tail and peel or scrape clean the carrots.
   c) Peel the turnip or swede, then cut it into large neat pieces (leave very small turnips whole).
   d) Trim the root end of the celery and remove any stalks that are past their best. Wash the celery thoroughly, then tie string round it if individual stalks are coming loose.
   e) Remove any spoiled leaves from the leeks, then trim off the root end. Cut a slit lengthwise through the leek, starting just above the root end. Wash the leeks thoroughly, then tie them together in a bundle.

6. After the meat has cooked for about 1½ hours, add the bouquet garni and celery to the saucepan and allow to cook for about 40 minutes.

7. Add the carrots, onions and swede or turnip and allow to cook for a further 10 minutes.

8. Add the leeks and simmer until all the vegetables and meat are cooked – about 15 minutes.

9. After the meat has been cooking for 1½ to 2 hours prepare the caper sauce, making sure that you have time to complete it before the main dish is ready.

10. Remove the leg from the saucepan and place it on a suitable metal tray. Cut the string and remove it.

11. Remove the vegetables ready for service:
    a) If large pieces of turnip or swede have been used, cut them into neat portions about the same size as the onions.
    b) Remove the string from the celery and divide it into portions about the same size as the carrots.
    c) Remove the string from the leeks, cut completely through the root end, and neatly fold them over to form lengths slightly shorter than the carrots.

12. Cover the exposed bone of the leg with a frill, then place the meat on the centre of the warm service dish.

Alternatively, carve the leg into slices and arrange on the serving dish. (Meat should be carved across the grain so that the meat fibres are shorter and therefore the meat tender and easy to chew.)

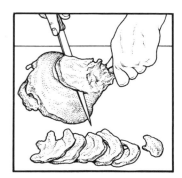

13. Neatly arrange the vegetables around the leg, then coat them with a little of the cooking liquor, seasoned to taste. Sprinkle with parsley, if required.

14. Serve the caper sauce in a sauceboat.

Boiled silverside of beef and dumplings

INGREDIENTS   SERVES 4

600 g	cured silverside	1 lb 8 oz
4	small carrots	4
4	small onions	4
	water or cold white stock to cover	
	bouquet garni	
	chopped parsley (optional)	

1. Soak the beef in cold water for 24 hours to remove excess salt.

2. Discard the soaking water and place the beef into a suitably sized saucepan.

3. Cover with the cold water or stock and bring to the boil. Skim if a scum forms.

4. Add the bouquet garni and allow the liquid to simmer until almost cooked (about 1½ hours).

5. Add the carrots and onions and simmer for about 10 to 15 minutes more (the timing will depend on their size and maturity).

6. Meanwhile, prepare the suet pastry (*see* box) and shape it into dumplings, using a rolling action of the hands.

7. Add the dumplings to the cooking liquid and simmer until cooked – a further 15 to 20 minutes.

8. Remove the beef from the pan and allow it to cool slightly.

Suet pastry

INGREDIENTS

50 g	plain flour	2 oz
25 g	suet (grated)	1 oz
30 ml	water	1 fl oz
	pinch of baking powder	
	pinch of salt	

1. Sieve together the flour, baking powder and salt into a mixing bowl.

2. Add the suet and mix through the flour.

3. Add the water and lightly mix to form a stiff paste.

9. Neatly carve the beef across the grain and arrange the slices carefully on the serving dish.

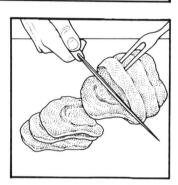

10. Garnish with the carrots, onions and dumplings and coat with a little of the cooking liquor. Sprinkle a little parsley over the dumplings or onions if desired.

11. Serve a sauceboat of the cooking liquor separately if required.

See: Video 2

Smoked haddock kedgeree

INGREDIENTS		SERVES 10
350 g	long grain rice	14 oz
1 kg	smoked haddock	2½ lb
10	hard-boiled eggs	10
500 ml	curry sauce (see box)	1 pt
150 g	butter or margarine	6 oz
	chopped parsley (optional)	
	seasoning	

1. Prepare the curry sauce (see box).

2. Place a saucepan on the stove with enough water to boil the rice – about 4 litres (8 pints). Add a little salt and bring to the boil.

3. Sprinkle all the rice into the boiling water and stir frequently until the water reboils.

4. Simmer slowly until the rice grains are cooked (15-20 minutes) stirring occasionally. The grains should be tender but still firm.

5. Wash the rice under cold running water to separate the grains.

6. Reheat the rice in very hot salted water, then drain thoroughly in a colander. Cover with a cloth, then dry the rice in a cool oven (or on a hotplate set low).

7. Meanwhile, lightly butter a shallow pan or fish kettle (with lid) and place the fish in the pan.

8. Barely cover the fish with fish stock or water, and place a piece of buttered greaseproof paper over the fish (see illustrations). Cover with lid.

9. Place on top of the stove and bring almost to the boil. Continue to cook slowly over low heat on top of the stove or in a moderate oven.

10. When cooked (about 10 minutes) drain the fish and remove the bones and skin.

11. Flake the fish and place it aside in a bowl.

12. Cut the egg whites into small dice and chop the yolks roughly.

13. Heat the butter or margarine in a large sauteuse and add the fish, eggs and rice. Toss the ingredients together and allow to reheat thoroughly. Also check the seasoning.

14. Neatly arrange the kedgeree in a warm service dish and sprinkle chopped parsley on top.

15. Serve accompanied by the curry sauce.

Curry sauce

INGREDIENTS		MAKES 500 ml (1 pint)
50 g	butter or margarine	2 oz
100 g	finely chopped onions	4 oz
1	clove crushed garlic	1
10 g	curry powder	½ oz
50 g	flour	2 oz
10 g	tomato purée	½ oz
500 ml	brown stock	1 pt
10 g	dessicated coconut	½ oz
10 g	sultanas	½ oz
25 g	mango chutney	1 oz
50 g	cooking apple	2 oz

1. Melt the butter or margarine in a saucepan.

2. Add the onions and garlic and cook gently until soft but not coloured – about 5 minutes.

3. Add the curry powder and cook for approximately 1 minute.

4. Mix in the flour and allow to cook over a low heat for 2 to 3 minutes.

5. Add the tomato purée and mix it in.

6. Away from the heat for the first stages, slowly blend in the hot stock returning to the heat and stirring smooth with each addition of liquid.

7. Bring the sauce to the boil and allow to simmer for 15 minutes. Skim as required.

8. Peel and finely chop the apple, and add it to the sauce together with the sultanas, chutney and coconut.

9. Simmer for a further 20 minutes then check consistency and seasoning.

Note: The sauce may be strained or liquidised if a smooth sauce is desired.

To make a circle of greaseproof paper
1. Fold a square or oblong sheet into half, then half again.
2. Fold again, diagonally, to form a triangle.
3. Repeat the folding two or three times until a narrow dart shape has been formed.
4. Place the point of the dart over the centre of the saucepan and mark the paper where it reaches the edge of the saucepan. Then trim the paper to this mark, and when opened out it will form a circle.

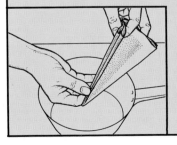

Scampi salad with mayonnaise

INGREDIENTS SERVES 4 (main course portions)

500 g	raw scampi tails (in their shells)	1¼ lb

Vinegar court-bouillon Makes 1 litre (2 pints)

1 l	water	2 pt
50 g	onion	2 oz
50 g	carrot	2 oz
25 g	celery	1 oz
25 g	leek	1 oz
50 ml	white wine vinegar	2 fl oz
5 g	salt	¼ oz
5	peppercorns	5
	sprig of thyme, bay leaf and a few parsley stalks	

Salad

A variety of salad vegetables may be used according to taste, e.g. spring onions, chives, radishes and red or green peppers, in this case:

2	tomatoes	2
1	hard-boiled egg	1
16	cucumber slices	16
	lettuce leaves or quarters (or curly endive or radicchio)	
	watercress	
1	lemon cut into wedges	1
100 ml	mayonnaise sauce (see box)	4 fl oz

1. Wash the shellfish tails in cold water.

2. Place all the ingredients for the court-bouillon into a saucepan and bring to the boil.

3. Allow to simmer for approximately 20 minutes.

4. Add the shellfish tails and simmer for 5 to 6 minutes depending on size.

5. Remove from the liquor and cool quickly. Note: If the shellfish is to be left to cool in the court-bouillon, then reduce the cooking time to 4 to 5 minutes, to allow for carry-over cooking during cooling.

6. When cold, remove the tails from their shells.

7. Inspect the tails and if there is one remove the sand vein, which will look darker than the flesh around it. Store the tails chilled until required for service.

8. Prepare the salad:
   a) Wash the lettuce and cress.
   b) Slice the tomatoes or cut into wedges.
   c) Slice or quarter the hard-boiled eggs.

9. Arrange the shellfish tails on the lettuce then neatly garnish with eggs, cucumber, tomatoes, cress and lemon pieces.

10. Serve accompanied with the mayonnaise sauce.

Mayonnaise sauce

INGREDIENTS MAKES 1 litre (2 pints)

5	egg yolks	5
½ tsp	English mustard (dry)	½ tsp
75-100 ml	white vinegar	3-4 fl oz
1 l	salad oil	2 pt
	squeeze lemon juice	
	salt and white pepper	

1. Place the egg yolks into a mixing bowl.

2. Add the salt and pepper and the mustard diluted in half the quantity of vinegar.

3. Whisk until thoroughly combined.

4. Add the oil in a thin stream while whisking continuously (*see* photograph). When the sauce becomes very thick, thin it as required using the remaining vinegar. The mayonnaise should be thick enough to hold its shape when placed on a serving spoon.

5. Finish with the lemon juice and check the seasoning.

Using frozen scampi
Scampi respond well to freezing and raw frozen scampi can almost always be used in place of fresh ones. Thaw them first in a cool room. This will not take long so don't be tempted to hurry the process by immersing them in water, as this will spoil both the taste and flavour.

Dressed crab with salad and mayonnaise

INGREDIENTS	SERVES 1 (main course portion)	
1 kg	*live crab*	2¼ lb
2 l	*court-bouillon (see previous page)*	4 pt
1	*hard-boiled egg*	1
50-75 ml	*mayonnaise (to bind)*	2-3 fl oz
5-10 g	*fresh white breadcrumbs*	¼-½ oz
	chopped parsley	

Salad

A variety of salad vegetables may be used according to taste, e.g. chicory, curly endive, beetroot and peppers etc. in this case:

2	*washed lettuce leaves*	2
2	*tomato quarters*	2
4	*cucumber slices*	4
1	*trimmed spring onion*	1
	salad cress	
	mayonnaise (see previous page)	

1. Submerge the crab in the boiling court-bouillon. Then bring back to the boil and simmer for 35 minutes.

2. Remove from the court-bouillon and set aside in a cool place. Alternatively, allow to cool and store in the court-bouillon (if you do this reduce the cooking time to 30 minutes).

3. Remove the claws and legs.

4. Pull back and detach the bottom pincer of each claw then crack the claws with the back of a knife and remove the meat. Also remove the meat from the legs if you have time to do so.

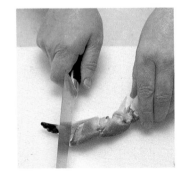

5. Place the white meat in a bowl ready for use.

6. Carefully pull open and remove the soft under-shell or purse.

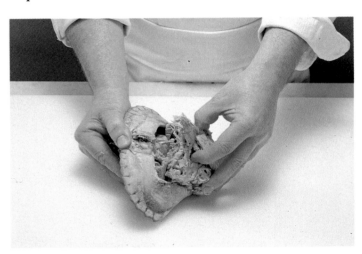

7. Remove the gills and discard. Also remove the hard piece of sac behind the eyes and discard.

8. Split open the purse with a knife and remove the meat using a fork or small spoon. Keep the white and brown meat separate.

9. Separate the white meat into shreds and inspect for any small pieces of broken shell.

10. Remove the soft dark meat and orange meat from the crab shell.

11. Thoroughly wash the shell, then break open by carefully pressing the outside of the shell along the natural line.

12. Rewash the shell and allow to dry.

13. Finely chop or sieve the egg yolk and white and keep separate.

14. Mix the soft dark meat and orange meat with enough white breadcrumbs and mayonnaise to form a paste. Check the seasoning.

15. Place the paste into both sides of the shell and smooth the surface with a palette knife.

16. Arrange the white meat in the centre then decorate over the top with lines of sieved egg yolk, sieved egg white and chopped parsley.

17. Arrange the lettuce leaves on the service dish then place the dressed crab on top of them.

18. Neatly garnish with the remaining salad vegetables and serve accompanied by a sauceboat of mayonnaise.

Spaghetti Italian-style

INGREDIENTS	SERVES 10 (main course portions)	
500 g	spaghetti	1 lb 4 oz
100 g	butter	4 oz
100 g	grated Parmesan cheese	4 oz
	salt and freshly milled black pepper to taste	

1. Place the spaghetti in a large saucepan containing about 5 litres (10 pints) of boiling salted water. Stir to separate the spaghetti.

2. Return to the boil (with a fairly vigorous bubbling movement). Cook for 12 to 15 minutes, stirring occasionally.

3. When it is cooked, drain the spaghetti in a colander. If it is sticky, wash or rinse it with very hot water and drain again.

4. Melt the butter in a sauteuse and heat until foaming, being careful not to let it burn.

5. Add the drained spaghetti and toss to coat thoroughly in butter. Also add half the Parmesan and season with the milled pepper.

6. Place the spaghetti on a serving dish. The remaining cheese can be sprinkled over the top of the spaghetti or offered separately.

Aspic

Aspics are used in many cold preparations to coat and/or decorate the food. They provide an attractive sheen and create a delicate flavour, which should add to the flavour of the dish, not mask or overwhelm it.
The cold decorated salmon trout recipe in Poaching/Practical Examples 4 requires a fish aspic (see box).

INGREDIENTS   MAKES 1 litre (2 pints)

1½ l	brown beef or veal stock	3 pt
150 g	lean minced beef	6 oz
50 g	leaf gelatine	2 oz
100 g	finely chopped onions, carrots, celery and leeks	4 oz
2	egg whites	2
10 g	tomato purée (optional)	½ oz
	½ bay leaf, sprig of thyme and parsley stalks	
3	peppercorns	3
	salt to taste	

1. Soak the leaf gelatin in cold water until it bends easily.

2. Mix together the minced beef, egg whites, vegetables, tomato purée and peppercorns.

3. Place into a saucepan, add the cold stock and thoroughly whisk together until combined.

4. Squeeze out the surplus water from the gelatin and stir into the mixture.

5. Place on a low heat and stir occasionally while the mixture is heating up, but do not stir after it has reached a temperature of 50°C (120°F).

6. Bring to the boil then slowly simmer for 1½ to 2 hours, leaving the crust undisturbed.

7. Carefully strain the aspic through a piece of muslin folded in two over a clean bowl or resting in a sieve, then skim off any surface fat. If the aspic is still not perfectly clear, strain again.

8. The strength of the aspic can be tested by placing a small amount on a plate and allowing it to cool in a refrigerator. Once set, the aspic should be of a melt-in-the-mouth consistency. If the aspic is too firm, a little clear stock or water can be added and the aspic retested. If it is too runny, add another leaf or two of gelatin (softened first) and repeat step 7.

9. Check the seasoning then put in a cold place. As soon as it is cool, place the aspic in a refrigerator. Use as required.

Fish aspic

For fish aspic, the list of ingredients is slightly different:

1½ l	fish stock	3pt
150 g	minced white fish trimmings	6 oz
50 g	leaf gelatin	2 oz
100 g	onions and leeks	4oz
	½ bay leaf, sprig of thyme and 3-4 parsley stalks	
2	egg whites	2
3	peppercorns	3
	salt to taste	

Otherwise follow the main recipe except for step 6 – fish aspic should be cooked for only 20 minutes.

✚ HYGIENE

Take great care when you are making and using aspic. The constant cooling and reheating necessary when you are using it to coat foods provide ideal conditions for harmful bacteria to multiply. Use fresh aspic each time.

Sweet jellies for dessert
In sweet jellies which are served for dessert, leaf or powdered gelatin softened in water acts as the setting agent. The base is flavoured with fruit juice, sugar, liqueurs or wines as required.

The amount of gelatin is important: too much and the jelly becomes over firm, too little and the jelly collapses. Getting the quantity right is usually a question of following the recipe.

Fruit jam

INGREDIENTS

1 kg	*fruit (apricots, cranberries, plums, damsons or peaches)*	*2½ lb*
1 kg	*sugar (see box)*	*2½ lb*
250 ml	*water*	*½ pt*
25 ml	*lemon juice*	*1 fl oz*

1. Wash and inspect the fruit. Remove any stalks, seeds, stones, spots of mould or deterioration.

2. Cut large fruits, e.g. apricots, plums and peaches, into pieces.

3. Place the fruit into a large saucepan or preserving pan then add the lemon juice and water (the jam will boil up to 3 or 4 times its original volume in step 6.)

4. Bring to the boil and simmer until the fruit is tender.

> **How much sugar, acid and pectin to use**
> How much sugar you use depends on the type of fruit; so does the amount of acid (lemon juice) and whether or not commercially produced pectin needs to be added. Strawberries, for example, need 1¼ kg sugar, 40 ml lemon juice and 250 ml liquid pectin. Blackcurrants and gooseberries need 1¼ kg of sugar.

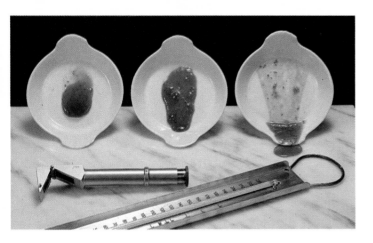

The jam in the centre has reached setting point. The example on the left has been boiled too long and the sugar concentration is too high. The example on the right has too much water left in the syrup so it should have been boiled for longer.

A sugar thermometer (at the front of the picture) gives more accurate results in sugar boiling than judging by eye. The temperatures the sugar solution should reach for different uses can be found in instructions on jam-making. The refractometer (also shown) measures the density of syrups (that is, how much sugar there is in the liquid) and can also be useful in deciding when the solution has boiled for long enough.

5. Add the sugar and stir until it has completely dissolved. (If the sugar is not completely dissolved before boiling, the finished jam may re-crystallise.)

6. Bring the jam to the boil and continue boiling rapidly until setting point is achieved.

7. Allow the jam to cool slightly and thicken then pour into sterile jars. (To sterilise the jars, rinse them out with boiling water.)

8. Quickly cover the surface of the jam with circles of waxed paper, then seal the jars with sterilised lids.

> **Setting point**
> To test if setting point has been reached drop a few spots of the boiling jam on to a cold dry plate and allow to cool. Lightly press with the fingers; the surface should wrinkle and hold its shape.

Redcurrant jelly

INGREDIENTS

1 kg	*redcurrants*	*2½ lb*
1 l	*water*	*2 pt*
800 g	*sugar*	*2 lb*

1. Wash the fruit and remove any stalks.

2. Place it in a saucepan, add the water and bring to the boil.

3. Allow to simmer until the berries are tender.

4. Strain the berries and cooking juice through a fine sieve into a clean bowl, pressing the berries to extract as much juice as possible. Then stretch a piece of fine muslin over a clean saucepan and strain the fruit juice through this.

5. Add the sugar to the liquor and reboil.

6. Boil the liquor until setting point is reached – *see* recipe for fruit jam.

7. Pour the jelly into sterile jars.

8. Quickly cover with circles of wax paper, then seal the jars with sterile lids.

Scotch broth

INGREDIENTS		SERVES 4 to 5
1 l	white stock, made with mutton bones	2 pt
	(see Introduction/Stocks)	
25 g	pearl barley	1 oz
50 g	onion	2 oz
50 g	carrot	2 oz
50 g	turnip	2 oz
25 g	celery	1 oz
25 g	leek	1 oz
	chopped parsley (optional)	
	salt and white pepper to taste	

1. Place the stock into a saucepan and bring to the boil.

2. Wash the barley, add to the stock and allow to simmer for about 1 hour. Top up with stock as required.

3. Wash and peel the vegetables then cut into small dice of about 3 mm (⅛ in.) as in the illustrations.

Dicing vegetables,
e.g. carrots.
Cut lengthwise into slices about 3 mm (⅛ in.) thick. (This step is not necessary for celery.)

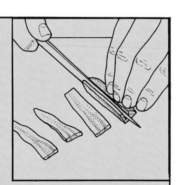

Cut lengthwise again to form sticks. Once you get practised, you can pile two or three slices on top of each other and cut through the pile in one go.

Gather a pile of sticks, turning them through a right angle so they are in a comfortable position to cut. Cut through the sticks, forming small dice of equal size (3 mm).

4. Add the onion, carrot, turnip and celery and simmer for 10 to 15 minutes.

5. Add the leeks then simmer until all the vegetables are cooked (another 10 to 15 minutes).

6. Skim off any surface fat then check seasoning and consistency.

7. When ready to serve, sprinkle with chopped parsley.

Cream of mushroom soup
Crème de champignons

INGREDIENTS		SERVES 4 to 5
50 g	butter or margarine	2 oz
50 g	flour	2 oz
100 g	white mushrooms	4 oz
75 g	onion	3 oz
25 g	celery	1 oz
25 g	white leek	1 oz
1 l	white chicken stock	2 pt
50 ml	cream	2 fl oz
	sprig of thyme and ½ bay leaf	
	salt and white pepper to taste	

1. Wash and prepare the vegetables:
   a) Leave 2 or 3 mushrooms whole (for garnish) and slice the rest of them.
   b) Roughly chop the onion, celery and leek.

2. Melt the butter or margarine in a saucepan.

3. Add the chopped onion, celery and leek and slowly cook them without colouring for 8 to 10 minutes.

4. Mix in the flour and cook for 4 to 5 minutes. Do not allow to develop any colour.

5. Slowly blend in the hot chicken stock, stirring smooth with each addition of stock.

Preparing mushrooms.
To slice, cut through the cap and stem to form slices in an umbrella shape.
  If the mushrooms are being used in a stew and need to be a sturdier shape, or are small, cut each in half and then in quarters.

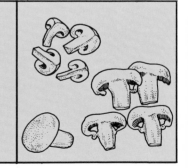

6. Bring to the boil then add all the mushrooms, both sliced and whole.

7. Skim off any surface fat and impurities and slowly simmer until cooked – about 45 minutes. Stir occasionally during cooking to avoid burning.

8. Remove the whole mushrooms from the soup and put to one side.

9. Pass the soup through a liquidiser or rub it through a sieve to form a purée. Then place into a clean pan.

10. Slice the whole cooked mushrooms then add them to the soup.

11. Reboil the soup then stir the cream into it.

12. Check seasoning and if after adding the cream the soup is still too thick, add a little hot stock or further cream.

Vichyssoise

INGREDIENTS		SERVES 4 to 5
15 g	butter or margarine	1/2 oz
75 g	onions	3 oz
200 g	leeks (white part only)	8 oz
300 g	potatoes	12 oz
750 ml	white chicken stock	1 1/2 pt
100 ml	cream	4 fl oz

sprig of thyme and 1/2 bay leaf
salt and pepper to taste
chopped chives and parsley

1. Wash and prepare the vegetables, then peel and chop the onions, dice the leeks, and peel and slice the potatoes.

2. Melt the butter or margarine in a saucepan then add the onion and leeks and slowly cook until soft but do not allow to brown – about 10 minutes.

3. Add the stock and bring to the boil.

4. Add the potatoes and allow to simmer until cooked – about 30 minutes. Stir occasionally during cooking to reduce the risk of burning and skim off any surface fat.

5. Remove the bay leaf then liquidise or force both the vegetables and the liquid through a sieve. Check the consistency and add a little more chicken stock if it is too thick.

6. Quickly chill the soup.

7. When serving, lightly whip the cream and fold through the soup. A low-fat cream or yogurt can be used instead.

8. Sprinkle the chives and parsley over the soup.

Dicing an onion.
Clean and peel the onion. Trim the root end carefully (if you trim off too much the onion will fall apart). Cut the onion in half from top to bottom and place each half flat side down on the chopping board. Slice the onion towards the root end (without cutting through the base so that the onion is still just held together). The size of the slices decides how big the dice will be.

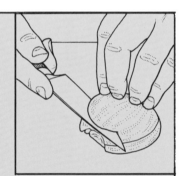

Cut a series of vertical slices towards the root (again not cutting through the base).

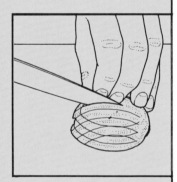

Now cut across the onion at right angles to form dice. If some of the dice are too big (this tends to happen with the slices that come from the curved outer edges), chop them smaller on the board.

Cleaning leeks. Trim off the green part and roots (taking care not to cut into the leaf bases). Remove any old outer leaves. Cut once or twice down the length of the leek, almost to the base. Fan out the leaves and wash under running water to free any dirt trapped inside.

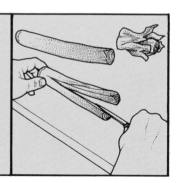

Consommé with profiteroles

INGREDIENTS   SERVES 20 to 25

6½ l	cold brown stock	13 pt
750 g	lean minced beef	1 lb 14 oz
500 g	finely chopped onions, carrots,	1 lb 4 oz
	celery and leeks in roughly equal quantities	
150 ml	egg whites	6 fl oz
50 g	tomato purée (optional)	2 oz
12	peppercorns	12

sprig of thyme, 2 bay leaves and parsley stalks
salt to taste

There are very many garnishes for consommé. In this case, profiteroles made from choux pastry have been used (*see* box).

1. Place all the ingredients except the cold stock into a bowl and thoroughly mix together.

2. Place the mixture into a large saucepan (a stockpot with a tap at the bottom is ideal), then add the cold stock.

3. Whisk thoroughly.

4. Place on a low heat and bring to the boil. Stir only when the liquid is beginning to heat – it should not be disturbed after it has reached 50°C (120°F).

5. Slowly simmer for 1½ to 2 hours without disturbing the crust.

6. Carefully strain the clear consommé into a clean pot through a piece of muslin folded double.

  If you are using a stockpot this is straightforward. If you are using a saucepan this process needs a little more care. The object is to disturb the crust as little as possible. Carefully make a hole where the crust is weakest, then ladle out the clear liquid from underneath and strain it.

7. Remove any surface fat with a piece of absorbent paper (a dish paper will do) then check the seasoning.

8. Ladle into consommé cups, then add between 5 and 10 profiteroles per portion and serve immediately.

Profiteroles

INGREDIENTS

100 ml	water	4 fl oz
40 g	butter or margarine	1½ oz
60 g	strong flour	2½ oz
70-100 ml	egg (1½-2 eggs) beaten lightly	2½-4 fl oz

1. Sieve the flour.

2. Place the water and fat into a small saucepan and bring to the boil.

3. Add all the flour in one go and mix thoroughly.

4. Stir over a low heat for about 1 minute. The mixture should leave the sides of the saucepan cleanly. If it doesn't, the quantities are probably wrong.

5. Allow to cool slightly. If the mixture is too hot then the eggs will coagulate.

See: Video 7 for sweet choux pastry

Broccoli with hollandaise sauce

INGREDIENTS   SERVES 8

| 800 g | broccoli | 2 lb |

hollandaise sauce (see *box*)

1. Wash the broccoli then trim off the stalks to within 50 mm (2 in.) of the flower heads.

2. Place enough water in a saucepan to partially cover the broccoli and bring to the boil. Lightly season with salt.

6. Add the beaten egg a little at a time while mixing the paste vigorously.

7. Scrape down the bowl occasionally to ensure even mixing.

8. Continue adding the egg until a soft consistency is achieved. *Important*: The mixture should still just be able to hold its shape when piped.

9. Place the mixture into a piping bag with a 2 mm (⅛ in.) plain tube.

10. Pipe out the pastry in very small balls of 5 mm (just over ⅛ in.) across on to a lightly greased baking sheet. (The picture shows a piping bag made of paper.)

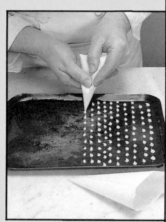

11. Bake at approximately 200°C (400°F) until crisp and golden brown. This will probably take no more than 4 minutes.

Note: Sweet profiteroles are made in more or less the same way except that a pinch of sugar is added with the flour. The quantity in this recipe would make 8 éclairs or choux buns or 16 sweet profiteroles.

3. Add the broccoli, cover with a lid and slowly simmer until cooked. Test the vegetable at regular intervals to avoid overcooking – it should be tender but firm.

4. Drain the broccoli thoroughly, taking care not to damage the delicate flower head and arrange neatly on a service dish.

5. Serve accompanied by a sauceboat of hollandaise sauce.

Hollandaise sauce

INGREDIENTS		SERVES 8 to 10
20 ml	white wine vinegar	¾ fl oz
2	egg yolks	2
250 g	butter	10 oz
	squeeze lemon juice	
	salt, pepper and pinch cayenne pepper to taste	

1. Melt the butter in a small saucepan over a gentle heat and allow it to become clear. A certain amount of water may separate from the butter.

2. Place the vinegar and egg yolks into a small sauteuse (*see* note below).

3. Place the sauteuse in a bain marie (a second larger saucepan containing water at just below boiling point) over an extremely low heat. Whisk continuously until a light and aerated result has been achieved. Great care must be taken that the mixture does not curdle. This will happen if it gets too hot so it may be necessary to remove the mixture from the heat from time to time. *Important:* the mixture should be whisked until the ribbon stage has been reached i.e. fluffy and stiff enough to show whisk marks. (This is called a sabayon.)

4. Remove from the heat and slowly whisk in the melted butter, taking care not to use any milky residue which may have separated from it.

5. Season the sauce and whisk through the lemon juice.

6. Place the sauce into a clean bowl and keep it warm (e.g. in another bowl of warm water) until required for service. (It will separate if kept too long.) In any case do not keep the sauce for more than an hour or two, because of the risk of food poisoning.

Note: Traditionally the vinegar together with crushed peppercorns are reduced down slightly in the sauteuse. 20 ml of cold water is added with the egg yolks and the sabayon prepared as described here. If this method is used, the sauce has to be strained through a piece of muslin before use.

What went wrong

Cloudy stock.

> 1. It was boiled too vigorously.
> 2. It was not skimmed effectively.

Vegetable garnish for boiled meat dish unevenly cooked.

> The vegetables should have been checked to find out when they were cooked. Any that are cooked ahead of the others should be removed and kept aside until the rest are ready.

Fruit jelly doesn't set.

> In a natural gel set this indicates that the amount of acid, sugar or pectin is not correct. Test a small amount first if you are in doubt.
>
> If you have opted for the gelatin method, a runny result indicates you have not used enough gelatin.

Boiled sugar solution turns back to crystals.

> Pan not absolutely clean. Undissolved sugar crystals have fallen into the solution from the side of the pan.
>
> To remove any stray crystals, wipe down the side of the pan and the thermometer with a clean brush dipped in water.

Boiled eggs discoloured.

> Overcooked. Watch timing carefully and chill in cold water immediately after cooking to prevent carry over cooking.

Thickened soup tastes burnt.

> Roux overcooked. Take more care at the vital first stage when the flour and fat are cooking.

Pasta is too soft.

> Overcooked because:
> 1. Cooked too long
> 2. Held too long before service
> 3. Reheated for too long.

Leeks fall apart during boiling.

> Root trimmed off too severely so that there is nothing to hold the leaves together. (Tie bundles of 4-6 leeks together when boiling.)

Cauliflower discolours.

> Either the result of over-cooking or the reaction of hard water on a substance called flavone in the cauliflower, causing it to yellow. A little lemon juice added to the cooking water will counteract this reaction.

Potatoes discolour.

> 1. Poor handling has caused bruising.
> 2. Storage in conditions which are too cold (below 4°C/40°F) has caused the potatoes to build up excess sugar. (If other potatoes have been kept in similar conditions, move them to normal room temperature for a short time. The discoloration will vanish.)
> 3. They have been peeled and not kept fully submerged in cold water.
> 4. They have been kept in an aluminium saucepan after peeling.

TEST YOURSELF

1. Identify two items that require:
   a) rapid boiling
   b) simmering
   c) cold water start
   d) boiling water start
For each item explain the reason.

2. List two advantages and two disadvantages of boiling as a method of cooking.

3. Identify the pan that should be used to boil sugar and give a reason.

4. Give one reason why shellfish is sometimes boiled in a court-bouillon?

5. Give one reason why pasta should be stirred during boiling?

6. List the advantages and disadvantages of blanching vegetables?

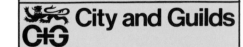 City and Guilds

Tips

Protect the vitamin content of vegetables at all stages:

– Don't prepare them until you need them.
– Use a sharp knife when preparing them.
– Don't soak them in cold water after you have prepared them (except for potatoes).
– Cook them for the minimum time, as close to service as possible.

When you are cooking large quantities of potatoes, put them in an empty pot. Carry the pot to the stove, then add the boiling water from another saucepan. If you add the potatoes to the boiling water, it is easy to splash and burn yourself.

When you are boiling cured meats, and have brought the cold water to the boil with the meat in it, always taste the water. If it is very salty, replace it with fresh cold water and bring to the boil a second time.

Think before you salt. Many customers are trying to cut down their salt intake for health reasons. If they are not and particularly like the taste of salt, they can always add their own.

When you are boiling meat or shellfish which is to be served cold, reduce the cooking time and allow the food to cool in the cooking liquid. The flavour and moistness will be improved.

> **CHEF'S TIP**
>
> Stop dumplings sticking together by splashing cold water over them when they have been removed from the cooking liquid.

Purée soups: 1) Vichyssoise 9) Crécy. **Thickened brown soups:** 2) Mulligatawny 6) Game. **Unpassed vegetable soups (not sieved or puréed):** 3) Minestrone 5) Scotch broth 14) French onion. **Clear soups:** 4) Consommé 11) Consommé with madeira. **Cream (roux-thickened) soups:** 7) Cream of tomato 8) Cream of mushroom. **Fish soup:** 10) Crab. **Garnishes:** 12) Toasted croûtes 13) Croûtons.

> **CHEF'S TIP**
>
> When serving plain boiled vegetables, you don't necessarily need to rely on a final brushing of butter to make them look good. Many customers are trying to cut down their intake of fat.

3 POACHING

Poached dishes are delicate in texture and flavoursome, which makes them attractive to the customer. The fact that poaching is a quick method of cooking means that it is also popular with caterers. A la carte menus often feature a high proportion of poached dishes.

Some fine examples of dishes in which poaching plays an important part are Eggs Florentine – poached eggs on a base of spinach coated with a cheese sauce, and often served as a starter, Sole Bonne Femme – poached sole in a white wine and mushroom sauce, either as a fish course in an elaborate menu, or as a main course in a simpler meal, Peach Melba – poached peaches with vanilla ice cream and raspberry sauce, a favourite among sweets, and Canapés Ivanhoe, a savoury dish of poached smoked haddock covered with white sauce and then browned under the grill.

▸▸▸ TO DO

List the foods served in your place of work or on a selected menu that could be poached instead of the way they are cooked at present. Pick out those which would have
a) improved flavour
b) reduced fat content.

Poaching may seem like a very simple method of cooking, but in fact a great deal of skill and care is needed to produce a successful and well-presented dish. The prime skill lies in selecting the right foods and matching suitable cooking liquids to them, so that the flavour of one does not mask the other.

For customers who are trying to keep the fat content of their diet low, poached dishes are an excellent choice provided that they are not covered in a rich sauce. The cooking method does not require fat and many of the items that are commonly poached are low in saturated fats. Poached fish, for example, is very easy to digest and is therefore useful in hospital catering.

Many thousands of kilograms of fish are sold to caterers and catering suppliers every working day at Billingsgate in London's East End.

3 POACHING

What happens

Poaching is a method of cooking food gently in not quite boiling liquid. The food is either partially or completely covered by the liquid, which is held at a few degrees below boiling point so that the food is moved about as little as possible and does not break up.

Poaching is a fast and successful method of cooking tender foods at low to moderate temperatures. This makes it different from the three other cooking processes that use liquid as a cooking medium: boiling, braising and stewing. Foods that require a long cooking time to make them tender and tasty, or which benefit from being cooked fast at high temperatures, are generally not suitable for poaching.

> Cooking food in a container which is then immersed in hot water is not true poaching. (Egg poachers – *see* Terms and Equipment – are an example of this.) Although the water is acting as a buffer between the heat source and the food, providing gentle heat transfer, the food itself is not in contact with the cooking liquid, a key factor in poaching.

Why use poaching?

The main use of poaching is for delicate foods which tend to fall apart when cooked by other methods. One of the best examples is fish. When poached, fish cooks very quickly to a tender, moist, flaked texture. What little connective tissue there is converts easily to gelatin. If cooked by the rougher action of boiling, the fish tends to overcook which means that it will get a rubbery texture and disintegrate easily. Other delicate foods are also badly affected by the buffeting they get in a boiling liquid.

If the food is completely covered by the cooking liquid, poaching is usually done on the top of the stove. The heat is conducted through the base of the saucepan (or for fish, a specially designed pan called a fish kettle) and distributed through the liquid by convection currents. The heat is then conducted through the food, cooking it. This is called *deep poaching*.

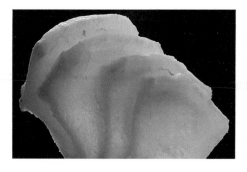

Fish is more suitable for poaching than meat for two reasons in particular:
1) fish protein coagulates or sets at a lower temperature than meat protein – 41°C (105°F)
2) the collagen that is partly responsible for toughness softens, i.e. changes to gelatin, faster and at a lower temperature. Meat needs a temperature of at least 100°C (212°F), provided by boiling, stewing or braising.

Cooking the sauce
When the liquid used in poaching forms the basis of a thickened sauce, the sauce will usually have to be cooked separately so that it can be boiled. This is because the temperature in poaching is not high enough to cook any starch used to thicken the sauce properly.

If the food is only partially covered by the cooking liquid, poaching is usually started in a saucepan on top of the stove, and when the liquid has reached the right temperature, the poaching process is often continued in the oven. Convection currents in the oven transfer the heat to the cooking container. This is called *shallow poaching*.

In many poached dishes the cooking liquid contributes to the taste of the finished dish, either by giving flavour to the food, or by forming the basis of an accompanying sauce, or both. Spices, herbs, salt, pepper, lemon juice, chopped onions or shallots, sliced mushrooms and cinnamon and sugar are some of the ingredients that can be used.

Shallow or deep poaching — which to use?

Large and medium-sized whole food items, large cuts of fish and all fruit are usually deep poached, i.e. completely covered in the cooking liquid. As the food has not been weakened by being cut up, it does not fall apart even though there is cooking liquid all around it. It will also cook through evenly.

With certain food items the skin is left on to provide further protection, provided that it will not slow down the cooking. So the skin of whole fish is left on, but the thick skin of some fruits is removed. As fruit tends to float, it is covered with a piece of paper to prevent the exposed surface drying out.

Shallow poaching, in which the liquid level generally comes about two-thirds of the way up the food, is used for particularly delicate whole foods, and thin or fragile cuts of food, which would break up if they were deep poached.

So that the uncovered portion of the food does not dry out, the food is covered with a piece of buttered or greased greaseproof paper and often a lid as well. There are many opinions as to exactly what covering to use. Some chefs use tin foil, but others say that tin foil should be avoided because it will make any wine used in the poaching liquid discolour, and the chemicals in some greaseproof paper may give the food a disagreeable flavour. Sometimes buttered brown paper is used. So there is no easy answer and you should always check on what method is preferred by the place where you are working.

In deep poaching the starting temperature is usually hot. This means that cooking will start immediately, so the overall cooking time can be kept to a minimum (always important with tender foods). With whole fish, though, the starting temperature has to be cold, because if it is placed in hot liquid, the flesh will shrink suddenly and unevenly and the fish will distort (the exception is 'blue' trout – *see* box).

Shallow poaching uses quite a small amount of liquid in relation to the food, so there is no need to preheat the liquid because it and the food will heat up quickly from cold.

In shallow poaching the liquid is normally used to form the basis of the sauce which will accompany the cooked food. We have made the level of liquid in this photograph lower than it would usually be so that you can see clearly that the fish is resting on chopped onion at the bottom of the cooking utensil. This helps to keep the fish in one piece, and adds flavour to the fish and the sauce. Any proteins which have dissolved into the liquid during cooking will remain in the sauce.

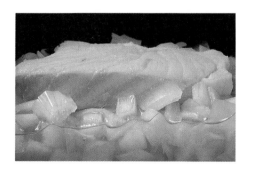

✚ HYGIENE

Poaching temperatures will allow the survival of certain types of bacteria, so it is important that any poached food, especially if it is decorated by hand, spends as little time as possible in a warm environment – because this would provide the perfect conditions for the bacteria to multiply and eventually to cause food poisoning. If the food is not going to be eaten immediately after cooking, cool it quickly, cover it, and put it in the refrigerator until it is needed. If the decorating itself takes a long time, e.g. a whole poached salmon for a buffet table, then try to work with the food on a bed of ice, and do the job as fast as possible. Often a simple bold design will be just as appealing as a complicated one that might take hours, and much more hygienic. Hand decoration also involves the risk of contamination by the bacteria commonly present on hands.

An exception to the rule of starting whole fish from cold is so-called 'blue' trout (or carp or pike). This effect can only be achieved with fish that are cooked within minutes of being killed and have not had their slimy surface layer washed off. The fish are placed in hot liquid containing vinegar which turns the slimy layer blue while the heat makes them distort.

▸▸▸ TO DO

Take a firm, fresh pear, remove the peel, cut it in half and remove the core. Heat 250 ml (9 fl oz) of water to just under boiling point in a small saucepan. In a second, similar-sized saucepan, bring an equal quantity of water plus 100 g (4 oz) of sugar to just below boiling point. Poach one half of the pear in each of the saucepans for 5 minutes, covering the fruit (which will float) with a piece of greased paper so that it does not dry out. Allow both halves to cool in the cooking liquid, then compare their texture and flavour. Which one is firmer and which has the better flavour?

3 POACHING

There are a limited number of foods that can be poached successfully. Because of the relatively low temperatures and short cooking times involved, items to be poached should be of the best quality and very fresh. Typically, foods suitable for poaching are of fine texture and delicate flavour. Often the food is cut into small, thin pieces, so that the heat penetrates quickly and evenly.

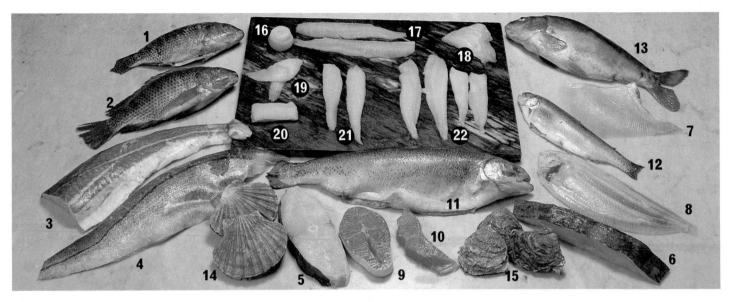

Round white: 1) Grey mullet (prepared) 2) Grey mullet (unprepared) 3) Cod fillet 4) Haddock fillet. **Flat white:** 5) Halibut steak (darne) 6) Turbot (tronçon) 7) Skate wing 8) Lemon sole. **Oily:** 9) Salmon steak (darne) 10) Cutlet of salmon (or half darne) 11) Salmon trout 12) Rainbow trout. **Round:** (freshwater) 13) Carp. **Molluscs:** 14) Scallops 15) Oysters. **Various cuts:** 16) Paupiette of lemon sole 17) Fillet of whiting 18) Suprême of cod 19) Cravate of lemon sole (folded into a loop) 20) Délice of lemon sole 21) Fillet of lemon sole 22) Fillets of plaice.

Why fish is good for poaching

The protein structure of fish makes it ideal for poaching, although strong-tasting fish like sardines are not often poached.

The setting or coagulation of protein, which is the reason why translucent raw fish turns opaque and firm as it cooks, happens much faster in fish than it does in meat. The process can be speeded up by the addition of acid, which is why lemon juice, wine or vinegar and onions or shallots are used in many poached fish recipes.

Small fish, either round or flat, can be poached whole, but there are many sorts of fish which are filleted before poaching. Fillets may be folded in half to form 'délices', or rolled up to make 'paupiettes'. If the fillets are large, they may be cut, on a slant, to form 'suprêmes'. Large fish can be filleted or cut (through the bone) into steaks: steaks from round fish are called 'darnes' and steaks from flat fish are called 'tronçons'.

Fish may also be made into 'quenelles'. The raw fish flesh is pounded to a smooth paste and cream and egg whites are mixed in with it. The resulting mixture is then shaped into small cigar shapes and poached in fish stock.

All these styles of presentation ensure an even shape which makes for even cooking.

Types of fish

Fish are sometimes divided up according to their condition when purchased: frozen, tinned, smoked, 'wet' (meaning fresh as opposed to salted) and sometimes by where they come from: sea or freshwater. (Freshwater fish are sometimes divided into river and lake fish.)

But perhaps the most useful way of classifying fish for caterers is:
1) by their shape, whether they are *flat* or *round*
2) by the general characteristics of their flesh, whether they are *white* or *oily*.

Flat fish such as sole and plaice are filleted in a different way from round fish such as cod, hake, whiting, salmon and herrings. The reason is quite simply to get the best-sized fillets in the easiest way.

The flesh of the last two examples, salmon and herrings, has a different and easily detectable characteristic. It is oily – there is more fat in its flesh than in white fish. Other oily fish are mackerel, tuna, anchovies and sardines, quite different in flavour and taste to white fish such as turbot and halibut.

For classification of shellfish, e.g. lobster, crab, scallops, *see* Boiling/Food Selection 6.

For caterers who have difficulty in obtaining fresh fish at the right time and price, the huge range of frozen fish now available offers a solution:

1. Prawns
2. Whole trout
3. Cockles
4. Codling
5. Monk fish tails
6. Mussels
7. Herring
8. Scampi
9. Salmon steaks

10. Breaded haddock
11. White crab meat
12. Smoked trout fillets
13. Scallops

Freezing does not improve the flavour and texture of fish, so fresh fish is always better if it is possible to get it. Deep-frozen fish starts to deteriorate after two to three months so always check the date stamp on the wrapping or packet.

Buying points

Wet fish
– The skin should be bright and have a good sheen. Dull or slimy skin is a bad sign. The scales should be firmly attached.
– The eyes should be bright and clear, not sunken or cloudy.
– The flesh should be smooth, firm and springy to the touch. After pressing with a finger, the dent should flatten out quickly.
– The smell should not be sour or unpleasant (although skate does occasionally smell of ammonia until it is cooked).
– The gills (if present) should be bright blood-red underneath when lifted.

Frozen fish
– The packaging should be undamaged and the fish itself completely firm.
– There should be no dull white patches (a sign of freezer burn caused by poor or over-long storage).

Why fish have white flesh
Most fish have white flesh, whereas most meat is dark. Chickens and turkeys have white breast meat and brown leg meat, while game is usually dark all over. This variation in colour depends on how much general work the muscle does. The more work, the darker the colour. The colour is due to a protein in muscles called myoglobin which stores oxygen. Fish are supported by the water they swim in so they do not require large amounts of oxygen for their muscles. As a result these muscles contain very little myoglobin, and their flesh is very often white.

The bright and glossy surfaces of the smoked fish on this stall are a sign of good quality and freshness.

Smoked fish should have a pleasant, smoky smell. Colour is not a good guide to quality, because some smoked fish is dyed and different degrees of smoking may have been used. But the colour should be even and the flesh of the fish firm to the touch.

Meat and offal

Red meat is almost never poached because the low temperatures and short cooking times are unsuitable for even the most tender cuts.

The very finest quality chicken breast can sometimes be poached, cut as a suprême (*see* Practical Examples 2). Chicken and veal may also be prepared and poached as quenelles (*see* Food Selection 1) or mousselines (which are larger), for which the meat is finely minced and therefore cooks much faster than it otherwise would.

It is important to remember, though, that what is sometimes described as 'poached chicken' on a menu has often actually been boiled, and cooked for a far longer time than would normally be associated with poaching, e.g. an hour for a 1½ kg young fowl.

Some of the internal organs (offal) of young animals, as they have a more delicate structure than the meat, benefit from the poaching process. Typical examples are calf and lamb brains and sweetbreads (the thymus or neck gland and/or pancreas of an animal).

Eggs

Eggs can be poached if they are cracked very carefully into almost boiling water with the heat reduced so low that there are no bubbles bursting. A little vinegar may be added to make the cooking water acidic. This helps the rapid coagulation (setting) of the egg white and so stops the egg spreading out in the cooking water. It also lowers the temperature at which the protein will set, resulting in a softer cooked egg.

A fresh egg has a very thick white. During storage, the natural ageing process causes the white to become more and more runny, so it is possible to tell quite easily if eggs are not fresh by the consistency of the white when they are cracked open. In stored eggs, the membrane that surrounds the yolk is weakened so the yolk breaks very easily. So if you want to poach eggs, make sure they are very fresh and then they should hold their shape when dropped into the poaching liquid.

Vegetables

Poaching is not usually used as a method of cooking vegetables. It is too slow and not hot enough for green and root vegetables.

Mushrooms, tomatoes, onions and shallots are used in many poaching recipes to provide a base for other foods and to add flavour either to the main dish or to the accompanying sauce. Shallots, which are a variety of onions, have a mild, subtle flavour and are good for this purpose, although spring onions can provide a cheaper alternative.

Fruits

A wide variety of fresh fruits are poached. They should be of uniform size and shape, without blemishes and with no discoloration. The cooking time varies considerably depending on the type of fruit. Strawberries, for example, have only to be covered with hot syrup to cook, while apples are brought almost to the boil and then allowed to cool in the poaching liquid.

The poaching liquid for fruit is usually a solution of water and sugar which has been brought to the boil to form a syrup. Lemon juice is normally added to help keep the fruit firm. The sugar also helps in this way, by strengthening the cell walls of the fruit.

Frozen fruits are generally unsuitable for poaching as the cell walls have often been broken down already by the freezing process, so they are too mushy. Bottled and tinned fruits will have been poached already as part of the preservation process.

Soft fruits deteriorate quickly so it is best to purchase only small quantities as required. Some fruits may be individually wrapped in tissue and packed into boxes with cardboard trays separating the layers of fruit. This cuts down the risk of bruising and disease being passed from one fruit to another. Modern transportation and storage ensures that most fruits are available throughout the year and means that caterers no longer have to rely on local produce.

Fruits can be classified under various headings:
Berries, e.g. strawberry, blackcurrant, grape.
Citrus, e.g. orange, lemon, lime.
Stone, e.g. peach, cherry, apricot.
Hard, e.g. apple, pear.
Tropical, e.g. pineapple, banana, kiwi.

Some fresh fruits for poaching: 1) Pineapple 2) Pears 3) Peach 4) Plums 5) Cooking apple (Bramley) 6) Dessert apple (Granny Smith) 7) Dessert apple (Red Delicious)

♟ CHEF'S TIP

Don't rinse berries until they are about to be prepared or served. The water will remove their thin protective layer of 'bloom' (a kind of wild yeast) and they will then deteriorate quickly.

Some dried fruits:
1) Prunes 2) Figs 3) Pears
4) Dates 5) Apricots
6) Apples 7) Peaches

Drying – reducing the water content of tissue to the point that very few microbes can grow in it – is one of the oldest methods of food preservation. Prunes, raisins and dates are still dried in the sun in many parts of the world, but forced hot-air drying is now widely used.

Dried fruit should be soaked before poaching so that the water content is replaced efficiently. The use of warm water reduces the time needed for soaking and produces a better texture and flavour than overnight soaking in cold water: two hours in water at about 80°C (176°F) should be enough.

Terms

In *shallow poaching* the food is only partially covered in liquid, which is often used as the basis of a sauce after the food has been cooked.

In *deep poaching* the food is cooked in enough liquid to cover it completely (although some food, like fruit, floats). Once cooked, the food is often allowed to cool in the liquid so that it can absorb any flavours that have been added. Some of the cooking liquid may accompany the finished dish, but it is never all used to form a sauce, as in shallow poaching.

A *fumet* is a concentrated fish stock often used when shallow-poaching fish. It results in a more flavoursome finished dish.

A *cartouche* is another name for the piece of greaseproof paper that is placed over shallow-poached foods while they are cooking. It helps keep the moisture in and so reduces the tendency of food to shrink while cooking. It is particularly necessary for dealing with fruit, which floats and so has a lot of its surface exposed to the air.

A *court-bouillon* is a vegetable stock made with water and wine or vinegar and used as cooking liquid – mainly for fish.

Equipment

Any saucepan or bratt pan used for boiling will also be suitable for deep poaching, so long as the food to be cooked will fit into it comfortably and can be removed easily.

Fish kettles are specially designed for poaching whole fish, and come in different shapes and sizes for the various types of fish. The lid fits tightly. A perforated drainer fits into the bottom of the kettle and has handles that will reach above the surface of the cooking liquid on either side. This is useful for removing the cooked fish. Fish kettles are made of stainless steel, aluminium or tin-lined copper.

Round or oval frying pans, sauteuses, and *plats à sauter (see* Book 1, Shallow Frying/Terms and Equipment) are often used for shallow poaching. Oval dishes made from tin-lined copper, fireproof china, or enamelled cast iron are also suitable.

IMPORTANT
If the pan or dish is to be placed in the oven as part of the cooking process, always make sure that its handles are heat proof.

Equipment hygiene

Always check the equipment you are going to use for cracks or defects that may hold bacteria or could even cause the equipment to break when it is being used. Report any defects to your supervisor and do not use a damaged piece of equipment. After cooking make sure that all the equipment used is thoroughly clean by washing it in hot water and detergent, rinsing it and finally drying it.

A vinegar court-bouillon, as shown above, complements the flavour of oily fish such as salmon, trout and skate, and shellfish (when the vinegar also has a tenderising effect). The ingredients – water, onion, carrot, celery, leek, parsley, bay leaf, thyme, peppercorns, salt and vinegar – are brought to the boil and simmered for 15-20 minutes.

The court-bouillon can be made either in the fish kettle, or separately in a saucepan allowing it to be strained into the fish kettle when cooked. This second method has the advantage of keeping the fish free of the vegetable ingredients which would need to be removed later. Either way, the court-bouillon is allowed to get cold before the fish is added.

Egg poachers and how to use them

An egg poacher is similar to an omelette pan but with a lid and a tray with circular cut-outs into which small round egg moulds are placed.

Put enough water in the pan to come up to but not over the egg moulds and heat the water until it simmers. Each mould is buttered and seasoned before the raw egg is broken into it. A lid is then placed on the pan of gently simmering water and the eggs are cooked until the white has set and the yolk is soft.

Though commonly called 'poached eggs' they are more correctly called moulded eggs (*oeufs moulés*) because the egg never comes into contact with water. The addition of butter in the cooking removes one of the health advantages of true poached eggs, namely that they are low in fat.

▶▶▶ TO DO

Make a list of the equipment available in the kitchen at your workplace, college or home which would be suitable for poaching:
1. two paupiettes of sole
2. a large trout
3. dried prunes.
Which method of poaching would you use for each (deep or shallow) and why?

3 POACHING

Essential points

The stages that you will be assessed on for the Caterbase module, *Poaching*, are covered by the steps in this section.

1. Prepare your work area, collecting the equipment and ingredients you will need, and removing anything that is not required.

> Make sure everything is spotlessly clean. Raw foods, particularly fish and meat, should always be kept separate: if you are preparing fish do not use a board that has been used for cutting raw meat.
>
> Select the type of container that is best for the food to be cooked, taking size and shape into account.

2. Prepare the ingredients as required for the dish you are cooking, or as stated in the recipe instructions.

> Fresh fish, if scaly, should be scaled before deep poaching as the skin is left on for the cooking. For shallow poaching the skin is removed (unless it is easier to remove it after cooking).
>
> Frozen fish must be defrosted before poaching (with the possible exception of small cuts). This will avoid uneven cooking, which can lead to a risk of food poisoning.
>
> Dried fruit should be soaked before poaching. Hard fruit and peaches should be peeled (peaches are blanched first to ease skinning). The stalks of pears are normally left on and the bottoms trimmed so that the pears will rest upright. Gooseberries are topped and tailed, as are blackcurrants. Other berries should have stalks removed. Stones can be removed from peaches, apricots, nectarines, plums and cherries after the fruit has been cut in half. Rhubarb is trimmed and cut into lengths of about 4 cm (or just under 2 in.). Green rhubarb should be peeled before cooking.

3. Prepare the cooking liquid – the amount and whether it is cold or hot will depend on the food being cooked. If the cooking liquid is being prepared in a separate container (e.g. as for a court-bouillon or a fish fumet) it will later need to be strained, usually cooled and transferred to the fish kettle, saucepan, sauteuse or whatever cooking container is being used.

> For whole or large pieces of fish, the deep poaching liquid should be cold to prevent the fish twisting or distorting.
>
> With small cuts of fish and flat fish, some preparation can be done in advance of shallow poaching. They are placed in the cooking container, usually resting on a base of chopped vegetables, then covered and chilled. When the time comes for the food to be cooked, the liquid is added (usually cold). This two-stage method is particularly useful for large banquets, or any event where as much as possible needs to be prepared in advance.
>
> Fruit is cooked in hot syrup, often with lemon juice added.
>
> Eggs are placed into hot liquid (water with a little vinegar).

4. Add seasoning and flavourings.

> Often these are already part of the cooking liquid, as in a court-bouillon or sugar syrup. Always take care not to spoil delicate flavours by over-seasoning or using too much of a liquid which has a particularly strong flavour, like vinegar.

5. Maintain the cooking temperature carefully.

> Remember one of the main differences between poaching and boiling, stewing or braising is that the temperature of the cooking liquid should *never* reach boiling point. This is to prevent the damage to the texture of delicate foods that can be done unless poaching is used.
>
> But also remember that you cannot usually cook the accompanying sauce in the same way. Any starch used to thicken it will not cook properly at poaching temperatures and will need to be prepared separately.

6. Take care that the food does not burn, stick or dry out.

Covering the food with paper (buttered or greased to prevent it sticking to shallow-poached food) will help ensure even heat distribution. A paper covering is also important when deep poaching food like fruit, which tends to float.

Keeping the container covered (using a lid or tin foil to cover an oval dish or deep tray) is another way of ensuring even heat distribution and making the temperature control easier.

7. Drain the food carefully, prepare any accompanying sauce and serve the whole dish as attractively as possible.

In deep poaching the food is often allowed to cool in the cooking liquid, which helps the flavours to develop more fully and keeps the food moist. It must then be carefully drained.

Careful draining is important whether the food is served hot or cold, as any cooking liquid left on the food will spoil the appearance of the sauce. Take great care in handling the food while draining because it may easily fall apart.

If fish has been cooked with its skin on, this should be removed before service. The centre bone can also be removed from fish steaks, using the point of a sharp knife to separate it from the flesh. The side bones should be removed from whole flat fish.

When reducing the sauce after removing fish which has been shallow poached, shake the pan gently from time to time and stir the liquid to prevent burning. If you are adding butter to enrich the sauce, do this at the last minute and do not allow the sauce to boil again, otherwise the butter fat will separate out and float to the surface, producing an unattractive effect.

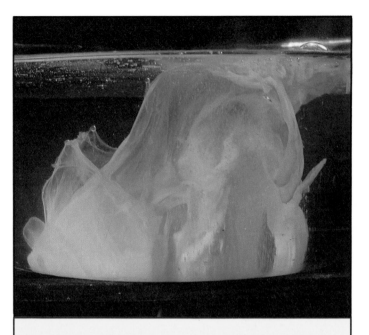

Neatness of shape in a poached egg is a test of the chef's skill. But it is only possible to perfect this skill with fresh eggs – as an egg ages it becomes more watery and the white will spread out in the water, rather than staying in an attractive shape.

Some recipes suggest cracking the egg into boiling water, explaining that the action of the boiling water will cause the egg white to wrap around the yolk. But in fact the convection currents are quite strong enough just below boiling point to produce this wrapping effect. Also, if you are poaching several eggs at the same time the fierce heat necessary to keep the liquid boiling while the eggs were added would mean that the first eggs would suffer badly from being cooked too fast.

♟ CHEF'S TIP

Instead of attempting to crack the egg directly into the hot water, break it into a cup first. Then let it slip gently into the water over the lip of the cup.

▸▸ TO DO

Cold decorated salmon trout can look wonderful when presented for service, but it takes some time to prepare. Read the recipe in the next section and work out the time you will need for each stage, including assembling the ingredients. How long in advance of service will you need to start work on the recipe?

If possible, prepare the recipe and time yourself doing it. You may choose to do this in a group.

Eggs florentine
Oeufs pochés florentines

INGREDIENTS		SERVES 10
10	fresh eggs (size 1 or 2)	10
	white wine vinegar	
1¼ kg	spinach	3 lb
50 g	butter or margarine	2 oz
750 ml	Mornay sauce (see box)	1½ pt
50 g	grated Parmesan cheese	2 oz
	salt and milled black pepper to taste	

1. Poach the eggs as follows:
   a) Fill a shallow-sided pan (a large plat à sauter/sauté pan is ideal) with water to a depth of 65 mm (2½ in.).
   b) Add the vinegar – 50 ml (2 fl oz) vinegar per litre (2 pt) of water.
   c) Place the pan on the stove and bring it to the boil.
   d) Reduce the heat so that the temperature falls just below boiling point.
   e) Carefully break each egg into the water so that the egg white wraps round the yolk.

   f) Allow each egg to cook until the white is set but the yolk still liquid (2½-4 minutes). Make sure that the temperature of the water is kept at just below boiling point.
   g) Carefully remove the eggs and place them into a bowl of water containing ice cubes until they need to be served.

2. Remove the stems from the leaves of the spinach and wash the leaves in cold water.

3. Place the spinach into a small quantity of boiling salted water, cover the pan with a lid, and boil for 3 to 5 minutes.

4. When cooked, cool the spinach quickly under cold running water, then drain it thoroughly in a conical strainer or sieve, squeeze it dry and form it into balls, one ball per portion.

5. Melt the butter or margarine in a sauteuse and then heat it until it foams. Add the spinach and cook it gently until it is hot enough for service. Season to taste.

6. Reheat the eggs in a saucepan of very hot (but not boiling) salted water for about 1 minute.

7. Neatly arrange the hot spinach on the serving dish.

8. Drain the eggs thoroughly and place them on top of the spinach.

9. Coat the eggs and spinach with the hot Mornay sauce, than sprinkle the grated Parmesan cheese on top.

10. Place the dish under a pre-heated overhead grill or salamander until the surface of the sauce turns golden brown, then serve immediately.

Mornay sauce

INGREDIENTS		MAKES 750 ml (1½ pint)
75g	butter or margarine	3 oz
75g	flour	3 oz
750 ml	milk	1½ pt
1	onion clouté (onion with bay leaf attached to it by a clove)	1
75g	grated cheese (Gruyère, and an equal amount of Parmesan, or a similar hard cheese to taste)	3 oz
	salt and ground white pepper to taste	

1. In a saucepan, gently heat the onion clouté with the milk for 5 to 8 minutes. (This is sometimes called infusing.)

2. Melt the butter or margarine in a second saucepan, then add the flour and mix.

3. Cook over a low heat for 4 to 5 minutes making sure that the mixture does not turn colour. This is making a white roux.

4. Remove the onion from the milk and set aside. Slowly blend the hot milk into the butter and flour mixture, stirring till smooth each time milk is added.

5. Put the onion clouté in the sauce and bring the sauce to the boil.

6. Reduce the heat and simmer it gently for 8 to 10 minutes. Skim off any surface fat or impurities that may rise to the surface.

7. Remove and discard the onion. Strain the sauce if any lumps have formed.

8. Check seasoning and consistency – the sauce should be thick, creamy and smooth enough to pour.

9. You have now made Béchamel sauce. To turn it into Mornay sauce, add the grated cheese, stirring until it is thoroughly melted.

Italian-style gnocchi

INGREDIENTS SERVES 20 (as first course or starter)

Gnocchi mixture

800 g	potatoes (floury variety)	2 lb
4	egg yolks	4
75 g	butter or margarine	3 oz
100 g	flour	4 oz
to taste	salt, pepper and nutmeg	to taste

Additional ingredients

100 g	butter or margarine	4 oz
1 l	tomato sauce (see box)	2 pt
75 g	grated Parmesan cheese	3 oz

1. Wash and peel the potatoes and remove any eyes. If the potatoes are large or of different sizes, cut them into even-sized pieces.

2. Boil the potatoes until they are tender, then drain them.

3. Mash the potatoes in a mixing bowl (or in the saucepan they have cooked in, then transfer to the bowl).

4. Mix the flour, egg yolks, butter or margarine and seasoning through the hot mashed potato until everything is properly combined.

5. Using the palm of one hand and the fingers of the other, mould the mixture into small balls – 20 mm (¾ in.) wide, putting a little flour on your hands if the mixture gets too sticky.

6. Lightly flatten the balls and draw the prongs of a fork across them to decorate them.

7. Place the gnocchi into salted water just below boiling point in a shallow-sided saucepan, then poach until cooked (approximately 6 minutes), making sure the water never boils.

8. Remove the gnocchi and drain them thoroughly in a colander.

9. Melt the butter or margarine in a sauteuse or plat à sauter.

10. Add the gnocchi and roll them in the hot butter.

11. Gently blend in the tomato sauce, taking care not to damage the gnocchi.

12. Arrange the gnocchi in a serving dish and sprinkle with the Parmesan.

13. Place under a pre-heated grill or salamander until golden brown (gratinate).

Tomato sauce

INGREDIENTS   MAKES 1 litre (2 pints)

100 g	butter or margarine	4 oz
100 g	flour	4 oz
100 g	carrots	4 oz
100 g	onion	4 oz
50 g	celery	2 oz
50 g	leek	2 oz
	1 clove garlic, sprig of thyme, 1 bay leaf and 3 or 4 parsley stalks	
50 g	streaky bacon	2 oz
100 g	tomato purée	4 oz
1 l	brown stock (see Introduction/Stocks)	2 pt
	salt and ground white pepper to taste	

1. Wash, peel and prepare the vegetables:
   a) Roughly chop the carrots, onion, celery and leek.
   b) Crush the garlic.

2. Cut the bacon into pieces about 1 cm (½ in.) long.

3. Melt the butter or margarine in a saucepan.

4. Add the bacon and vegetables and cook without allowing to colour for 6 to 8 minutes.

5. Add the flour and mix in.

6. Cook the roux over a low heat for about 5 minutes, stirring regularly so it does not burn.

7. Add the tomato purée and mix in.

8. Slowly blend in the hot stock, stirring smooth with each addition of stock.

9. Bring to the boil and allow to simmer slowly until the flavours have fully developed – about 1 hour. Stir occasionally during cooking to prevent sticking and burning. Also skim the sauce if any scum forms and top up with additional stock if it gets very thick.

10. When cooked, strain the sauce or pass it through a liquidiser.

11. Check consistency (which should be similar to that of double cream) and season to taste.

Basic steps in preparing chicken

This information will help you to gain the Caterbase module, *Preparing Poultry*, and will also be useful in dealing with pheasant and grouse.

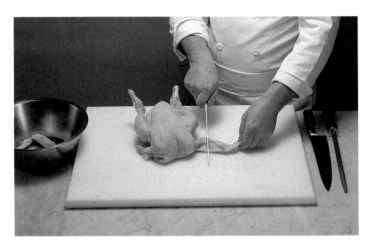

Nowadays most poultry is delivered to catering establishments already plucked and cleaned. If the giblets (internal organs) have been left (look for them in the chest cavity), they should be removed.

If you are using a freshly killed bird, perhaps from a local farmer, first remove all the feathers. Pull them out carefully to avoid damaging the skin (work somewhere well apart from other food as the feathers will get everywhere). Start with the breast, followed by the back, wings and legs.

Rotate the bird briefly over a naked flame (the burner on a gas stove will do) to singe off any small remaining hairs. Remove any remaining feather stubs with the tip of a small knife.

Then remove the head. Holding it firmly with one hand slit along the skin of the neck and fully expose the flesh on the neck. Push the skin back and cut through the neck close to the body. Strip out the gullet, crop and windpipe from the neck cavity and discard.

Turn the bird on its back. Make a small slit above the vent (just below the parson's nose). It is best to pinch the skin up so that you do not puncture the intestines. Remove any fat from around the opening, then insert two fingers into the bird and work around the edges of the cavity to free all the internal organs from the ribs.

Squeeze the chicken to force the entrails towards the opening. Grip them firmly and withdraw.

Check that you have removed all the innards. Then wipe around the inside of the bird with a clean cloth. (Don't wash the bird unless it is to be cooked immediately.) The neck may be kept for use in stocks. Sometimes the heart, liver and gizzard are also reserved for use in other dishes. The other waste must be cleared away at once and the board and bench thoroughly washed before you continue work.

After all this has been done remove the wishbone. Lift open the flap of flesh, scrape down each side of the breast to expose both halves of the wishbone. Slip the blade of the knife behind the bones. Finally work up the bones with the fingers to free them from the flesh, when you reach the flat piece which joins the two halves, twist the wish bone to detach it completely. Replace the flap of flesh. Remove the winglets cutting through the middle of the first joint from the chicken.

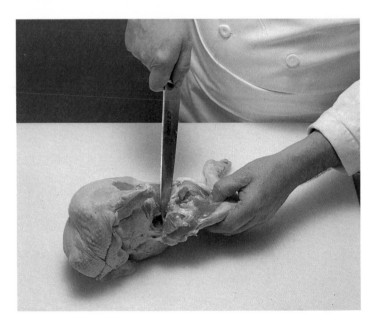

Remove each leg by folding the leg back away from the carcase, cutting it carefully away as you do so. Cut around the 'oyster' of flesh underneath the carcase so it comes away with the leg. When you have reached the ball joint, pull the leg back firmly and cut through the joint.

If you are preparing the chicken for shallow frying or stewing:

Cut along the length of the breast, parallel to the breast bone and about halfway between the breast bone and the wing joint. (The aim is to produce four equal-sized portions from the breast.) Cut down through the flesh until you reach the wing joint. Cut through this.

See: Video 4

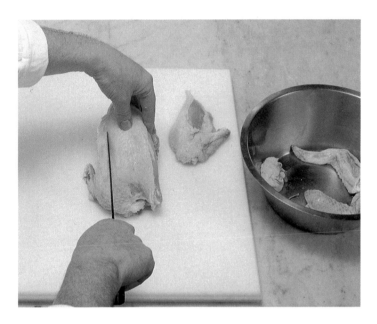

Hold the chicken by the parson's nose in an upright position, and using a heavy knife chop down between the carcase and the breast.

If you are preparing suprêmes (whole breast portions):
Remove the skin from the breast. Cut down the side of the breast bone using a filleting action so that the flesh is all removed from the carcase, then down through the wing joint to detach the suprême.

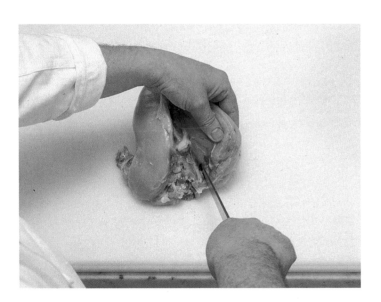

Chicken prepared for shallow frying or stewing:
The breast is then cut in half, diagonally through the centre using a firm pressing action with the knife so that you cut through the breast bone cleanly.

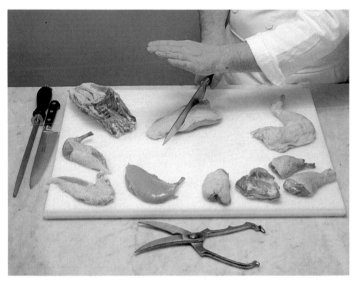

In this photograph the remaining lower half of the carcase is shown top left. This can be cut into three equal pieces and used as part of the final presentation. The carcase pieces are arranged in a Y shape and the rest of the chicken is reformed on this base. The carcase pieces are *not* served to the customers.

The first two cuts from the chicken breast are shown bottom left. The flesh has been scraped away from the bone in the top sample (the custom in high-class service).

The leg pieces are shown on the right of the photograph, also prepared in different styles. At the top is the whole, untrimmed leg. This is then cut in two through the middle joint. The leg below the bottom knuckle is always removed (*bottom right*) from the lower part of the leg; in high-class service the flesh near the knuckle is also cut away and the bone scraped clean (*centre right*). The bone from the top half of the leg is also removed in high-class service (*centre*).

The trimmed suprême, with the flesh trimmed away from the bone, is shown centre left.

The poultry sécateurs at the foot of the photograph are used sometimes for jointing and trimming poultry.

Poached suprême of chicken with asparagus
served with braised rice

INGREDIENTS		SERVES 20
20 × 175 g	*suprêmes of chicken*	20 × 7 oz
25 g	*butter or margarine*	1 oz
100 g	*finely chopped shallot or onion*	4 oz
250 ml	*dry white wine*	½ pt
750 ml	*chicken stock*	1½ pt
500 ml	*cream*	1 pt
1½ l	*chicken velouté (see note below)*	3 pt
60	*asparagus spears (3 tips per portion) (900 g/2¼ lb)*	60

1. Lightly butter the inside of a large plat à sauter or sauteuse (alternatively a bratt pan may be used).

2. Sprinkle the chopped shallots or onions over the base of the pan then place the suprêmes on them.

3. Add the white wine and then the stock so that the suprêmes are just covered.

4. Cover with a piece of buttered paper, place the lid on the pan and bring the liquid almost to the boil.

5. Allow it to poach over a low heat or transfer the pan to a moderate oven until cooked – about 15 minutes.

6. Remove the suprêmes, cover them with the cooking paper, and keep them hot on a suitable dish or tray in a warm oven or a hot cupboard.

7. Boil the cooking liquor vigorously so that it reduces to a third of its original volume, then add the cream.

8. Further reduce the liquor by two-thirds, then add the velouté.

9. Bring the liquor to the boil and then allow it to simmer for 2 to 3 minutes.

10. Check consistency (the liquid should be thick and creamy) and seasoning.

11. Meanwhile prepare and cook the asparagus:
    a) Wash the asparagus spears and peel the lower half of the stalks if necessary. Tie them into bundles.
    b) Put the bundles into boiling salted water so that they are covered and simmer them until cooked – about 10 minutes.
    c) Trim each spear to leave the tip and a short length of stalk.

12. Coat a serving dish with a little of the completed sauce then neatly arrange the suprêmes in the dish.

13. Place on top of each suprême 3 hot asparagus tips, then coat with the sauce and serve. Alternatively place the asparagus spears in a neat pile alongside the suprême.

For chicken velouté, follow the fish velouté instructions opposite, but use chicken stock instead of fish stock.

Braised rice
Riz pilaff

INGREDIENTS		SERVES 20
500 g	*long grain rice*	1¼ lb
100 g	*butter or margarine*	4 oz
250 g	*shallots or onions*	10 oz
900 ml	*chicken or vegetable stock*	1¾ pt
	salt and milled pepper to taste	

1. Peel and finely chop the shallots or onions.

2. Melt half the butter or margarine in a sauteuse or plat à sauter.

3. Add the shallots or onions and cook gently for about 3 minutes until they are soft, taking care that they do not colour but remain pale and translucent. This process is known as 'sweating'.

4. Add the rice and sweat for a further 3 minutes. Stir frequently, making sure that it does not stick or burn.

5. Stir in the chicken stock and bring to the boil.

6. Cover the food with a circle of buttered greaseproof paper, then put the lid on.

7. Place in a hot oven – 220°C (425°F) – for about 15 minutes. When cooked, the rice should have absorbed all the stock leaving the rice grains dry and easy to separate.

8. Stir the remaining butter through the rice with a fork.

9. Check seasoning and serve as soon as possible.

Poached suprême of halibut Bréval style
Suprême de flétan Bréval

INGREDIENTS		SERVES 4
4 × 150 g	*halibut suprêmes*	4 × 6 oz
5 g	*butter*	¼ oz
25 g	*finely chopped shallot or onion*	1¼ oz
100 g	*sliced white mushrooms*	4 oz
100 g	*tomato concassé (skinned and*	4 oz
	chopped tomato flesh)	
	chopped parsley	
50 ml	*dry white wine*	2 fl oz
150 ml	*fish stock (see Introduction/Stocks)*	6 fl oz
	squeeze lemon juice	
300 ml	*fish velouté (see below)*	12 fl oz
50 ml	*whipping or double cream*	2 fl oz
8	*fleurons (puff pastry crescents)*	8

1. To produce suprêmes, lay a fillet of halibut on a chopping board presentation side upwards, then cut neat slices at a slant across the fillet.

2. Butter the base of a dish or pan suitable for cooking fish and add the shallots, mushrooms, tomato concassé and some of the chopped parsley.

3. Place the suprêmes, presentation side up, in the dish and sprinkle on the remaining chopped parsley.

4. Add the wine, lemon juice and enough fish stock to bring the liquid to two-thirds the height of the suprêmes.

5. Cover with a piece of buttered greaseproof paper, put the lid on the pan, and place the pan over the heat.

6. Bring almost to the boil then transfer to a moderate oven 175°C (350°F). Cooking time: about 6 minutes.

7. When cooked, remove the suprêmes to a suitable dish or tray and keep warm in a warm oven or hot cupboard covered with the cooking paper.

8. Boil the cooking liquor vigorously until it has reduced to a thick and concentrated state.

9. Add the fish velouté (*see* box) and bring to the boil.

10. Meanwhile whip the cream until stiff.

11. Remove the sauce from the heat and lightly fold the whipped cream through it.

Sometimes a warm egg and butter mixture (sabayon) is used instead of the cream. If so, prepare a sabayon as explained in Boiling/Practical Examples 6, using white wine or fish stock in place of the vinegar.

CHEF'S TIP

A border of piped and duchesse potato browned under a grill may be used as a garnish in place of the fleurons.

12. Check seasoning, then coat the base of a serving dish with a little of the sauce.

13. Arrange the suprêmes on the dish, presentation side upwards, then coat them with the remaining sauce.

14. Place the dish under a pre-heated grill or salamander and allow to develop a good golden brown colour.

15. Garnish with the fleurons and serve.

Alternatives
Halibut is quite an expensive fish and can be difficult to obtain. This recipe can also be used for other white fish, such as sole or plaice, either whole (if small) or in any of the cuts: fillets, suprêmes, steaks, etc.

Fish velouté

INGREDIENTS		MAKES 1 litre (2 pints)
100 g	*butter or margarine*	4 oz
100 g	*flour*	4 oz
1 l	*fish stock (hot)*	2 pt
	salt and ground white pepper to taste	

1. Melt the butter or margarine in a saucepan, then add the flour and mix together.

2. Cook over a low heat for 4 to 5 minutes to make a white roux making sure that the mixture does not turn colour (this happens if the heat is too fierce).

3. Slowly blend in the hot fish stock stirring till smooth with each addition of stock.

4. Bring to the boil and slowly simmer for 8-10 minutes. (Traditionally velouté took 1 hour to cook, but modern flour now makes this unnecessary.) Skim off any surface fat or impurities that rise to the surface.

5. Strain the sauce if lumps have appeared.

6. Check seasoning and consistency (it should be smooth and creamy).

Cold decorated salmon trout

INGREDIENTS   SERVES 4 to 6

1¼ kg	whole salmon trout	3 lb
4 l	cold vinegar court-bouillon	8 pt
	(see *Terms and Equipment*)	
1 l	fish aspic (see *Boiling/Practical Examples 4*)	2 pt

Garnish

100 ml	fish chaudfroid sauce (see *opposite*)	4 fl oz
1	mushroom	1
6	cooked asparagus tips	6
6	radishes	6
1	cucumber	1
4	hard-boiled eggs	4
1	leek	1
18	cooked and peeled prawn tails	18
6	large whole prawns	6
	(cooked, shells removed from tails)	
250 ml	fish aspic	½ pt
	mayonnaise sauce see *Boiling/Practical Examples 2*)	
	anchovy essence (bottled)	

1. Prepare the fish for cooking (*see* Book 1, Grilling/Practical Examples).

2. Place the fish on the perforated rack of a fish kettle and add the cold court-bouillon until the fish is covered. Cover with a lid.

3. Place the fish kettle over heat and bring the liquid almost to boiling point, skimming it if a scum forms.

4. Poach the fish for 10 to 15 minutes, then remove it from the heat and, leaving it in the cooking liquor, cool as quickly as possible. If this stage takes too long, the fish will go on cooking in the warm liquid and will overcook. The fish can be kept chilled in the liquid until it is to be skinned but never keep for longer than a day or so.

5. Remove the fish from the court-bouillon and drain.

6. Carefully remove the skin with a palette or filleting knife and scrape the brown surface off the flesh. Also remove the base of any fins along the back and belly. Finally check the fish and remove any remaining bits of loose skin or flesh.

7. Place the fish on a wire cooling tray resting in another tray and refrigerate until ready for decorating.

8. Carefully pour an even layer of aspic about 4mm (⅛ in.) thick on to a suitable fish-serving dish. Place in the refrigerator to set.

9. Prepare the garnish (*see* opposite).

10. Coat the fish with a layer of aspic.

11. Place the plaque on to the fish, then carefully peel off the dampened paper. Place the decorated mushroom in the centre of the plaque.

12. Decorate the fish with the garnish of strips of leek leaves, slices of cucumber and radish.

13. Glaze the fish and its decorations with a further layer of aspic and allow to set.

14. Carefully transfer the decorated fish from the wire cooling tray to the fish service dish.

15. Neatly arrange the rest of the garnish (egg, asparagus tips, cucumber barrels and aspic diamonds) around the fish and serve.

Preparing the garnish

Plaque of chaudfroid sauce

1. Prepare a fish velouté as described on the previous spread but replace half the fish stock with fish aspic.

2. Add 200 ml (8 fl oz) cream. This is called a chaudfroid sauce.

3. Cool and reserve for use.

4. Shape a template or mould using a margarine or butter border 55 mm (¼ in.) deep on top of a sheet of silicone paper. (Silicone paper is often used in bakery and confectionery work because of its non-stick properties.) To get a perfectly round shape, use a suitable pastry cutter or, alternatively, choose a different shape which you can judge by eye.

5. Stir the chaudfroid sauce over iced water until it is almost setting, then pour it into the butter mould you have just made. Place in a refrigerator to set.

6. When set, carefully remove the border of butter or margarine around the set chaudfroid.

7. Turn the plaque out on to a second piece of dampened silicone paper and peel off the first sheet.

The eggs

1. Boil the eggs for 8 to 10 minutes. Cool immediately under running water. Remove the shells.

2. Halve 3 of the eggs in a serrated fashion (*see* photograph). Cut the fourth egg in half from top to bottom. Remove the yolks of all 4 eggs.

3. Chop the yolks finely (or press through a sieve), then mix in a little anchovy essence and mayonnaise to hold together or bind them.

4. Pipe the mixture through a star tube into the hollows of the six serrated egg halves. Coat with aspic and refrigerate.

5. Cut thin strips about 2 cm (¾ in.) long from the white of the fourth egg, and keep to one side.

Asparagus tips

1. Trim off excess stalk to leave a neat length that will fit around the edge of the fish. Lay a strip of egg white towards the tip and another towards the end, forming bands.

2. Coat with aspic and set aside in the refrigerator.

Cucumber slices and barrels

1. Thinly slice about 2 cm (¾ in.) of the cucumber. Set aside.

2. Peel the remainder of the cucumber. Cut into 3 lengths about 5 cm (2 in.) long. Then cut each of these in two with a serrated cut to form 6 barrels about 25 mm (1 in.) long. Remove the seeds from the centre and place the barrels in boiling water for 30 seconds. Quickly cool under running water. Drain.

3. Arrange the prawn tails neatly in the cucumber halves, so they are hanging over the edge.

4. Coat with aspic and set aside in the refrigerator.

Aspic diamonds

Pour an even layer of aspic about 5 mm (³⁄₁₆ in.) deep into a shallow tray. Place in a refrigerator to set. Make a series of parallel cuts diagonally across the aspic about 8 mm (⅓ in.) apart and a second series of cuts across these to form diamond shapes in between. Loosen the aspic diamonds from underneath with a palette knife. Keep chilled until required.

Leek leaves and slices of radishes

1. Select 3 unblemished leaves from the leek, place in boiling water for 10 seconds. Cool quickly under running water.

2. Cut into thin strips.

3. Cut the radishes in half and thinly slice them to form half circles.

Mushroom

1. Slice off the mushroom stalk and the dome to form a thick, flat, disc shape.

2. Quickly brown the top of the mushroom on a griddle or solid top stove.

3. Make a shallow cut around a design of your choice (a fish shape is shown in the photograph on the Problems, Tips and Tasks spread). Carefully cut away the surrounding brown surface to leave a brown fish against a white background.

Peach Melba

INGREDIENTS   SERVES 4

2	*large peaches*	2
	Poaching syrup	
500 ml	*water*	*1 pt*
200 g	*sugar*	*½ lb*
½	*lemon*	*½*
200 ml	*Melba sauce* (see *box*)	*8 fl oz*
200 ml	*vanilla ice-cream (4 medium scoops)*	*8 fl oz*
	Chantilly cream (see *box*)	

1. Prepare the peaches as follows
   a) Blanch the peaches by placing them in a wire basket and submerging it in boiling water.
   b) After 5 seconds test them to see whether the skins can be peeled off – if the skins still do not lift off easily, submerge the peaches for another 5 seconds.
   c) Then place them into cold water to cool.
   d) Remove the skins.

2. Carefully halve the peaches and remove the stones. Peaches which are to be served on their own can be poached whole (as in the illustration).

3. Prepare the sugar syrup: place the water, sugar and juice from the lemon into a small saucepan and bring to the boil. Simmer until the sugar has dissolved.

4. Place the peach halves in the syrup.

5. Cover the peaches (they will float otherwise) with a circle of greaseproof paper (sometimes known as a cartouche) and poach the fruit until it is cooked taking care not to let the liquid boil (8 minutes is a general guide although the cooking time varies considerably depending on the ripeness of the fruit.)

6. Allow the peaches to cool in the syrup.

7. Meanwhile prepare the Chantilly cream (*see* box).

8. Portion the ice-cream into individual serving dishes (e.g. coupes). Drain the peaches, then place one half on each serving of ice cream.

9. Coat with Melba sauce (*see* box) and pipe rosettes of Chantilly cream around the peaches to decorate. This stage needs to be completed fast so that the ice-cream does not melt before being served.

Melba sauce

INGREDIENTS   SERVES 4

200 g	*raspberries*	*½ lb*
50 g	*sugar*	*2 oz*
50 ml	*water*	*2 fl oz*

1. Place the ingredients into a saucepan and bring to the boil.

2. Simmer for 5 minutes then pass through a fine strainer.

3. Cool and store chilled until required for use.

Pears with butterscotch sauce

INGREDIENTS		SERVES 4
4	*medium pears*	4
½ l	*poaching syrup*	1 pt
	(see *Peach Melba/Step 3*)	
200 ml	butterscotch sauce (see *box*)	8 fl oz

1. Peel the pears leaving the stalks attached.

2. Trim the bottoms so that the pears will sit upright.

3. Store in water with lemon juice added until ready for poaching.

4. Bring the syrup to the boil in a suitable saucepan.

5. Submerge the pears in the syrup and place a circle of greaseproof paper over the top (they are likely to float).

6. Allow the pears to poach until cooked. The cooking time will vary depending on the ripeness of the fruit (8 to 10 minutes is a guide.)

7. Allow the pears to cool in the syrup.

8. When ready for service, drain the pears and arrange them in a service dish. Neatly coat them with the butterscotch sauce.

Butterscotch sauce

INGREDIENTS		SERVES 4
100 g	*granulated sugar*	4 oz
50 ml	*water*	2 fl oz
100 ml	*double cream*	4 fl oz

1. Place the sugar and water into a heavy pan. An unlined copper pan is most suitable, because it has a very smooth surface. (Aluminium pans tend to develop tiny irregularities in the surface and when undissolved sugar crystals are trapped in these they cause the sugar mixture to re-crystallise.)

2. Bring the sugar and water to the boil over a low heat stirring occasionally. Ensure that there are no undissolved sugar crystals. Wipe down the sides of the pan with a clean brush dipped in water to remove any splashes of sugar.

3. Then boil the mixture quickly. Do not stir. Do not shake the pan.

4. When the mixture has turned a golden brown colour – it will do so at a temperature of 155°C (311°F) and a sugar thermometer can be used to find out precisely when this stage has been reached – take the pan off the heat and whisk the cream through the mixture, dribbling it in a little at a time.

5. Allow to cool. Stir before use. If the sauce is too thick, add a little more cream.

Chantilly cream

INGREDIENTS		SERVES 4 to 6
125 ml	*double or whipping cream*	5 fl oz
25 g	*caster sugar*	1 oz
	few drops vanilla essence	

1. Place the ingredients in a cold basin (glass, stainless steel or china) and whisk until the cream stands in soft peaks.

2. Set aside in the refrigerator (covered) until required for use.

△ SAFETY

When the cream is added, this may cause drops of extremely hot sugar to spit out of the pan. Cover the arm and hand you are using to hold the pan with a thick, dry kitchen cloth and keep your pouring/whisking hand safely at a distance the moment there is any sign of spurting.

3 POACHING

What went wrong

Poached fish has a tough, rubbery texture.

The temperature of the cooking liquid was too high, causing the flesh to toughen and shrink.

Food breaks up.

Cooking time too long, or temperature too high causing flesh to break up.

Fruit discolours.

White fruits such as apples and pears rapidly discolour if exposed to the air after peeling. They must be immersed in the cooking liquid immediately after preparation, and a circle of greaseproof paper (or cartouche) placed on top as the fruit will tend to float.

If fruit is to be kept for any length of time after preparation, it should be placed in acidulated water (i.e. water with lemon juice added) to prevent discoloration.

Poached eggs are a poor shape or stuck to bottom of pan.

Temperature of water too low or eggs were not fresh.

Sauce watery, running off the food.

Food was not drained properly after poaching and before adding sauce. Sauce may also run off if it is too thin.

Cream separates.

Cooking liquid was reduced too much after the cream had been added. To avoid this, shake the pan gently or stir from time to time while reducing the sauce to ensure an even reduction.

Fish sticks to the bottom of the pan or the covering sticks to the fish.

The pan or paper has not been properly prepared. Both should be greased thoroughly with butter or margarine.

Sauce lumpy.

If it is a flour-based sauce, then it is likely that the liquid has been added too quickly or that too much flour was used in relation to the butter or margarine, or that the sauce was not stirred thoroughly enough.

The problem can be corrected by forcing the sauce through a fine strainer and bringing it back to the boil for a minute or so.

Sauce too thick or too thin.

If it is too thick, more liquid (cream, stock, etc. as appropriate) can be added.

If it is too thin, it can be reduced by boiling vigorously. Alternatively, blend a small amount of butter and flour in equal quantities to form a smooth paste (this mixture is known as a beurre manié). The sauce should be taken off the heat, the beurre manié added and thoroughly whisked in before the sauce is brought briefly to the boil again.

Sauce does not brown evenly under the grill.

1. The sauce is too thick or too thin, or the velouté base was not cooked thoroughly.
2. Not enough care was taken in judging the quantities of cream, or egg yolks or butter which were added.
3. Cheese that should have been sprinkled on top was missed out.
4. The grill was not at the right temperature. (Grills should be pre-heated before use.)

Sauce discoloured.

1. Poor quality stock or velouté was used.
2. Inadequate attention was paid to quantities of cream, etc. that should be added.
3. The roux was burned.
4. Aluminium pan was used for making a light-coloured sauce and a metal spoon was used for stirring it.

Tips

To test whether fish is cooked enough, press gently with the back of a teaspoon. It should give under the pressure and not spring back. If it springs back as if you were pressing a sponge, the fish is not yet cooked. If the fish breaks up, it is overcooked. When the fish is cooked correctly it can be easily taken off the bone.

If you are poaching very sour fruit, increase the sugar content of the cooking liquid.

Before browning a dish with a sauce under the grill or in the oven, test a small sample on the back of a fireproof saucer or dish to see that it browns satisfactorily.

If you are using powdered gelatin to make an aspic, sprinkle it over a small quantity of cold stock or water (whichever is appropriate to the recipe) and let it soften for a few minutes before blending it into the rest of the liquid. Soak leaf gelatin in cold water for about 10 minutes before use.

When you are poaching eggs, remember that the fresher the eggs the less vinegar you need to add to the water.

To prevent a skin forming on a sauce when it is cooling, place small pieces of butter on the surface (or brush over with melted butter). Alternatively a sheet of greaseproof paper can be used or a thin film of milk, stock or water (as appropriate, depending on what liquid has been used in the sauce) can be floated over the surface.

If you cannot serve a hot fish dish immediately after poaching, keep the fish (covered with a piece of cooking paper) in a hot plate or warm oven, and don't add the sauce until the last minute.

TEST YOURSELF

1. Explain the difference between shallow and deep poaching, and give two examples of foods suitable for each method.

2. Choose two further examples of food suitable for poaching and state what temperature the poaching liquid should be at when you start cooking.

3. Give three reasons why fish is suitable for poaching.

4. Identify two points that should be looked for when purchasing fresh fish.

5. Why is the temperature of the poaching liquid so important?

6. Name three items of equipment that are associated with poaching.

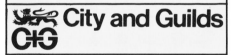
City and Guilds

The poached salmon trout in all its glory!

4 STEWING

Many customers have the impression that stewing is just a way of producing a nourishing but very economical meal that uses every scrap of meat, no matter how tough, and can include vegetables that are so old that they couldn't be used in any other way.

In fact, stewing has had such a bad name that it is hardly mentioned on menus even though a wide variety of delicious dishes are prepared this way.

▶▶▶ TO DO

Visit, or get information from:

a) a local hotel offering a fixed-price menu which changes daily

b) a self-service restaurant in an office or factory

c) a hospital or school.

List the number of dishes offered by each over the course of a week which have probably been stewed. Note the description used on the menu to tempt the customer to order the dish. Suggest reasons for any variation in the number of stewed dishes offered by the different establishments. For example, are more stewed dishes on offer in the restaurant or in the school/hospital?

Curries, hot pots, coq au vin and chilli con carne are enjoyed in many different establishments from schools to high-class restaurants, and they are all cooked by the same method as a plain beef stew. A whole range of tempting descriptions for menus has grown up:

- hearty and sustaining

- richly flavoured

- cooked to perfection

- traditionally cooked to add flavour.

To earn these descriptions, a stew needs to be made from well chosen but not necessarily expensive ingredients. The emphasis should be on careful preparation and cooking – good stews cannot be prepared in a few minutes.

4 STEWING

What happens

In the stewing process, pieces of food are gently simmered in a small amount of liquid. This liquid forms part of the finished dish and, with the help of other ingredients added in the cooking process, contributes to the overall flavour.

The food needs to be stewed in small pieces, so it is only quite small food items, e.g. chicken legs, that can be cooked whole.

Sometimes just one food item is stewed, but more often a stewed dish will contain several types of food.

Stews are usually begun on top of the stove and, once the cooking liquid has been brought to the boil, transferred to the oven where it is easier to maintain an even, gentle heat. However, some chefs choose to cook stews entirely on top of the stove, especially if they are adding ingredients during the cooking process.

If the food needs to be stewed for a long time, the container should be covered with a tight-fitting lid. This reduces loss of liquid by evaporation, and means that the amount of cooking liquid can be kept to the minimum. The smaller the amount of cooking liquid, the greater the concentration of flavour in the finished dish.

With only a little, often thick liquid, there is a danger of burning the food, particularly at the base of the pan, and finishing the cooking in the oven reduces this risk.

Additional ingredients are usually added for flavour:

– herbs and seasonings

– vegetables, which both add flavour and provide contrasts of colour and texture in the finished dish.

Sometimes these ingredients are removed from the stew once they have released their flavour.

See: Video 2

▶▶▶ TO DO

Look for the meats described as suitable for stewing in a supermarket or a butcher. Note the price per kilo (or pound), the appearance of the meat and the fat content. Compare these with a joint of meat described as suitable for roasting.

Examine the stewing meat carefully and identify (with the help of your supervisor or tutor if necessary) the meat fibres, the collagen and any elastin.

The cooking liquid

– provides a moist, slow heat for the food to cook in, which makes stewing an ideal cooking method for tough meats and vegetables (providing they are cooked for long enough).

– adds flavour to the food, e.g. if white or brown stocks, thick sauces, wine or brandy, etc., are used. This flavour-enhancing role means that stewing is also used for cooking meats, fish and vegetables which are not tough but which benefit from moist, gentle cooking over a short time, in a well-flavoured liquid.

– absorbs flavours produced by the food during cooking and helps preserve nutritional value by retaining vitamins and minerals that have escaped from the food.

The cooking liquid is always thickened.

In some stews it is thick at the start of cooking (either a sauce is used or a roux is made to thicken the liquid as it is added).

In other stews, ingredients are used which break down during cooking and have a thickening effect.

Sometimes the liquid is not thickened until after the food has finished cooking.

Brown and white stews

Brown stews are almost always thickened at the start of cooking, when the browning effect is also created. Shallow frying or brief cooking in a very hot oven is used to create the browning before stewing. (The temperatures in the stewing process are no higher than the boiling point of water so they cannot cause browning.) Often flour is added directly after the browning has been done — so that the liquid will thicken when it is added.

White stews need more careful treatment. If the meat is of rather poor quality the impurities it releases during cooking must be skimmed off, otherwise they will discolour the cooking liquid and create unpleasant flavours. The other thing to remember with less good quality meat is that the cooking liquid should not be thickened until after the meat is cooked, because it is far easier to remove impurities from a thin liquid than from a thickened one.

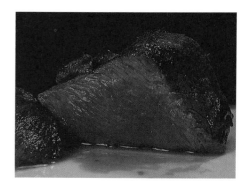

Frying meat in hot oil or placing it in a very hot oven enriches its colour and flavour. It used to be thought that these processes somehow sealed the meat, preventing the juices from escaping, but in fact this does not happen.

Meat is the muscle of animals. Muscles are made up of many bundles of long fibres held together (and attached to the bone) by connective tissue. The thickness of the fibres and the amount of connective tissue depends on the age of the animal and the amount of work a particular muscle does. Older animals and well-used muscles tend to produce coarser fibres and more connective tissue (as in tougher cuts of meat), but often the flavour is richer. There are two types of connective tissue: collagen, which is white, and elastin, which is yellow.

During cooking various changes happen to the fibres and connective tissue, which is why cooked meat both looks different to raw meat and has a firmer texture. The proteins in the fibres clump together (coagulate) and shrink, so the meat gets smaller and juices are squeezed out. This effect stops by the time the meat reaches 77°C (170°F). The collagen slowly changes to gelatin, which is soft and easily digested. The elastin, on the other hand, is not affected by heat and so has to be removed before cooking.

Stewing is an ideal method for cooking tough cuts of meat, because the long slow process means that all the collagen has been converted to gelatin before the fibre proteins have become hard and tough.

Muscle tissue is made up of many individual fibres. As soon as the fibres are heated they begin to shrink in width and once the temperature is over 54°C (130°F) they start to shorten. Above 77°C (170°F), they will have shrunk as much as they can and will begin to break, as the picture above shows. The magnification in the photograph below is 200 times and clearly shows the fibres breaking up.

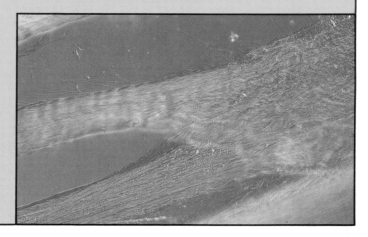

4 STEWING

Choosing meat for stewing

It is just as important to select meat of good quality for stewing as it is in any other cooking process. But it is true that stewing is a very good method for cooking meats that are too tough to roast or shallow fry. For example, this will include cuts of meat from the most exercised parts of the animal. On the other hand, stewing should never be used as a way of using up or disguising meat that:

– smells unpleasant, looks the wrong colour or has a soft, spongy texture as a result of being stored too long or at the wrong temperature

– has too much fat in relation to the amount of meat

– has fat which is discoloured or too soft (it should be white and firm)

– has gristle or sinew which cannot be easily separated from the meat.

▸▸▸ TO DO

Ask at your workplace if you can use a piece of stewing meat (or you could buy a small amount). Weigh the meat. Trim off any fat and gristle and cut the meat up into 20-25 mm (¾ in.) cubes. Weigh the cubes of meat. Work out the weight of the bits you are throwing away. Then work out the cost per kilo of the cubes of meat (based on what the meat originally cost). The meat can then be put away in the refrigerator and used for the To Do exercise on the Method page.

Preparation points

1. Cut away any bones. These can be put aside in a refrigerator or cold room and later used to make stock. Small bones are sometimes left in the meat, for example when cutlets from the neck of lamb or mutton are being used.

2. Remove any skin.

3. Trim off all gristle or sinew.

4. Remove as much fat as possible.

5. Cut the meat into suitably sized pieces. Most stews are made with cubes of meat of about 20-25 cm (¾ in.), but neck (or scrag) of lamb and mutton is cut into small cutlets.

Sides of lamb at Smithfield Market, London.

✚ HYGIENE

Apart from taking normal precautions over personal hygiene and cross-contamination (*see* Introduction/Safety and Hygiene), there is one kind of bacteria (*Clostridium perfringens*) which can present a risk in stewing. Its spores can live on meat and vegetables, and they are not destroyed during normal cooking. If stews are allowed to cool slowly, the bacteria may grow and reproduce to dangerous numbers.

So it is important that stews are kept at temperatures above 63°C (145°F) during extended service periods. If any is left over, it should be cooled quickly and put into a refrigerator.

✳ NUTRITION

Red meat has a high proportion of saturated fats, which are thought to be a contributory factor in heart disease. So you should always choose lean cuts and remove as much fat as possible. There are a number of things you can do to cut down the fat even further:

1. Use polyunsaturated fats or oils for the shallow frying stage and to make the roux (which will be used to thicken the sauce).

2. Replace a little of the meat with extra vegetable garnish, especially pulses (for example, lentils). This will also increase the fibre content of the meal. Avoid glazing vegetables in butter (which is done to give them a shiny appearance).

3. Skim off any fat that rises to the surface during cooking.

4. Instead of using butter and flour (beurre manié) as a thickening paste, use *fromage frais* and flour for a low-fat version, as described in Braising/Problems, Tips & Tasks.

5. Some recipes suggest adding butter or cream as a finishing touch. This can be left out or *fromage frais* used instead. Yogurt can also be used, but has to be added at the last minute — otherwise it will separate.

Cuts suitable for stewing come from the most exercised parts of the animal:

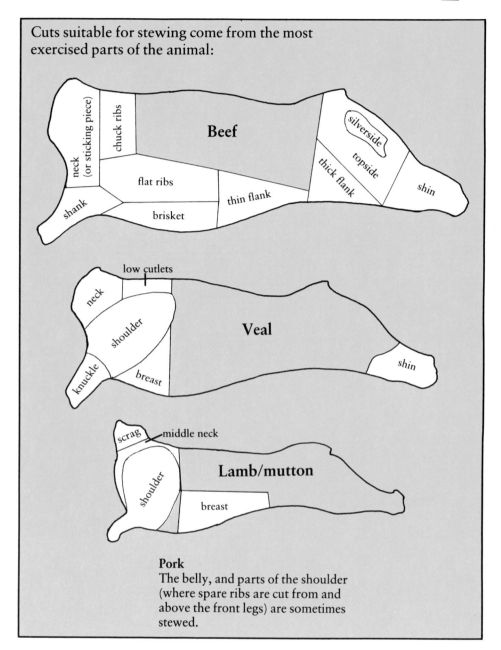

Pork
The belly, and parts of the shoulder (where spare ribs are cut from and above the front legs) are sometimes stewed.

On the left of the photograph is a range of cuts of beef suitable for stewing: diced shin (*top left*), diced thick flank (*bottom left*), chuck steak – a slice and some cubes (*top right*), topside – cut as carbonnades or small escalopes, a cut more commonly used in braised dishes (*bottom right*).

On the right are mutton cuts suitable for stewing: middle neck cutlets (*left and right rows*), scrag (*centre row*).

4 STEWING

Poultry

Chicken is not a tough meat like the cuts of beef, veal, lamb and mutton listed as suitable for stewing on the previous spread, and faster cooking processes like roasting and shallow and deep frying will make it tender enough to eat. But stewing does give poultry a richer flavour, which is why dishes like coq au vin (*see* Practical Examples 1) and chicken curry are so popular.

Chickens for stewing should be 4-8 months old and weigh between 1½ and 2 kg (3½-4 lb). Farm-reared duck 3-8 months old is sometimes stewed. Boiling fowl, young or baby chickens are not suitable. Turkey is not usually stewed.

▶▶▶ TO DO

Look at some vegetarian cook books and pick out some of the recipes that use the stewing process to cook vegetables and pulses. Choose whichever recipe appeals to you most, note the quantities of all the ingredients you will need and work out the cost of preparing the dish, using supermarket prices. What is the cost per serving? If you work in an establishment where food is served, discuss with your supervisor/tutor whether such a dish would appeal to your customers and how much would be charged for it.

On the left of the photograph is a rabbit prepared for a stew: front legs (*top left and right*), back legs divided into two (*bottom left and right*), forequarter (*top centre*), saddle (*bottom centre*).

On the right are two types of preparation for chicken. A plain method has been used for the wing and breast in the top row and the thigh and drumstick in the third row. In the second and fourth rows the same joints have been prepared for high-class service (knuckles chopped off and bones trimmed clean).

Game

Rabbit and hares are suitable for stewing and, as the picture shows, all the meat is used in a stew. Both can be bought fresh from early autumn through to spring (hare from August, rabbit from September). Young, well-fleshed animals are best:

– the ears should tear fairly easily

– the bottom jaw of a rabbit should break easily

– the claws of a hare should be hidden under the fur of the paws and should be flexible, not brittle.

Wild rabbits and hare are usually hung for a while before being used so that the gamey flavours can develop – how long will depend on how strong the taste should be, but between 2 and 9 days is usual.

Venison (which is the name given to all game with horns and fur, e.g. deer) makes quite a strong-flavoured stew. The leg is occasionally used because it is lean and needs very little trimming, but more economical cuts for stewing are the shoulder, neck and breast (as with lamb and mutton).

Game birds, such as pigeon, pheasant, grouse, partridge, guinea fowl and wild duck can be stewed. They are usually roasted first, then cut up into portions and stewed in some kind of cooking liquid. Some game, e.g. venison and hare, tends to be marinaded before being stewed, in the same way as it would be if braised (*see* Braising/Insight).

Offal

Tripe can be cut into pieces and stewed. Oxtail and ox liver can also be used, although when they are cooked in a sauce they tend to be described as 'braised'.

Fish

Eels and mussels can be simmered and then served in their cooking liquid in some recipes, e.g. eels à la bordelaise and moules à la marinière.

The Mediterranean speciality, bouillabaisse, is a kind of fish stew. The fish is cut into small pieces, simmered and then served in the cooking liquid. True bouillabaisse contains some Mediterranean fish that are not easily available in Northern Europe, such as *rascasse, chapon* and *rouquier*, but pike, mackerel and trout can be substituted for these. Other fish used for bouillabaisse include whitings, red mullet, John Dory, small conger eel and crawfish (or spiny lobster), which can be bought reasonably easily in Britain.

Vegetables

Vegetables are used in all meat, poultry and game stews to add to the flavour. Which vegetables you choose depends on the particular flavour you are aiming for. Carrots, celery, onions, leeks, mushrooms and garlic are the most frequently used.

In many stews the vegetables stay in the liquid to help thicken and/or enrich it, for example, potatoes, onions, celery, leek and cabbage in an Irish stew.

Sometimes vegetables are stewed in their own right to form complete dishes. Ratatouille (onions, tomatoes, aubergines, green peppers, courgettes and garlic) is sometimes classed as a stew – the tomatoes and onions are usually cooked first so that they create enough sauce to cook the remaining vegetables in. Marrow and pumpkin can be cooked in a similar manner. Vegetable curries often include vegetables such as cauliflower, parsnip and French beans.

Some vegetable dishes served with main-course dishes are stewed although they would not be described in this way on the menu, e.g. shredded cabbage, French-style peas (peas with button onions and shredded lettuce). In the case of French-style peas, the liquid is thickened to form a sauce.

Pulses that can be stewed either on their own or with meat and other vegetables include: haricot beans, lentils, chick peas and red kidney beans. Red kidney beans are an essential ingredient of chilli con carne. They can also be added to some dishes such as ratatouille to produce a more substantial main-course dish.

Preparing hare and rabbit

To skin
1. Trim the paws off the front and back legs.
2. Remove the skin off each back leg by making a slit through the skin on the inside of the thigh. Push two fingers through this slit and work around the leg to free the flesh from the skin. Then pull the leg up through the slit in the skin.
3. Hold both back legs and lift the animal up above the work surface so it is hanging freely. Then peel the skin down over the body and head (removing the ears when you come to the head).

To draw
4. Place the animal on its back and slit the belly open lengthwise, from the lower belly to the start of the rib cage.

5. Remove the intestines and throw them away immediately. Remove the lungs, liver and heart and place them in a basin with the blood which will run from the cavity. (Hare blood is saved and used in some recipes.)

To joint
6. First the head is cut off and thrown away. Then any loose flaps of flesh at the bottom of the rib cage are trimmed off.
7. The legs are removed. If the front legs are small they are left whole. The back legs are usually cut in two.
8. Trim off any sinew from the back of the animal.
9. Cut the body up into between four and eight pieces depending on its size, allowing two pieces per portion.

The photograph shows a range of vegetables which enhance the flavour of stews. *Clockwise, from top left*: onions, yellow, green and red pepper, courgettes, carrots, celery, leeks, baby corn, tomatoes, mushrooms, okra (or ladies' fingers), garlic and aubergine.

So-called 'stewed fruit' – sometimes offered on breakfast menus – will almost certainly have been cooked at poaching temperatures for a short time and is not in fact stewed.

Apples are sometimes used in curries to help thicken and flavour the liquid.

Terms

In *stewing* the food is cut up into pieces (unless it is already small) and simmered in a small amount of liquid. Cooking takes place either on top of the stove or in the oven. The liquid is later served as part of the finished dish.

In *brown stews* the main food item and any vegetables added as part of the recipe are first *seared* or *browned*, usually by shallow frying. Brown stock is used (*see* Introduction/Stocks).

A *ragoût* (from the French) is another name for stew, though it is usually used of brown stews.

A *navarin* is a brown stew of mutton (and occasionally of lamb) made with onions and potatoes and sometimes also with carrots, turnips and peas.

Preparing a brown roux
The fat has been melted, flour added and thoroughly mixed in. In the preparation of a brown roux this mixture is cooked until it turns an even brown colour (around 8 to 12 minutes). It must be stirred frequently to prevent burning and speckling.

The roux is then allowed to cool slightly to prevent it spitting when the hot liquid (brown stock in this photograph) is added, a little at a time. After each addition of liquid the mixture is thoroughly blended.

White stews are usually made from white meats, such as chicken, rabbit, veal, pork and lamb. A distinction is normally made between two types of white stew:

1. If the meat is not of very good quality, the cooking liquid is not thickened until after the meat is cooked (so that impurities can be removed first). There is no first stage of shallow frying, but the meat is *blanched* (placed in cold water and brought to the boil) and *refreshed* (washed off with cold water) to remove the impurities, before stewing begins. The vegetables are added to the stew raw and on the whole provide flavour rather than colour. This kind of white stew is called a *blanquette*. The liquid is thickened when the meat is almost cooked. At this point the cooking liquid is strained off, added to a roux (flour combined with fat and cooked briefly) and cooked without browning. This type of sauce is called a *velouté*.

2. Making white stew with high-quality meat is done in almost the same way as a brown stew, by cooking the food in a thickened stock. The meat and vegetables are briefly shallow fried first but extremely gently so that they do not go golden brown (this is called *sweating*). This stage adds flavour and forms the basis of the roux. This kind of white stew is called a *fricassée* and if vegetables are added they tend to be put in quite late on in the cooking and play an important part in the final appearance of the dish.

A *liaison* of egg yolk and cream beaten lightly together is often added to blanquettes and fricassées just before service, to lighten the colour and add to the flavour.

A *roux* is a mixture of fat and flour which is gently heated and blended together to form the base for a sauce.

Equipment

Saucepans are ideal for making small quantities of stew (although you should always check that the handles are ovenproof). In kitchens catering for large numbers, *bratt pans* are excellent for stews that require preliminary shallow frying. Operated by gas or electricity they can reach temperatures above 300°C (575°F) so they brown the food very fast.

Steam-jacketed kettles or *boiling pans* cannot heat their contents above 100°C (212°F) and so are suitable only for stews that do not need a browning stage: blanquettes, Irish stew and vegetable stews.

Copper (tin-lined) and aluminium saucepans with a selection of ladles that are useful for adding stock and skimming. Stainless steel saucepans and various types of ovenware are also suitable for stewing. In all cases it is important that the pan has a tight-fitting lid and that it is large enough to take the quantity of stew being cooked without any danger of spilling. On the other hand the pan should not be too big, otherwise extra cooking liquid will be needed to keep the food covered.

△ SAFETY

Large containers holding hot food and liquid can be dangerous if they are not handled very carefully. Do not push or pull the pan suddenly or the contents may splash out. It may be a good idea to remove the lid before lifting the container so that the level of the liquid is clearly visible. Two-handled pans may need two people to move them safely.

▶▶▶ TO DO

This activity will show how different kinds of stewing produce differences in texture, flavour and appearance. In each case you will be stewing a chicken drumstick in a covered saucepan until it is cooked (about 40 minutes) either in the oven or on top of the stove.

First collect the ingredients you will require: 4 chicken drumsticks, about ½ litre (l pt) of white stock and ½ litre (1 pt) brown stock, 25 g (1 oz) fat, 25 g (1 oz) white flour, and the following vegetables washed and roughly chopped – 3 onions, 3 carrots, ½ head of celery and 1 medium-sized leek.

1. Place the chicken leg in cold water, bring it to the boil, throw away the water and refresh the chicken leg under cold running water. Then place it in a saucepan, add one third of the vegetables and add enough white stock to cover.

2. Sweat the chicken leg (without allowing it to colour) in half of the fat.

Add half of the flour and make a roux. Gradually, add enough hot white stock to cover.

3. Brown the chicken leg and one third of the vegetables in half of the fat. Add half of the flour and make a brown roux. Add enough hot brown stock to cover.

4. Cover the chicken leg and one third of the vegetables with cold brown stock. Bring to the boil and simmer.

Note the overall length of the cooking time for each dish. Compare the finished results for flavour (both the cooking liquid or sauce and the chicken), appearance and texture.

If possible, do this activity as part of a group of four, with one person doing each variation. Discuss how the steps you have taken compare with the methods used for brown and white stews and why you think the results are so different.

▼ CHEF'S TIP

Using a metal spoon for stirring in a metal pan can cause discoloration of the sauce or stock (especially if an aluminium pan is used) so plastic or wooden spoons should be used. Many chefs use a spatula when making a roux (as in the photograph on the opposite page). The shape of the blade (with straight edges) makes it easier to keep food from sticking to the bottom of the pan and burning.

Essential points

Here are the most important steps you need to follow in the preparation of any stew. These instructions will help you with the Caterbase module, *Braising/Stewing*.

1. Make sure your work area is clean and ready for use.

2. Collect together the ingredients and equipment you will need (checking that it is clean and complete, e.g. that saucepans have lids).

> Stocks are usually essential to make good stews, so check before starting that if the recipe requires stock, it is available.
> If you will be using the oven, make sure it is preheated to about 180°C (360°F). If you are using a bratt pan or steam-jacketed kettle, check that it is ready for use.

3. Make sure you are familiar with the details of the stewing recipe you are following.

> Prepare the main food item and vegetables. Then, depending on the type of stew you are cooking and the recipe:
> — marinade the meat (usually only necessary for game, e.g. venison and hare)
> — blanch and refresh the meat (for a blanquette or Irish stew)
> — sweat the main food item and base vegetables (for white stews except blanquettes)
> — brown or sear the main food item and base vegetables (for brown stews and many speciality stews such as curries and goulash)
> — if pulses (e.g. beans or lentils) are being used in the stew they may need to be soaked in advance.

The onion and garlic in this picture are being sweated, which means being shallow fried very gently over a low heat without browning.

▶▶▶ TO DO

Remove the fat and sinew from 250 g (10 oz) of stewing meat and cut the meat into 20 mm (¾ in.) dice. Alternatively, use the meat you have prepared in the To Do exercise on Food Selection 1. Divide the meat accurately into 2 portions. Using small saucepans with lids, and in each case ¼ litre (½ pt) of liquid:

1. Place one portion into boiling brown stock.

2. Place the other portion into cold water and bring to the boil.

3. Cover the saucepans with lids and transfer both of them to a moderate oven set at 180°C (360°F). After one hour remove them from the oven.

4. Strain off the cooking liquid, measure how much is left and taste it in each case.

5. Weigh the portions of cooked meat. Taste a sample of each. Note the colour and texture. Calculate the loss of weight, and note down any differences between the two samples.

4. Add the cooking liquid to cover the food, then seasonings and flavouring as required. Cover with a lid, bring to the boil and then continue to simmer (in the oven, bratt pan or steam-jacketed kettle).

5. Check the cooking from time to time.

> Skim to remove any fat or impurities that rise to the surface.
>   Stir to prevent burning, particularly if you are using a bratt pan or cooking in a saucepan on top of the stove.
>   Add more cooking liquid if it has reduced too quickly, and the food is drying out.
>   Work out when any vegetable garnish needs to be added so that it will be cooked (but not overdone) at the same time as the main food item. Items that take a short time to cook should be put in late on so that they stay as intact as possible.
>   With a fricassée, the meat is removed from the cooking liquid when it is almost cooked. The liquid is then strained off, thickened with a roux and finally poured over the meat so that cooking can be completed in the liquid.

To skim the scum (impurities) and fat off a stew carefully hold a ladle just beneath the surface of the liquid and move it forward and from side to side under the scum. Lift the ladle up and transfer the scum to another saucepan or bowl, then throw it away.

6. When the food and garnish are cooked, remove from the heat. If necessary, adjust the consistency of the sauce and the seasoning.

> Meat should be easy to penetrate with a cocktail stick, and should also come away from the bone easily (e.g. a cutlet or chicken joint).
>   With blanquettes and fricassées the liaison of cream and egg yolks or other finishing touches such as yogurt are added at the last moment.
>   The sauce should be just thick enough to coat the food.

7. Transfer the stew to a warm service dish and serve immediately.

This veal has been put into cold water and brought to the boil (called blanching) to remove any impurities. Once the water has boiled for a few minutes, the saucepan is transferred to the sink and cold water run into it until all the scum has been washed off. A conical sieve is sometimes placed in the pan under the source of the water to break the force of the stream and prevent the meat spilling out into the sink.

Coq au vin

INGREDIENTS SERVES 12

3 × 1.6 kg	*drawn and cleaned chickens*	3 × 3½ lb
100 g	*butter or margarine*	4 oz
75 ml	*oil*	3 fl oz
2	*cloves garlic*	2
100 g	*onion*	4 oz
750 ml	*red wine*	1½ pt

sprig of thyme, bay leaf & parsley stalks
salt and freshly milled black pepper to taste

Thickening ('beurre manié')

50 g	*butter*	2 oz
30 g	*flour*	1¼ oz

Garnish

300 g	*piece of lean bacon*	12 oz
250 g	*button mushrooms*	10 oz
250 g	*button onions*	10 oz
6	*slices of white bread*	6
	chopped parsley	

1. Joint the chicken ready for sautéing (*see* Poaching/ Practical Examples 2).

2. Wash and peel the onion, then finely chop it. Peel the garlic, roughly chop, then add a little salt and crush with the blade of a knife.

3. Heat two-thirds of the butter and oil in a large sauteuse or plat à sauter or saucepan, then shallow fry the pieces of chicken (including the carcase cuts) on all sides until they have turned a good brown colour.

4. Drain off any excess fat, add the onions, garlic and herbs and continue cooking for 3 to 4 minutes.

5. Add the wine to barely cover the chicken and bring to the boil.

6. Cover with a lid and slowly simmer in the oven until cooked – for about 20 minutes at 180°C (360°F). The cooking time will depend on the quality of the chicken.

7. Meanwhile prepare the garnish:
   a) Cut the bacon into 15 mm (½ in.) cubes (these are called lardons).
   b) Place the lardons in a saucepan, cover with cold water and bring to the boil.
   c) Simmer for 10 to 15 minutes then refresh under cold running water. Drain ready for cooking.
   d) Wash and peel the onions.
   e) Wash the mushrooms.

f) Heat most of the remaining butter and oil in a sauteuse – leaving enough to shallow fry the croûtons in step (j) – then add the button onions and shallow fry until light brown.
g) Add the blanched lardons and mushrooms and continue cooking for 2 to 3 minutes.
h) Cover the garnish with a lid and complete the cooking in the oven for 5 to 10 minutes.
i) Trim the crusts off the bread, and cut each slice in half. Then trim these halves into heart shapes so you have 12 croûtons.
j) Shallow fry the croûtons in the remaining butter and oil until they are crisp and golden brown on both sides.

8. Cream together the butter and flour until light and smooth (this is called 'beurre manié').

9. When the chicken is cooked, remove the pieces of chicken and neatly arrange in a warm service dish. Each portion should include one piece of breast and one piece of leg. If the chicken pieces are being reformed in the shape of the chicken (*see* photograph opposite), the carcase pieces are used to form the base. Keep hot in a warm oven or hot cupboard.

10. If there is too much cooking liquid left and it is likely to swamp the chicken pieces, boil it down quickly taking care to stir it from time to time so that it does not burn at the bottom. Then blend in the beurre manié, a little at a time, shaking the pan (or stirring the sauce), until the sauce is thick enough to coat the chicken pieces smoothly.

11. Distribute the mushrooms, bacon and onions neatly over and around the chicken. Then strain the sauce over the chicken.

12. Sprinkle, if required, with chopped parsley. Dip the tips of the croûtons in chopped parsley and arrange them around the dish.

Veal blanquette
Blanquette de veau

INGREDIENTS		SERVES 4
500 g	*stewing veal*	*1¼ lb*
½ l	*white veal stock*	*1 pt*
1	*carrot*	*1*
1	*onion*	*1*
sprig of thyme, 1 bay leaf, 1 clove and parsley stalks		
25 g	*butter or margarine*	*1 oz*
25 g	*flour*	*1 oz*
100 ml	*cream*	*4 fl oz*
salt and white pepper to taste		
pinch chopped parsley (optional)		

1. Trim off any excess fat and sinew from the veal and cut it into cubes of about 20 mm (¾ in.).

2. Wash and peel the carrot and onion.

3. Place the meat in a saucepan, cover it with cold water and bring to the boil.

4. Refresh the meat under cold running water until all the scum has washed away. Drain the meat ready for cooking.

5. Place the meat into a clean saucepan and cover with the stock.

6. Fix the bay leaf to the side of the onion by piercing it with the clove. Add it, the carrot and the herbs and bring to the boil.

7. Cover with a lid, and slowly simmer in the oven until almost cooked – 1 hour approximately at 180°C (360°F). Top up with stock and skim as necessary during cooking.

8. Melt the butter or margarine in a separate saucepan, add the flour and mix together to form a roux. Allow the roux to cook for 3 to 4 minutes without developing any colour.

9. Drain off the cooking liquid from the meat and vegetables. Discard the vegetables and herbs and place the meat into a clean saucepan. Keep it warm to one side of the stove.

10. Add the cooking liquid to the roux a little at a time stirring in thoroughly. Simmer for 8 to 10 minutes.

11. Strain the sauce over the meat and bring back to the boil. Simmer for 5 to 10 minutes until the meat is cooked.

12. Mix in the cream and adjust the seasoning if necessary.

13. Place the stew into a warm serving dish.

14. Sprinkle with the chopped parsley (if required) and serve at once.

FOODCRAFT

See: Video 2

Coq au vin – the finished dish.

Irish stew

INGREDIENTS   SERVES 30

4½ kg	boneless stewing mutton or lamb	10 lb
3 kg	potatoes (or potato trimmings)	6½ lb
750 g	onions	1 lb 10 oz
750 g	celery	1 lb 10 oz
750 g	white leeks	1 lb 10 oz
450 g	white cabbage	1 lb
4-6 l	white mutton stock or water (to cover)	8-12 pt
	salt and pepper to taste	

Garnish

675 g	potatoes	1½ lb
450 g	button onions	1 lb
	chopped parsley	

1. Remove any excess fat from the meat, then cut it into cubes of about 20 mm (¾ in.).

2. Wash and peel the vegetables in the main recipe, cut them into small pieces or finely slice them.

3. Place the meat in a saucepan, cover it with cold water and bring it to the boil.

4. Refresh the meat under cold running water until all the scum has washed away. Drain the meat ready for cooking.

5. Place the meat into a clean saucepan and cover it with the cold stock or water.

6. Bring it to the boil. Skim any scum off as it forms and wipe around the sides of the saucepan if impurities collect there.

For some recipes, such as Irish stew, the vegetables can be cut into shapes known as 'paysannes': small squares, rounds or triangles as shown in the photograph. If they are added late on in the cooking process, they will improve the overall look of the stew.

7. Add the small pieces of potatoes, onions, celery, leek and cabbage to the saucepan, cover with a lid and cook in a medium oven at 180°C (360°F) until the meat is almost cooked – approximately 1¼ hours. The vegetables should break up and thicken the stew. From time to time remove the stew from the oven and skim off excess fat or impurities that have risen to the surface.

8. Meanwhile prepare the garnish. Wash and peel the button onions and the potatoes. Cut the potatoes into small cubes of 20 mm (¾ in.) or into small balls or barrel shapes and cover with cold water until required.

9. Add the button onions and simmer for approximately 10 minutes.

10. Add the shaped potatoes and complete the cooking – this will take about 15 minutes.

11. Check the seasoning.

12. Transfer the stew to a warm serving dish and sprinkle with the chopped parsley.

👨‍🍳 CHEF'S TIPS

Irish stew can be cooked on top of the stove, which makes it easier to skim regularly.

There are different views on which vegetables should be used in an Irish stew. Some recipes use only onions and potatoes, others add turnips and pearl barley.

Pickled red cabbage is a popular accompaniment to Irish stew.

Marrow provençale
Courge provençale

INGREDIENTS   SERVES 4

500 g	marrow	1¼ lb
50 ml	vegetable oil	2 fl oz
75 g	onion	3 oz
1	clove garlic	1
12	tomatoes	12
	salt and freshly milled black pepper to taste	
	pinch chopped parsley (optional)	

1. Peel the marrow then cut it in half (lengthways) and scoop out the seeds.

2. Cut the marrow into pieces about 25 mm (1 in.) square. Large marrows can be divided into wedges and then cut into slices about 5 mm (¼ in.) thick.

3. Prepare the other vegetables:
   a) Wash, peel and chop the onion (but not too finely).
   b) Peel and roughly chop the garlic, sprinkle it with salt, then crush it with the blade of a knife.
   c) Remove the stalks from the tomatoes and then plunge them into boiling water for 10 to 20 seconds to loosen their skin, then immediately cool under cold running water. Remove the skins, cut the tomatoes in half, scoop out the pips and roughly dice the flesh.

4. Heat the oil in a sauteuse or plat à sauter. Add the onion and garlic and cook for 2 to 3 minutes without allowing to colour.

5. Add the pieces of marrow, and cook without colouring for another 6 minutes.

6. Add the chopped tomato and cook slowly in a moderate oven, 180°C (360°F) for approximately 45 minutes.

7. Check the seasoning.

8. Place into a warm serving dish and sprinkle, if required, with the chopped parsley.

> The liquid released by the vegetables in this recipe means that it is not necessary to add liquid at the start of cooking (as you do with most stews).

Peas French style
Petits pois à la française

INGREDIENTS		SERVES 4
1 kg	fresh peas	2¼ lb
5 g	butter	¼ oz
12	button onions	12
½	small lettuce	½
	pinch caster sugar	
	pinch salt and pepper	
	Beurre manié	
20 g	butter	¾ oz
10 g	flour	¼ oz

1. Remove the peas from their pods and wash.

2. Peel and wash the button onions.

3. Wash the lettuce, then drain it well and finely shred it.

4. Place the peas, butter, onions, shredded lettuce and sugar into a saucepan.

5. Barely cover with water and bring to the boil.

6. Cover with a lid and transfer to the oven until cooked for about 30 to 45 minutes at 180°C (360°F).

7. Meanwhile cream together the butter and flour until the mixture is light and smooth.

8. Remove the peas from the oven and blend in the beurre manié, a little at a time (while shaking the saucepan) until the mixture thickens.

9. Check seasoning then transfer to a warm service dish and serve immediately.

> **CHEF'S TIP**
> If using frozen peas, first cook the button onions and shredded lettuce. Add the frozen peas just before step 7.

What went wrong

Stew looks light brown when it should be a rich brown.

1. The meat and/or base vegetables were not browned enough before the roux was made.
2. The stock was too pale in colour.
   The colouring can be corrected by careful use of gravy browning.

Stew is light brown when it should be white.

1. The stock was too dark.
2. The meat and vegetables were allowed to colour too much in the shallow frying stage before the roux was made.
3. The roux was overcooked.
4. The stew has been burnt during cooking.
   The addition of cream, yogurt, fromage blanc or quark (a soft cheese made from skimmed milk) will lighten the colour as well as add flavour, although it cannot disguise a burnt taste.

Stew is grey when it should be white.

1. The meat was not blanched properly or not thoroughly refreshed.
2. The stew was not skimmed during cooking.

The meat and/or vegetables are overcooked.

1. Cooking went on too long.
2. The speed of cooking was not checked or checked too late.
3. The stew was kept warm for too long between cooking and service.
4. The garnish was added too soon. If the garnish has cooked too quickly, it should be removed from the stew and can be kept aside (covered) for a short time in a warm oven or hot cupboard.

The meat is undercooked or tough.

The quality of meat used was not as good as the recipe timings allowed for.

The sauce is too thin.

There was too much liquid in relation to the quantity of roux or thickening vegetables. *See* tips.

The sauce is too thick.

1. Too much roux was made.
2. Not enough liquid was added.

The sauce is bitter in taste.

1. The roux and/or the stew as a whole was overcooked.
2. The stew was kept warm for too long after cooking and before service.

The sauce is greasy.

1. The stew was not skimmed adequately.
2. Fat was left on the meat when it was prepared.
3. The stew was kept standing for too long between cooking and service.

The sauce has curdled.

The stew was boiled after the egg yolks had been added (as part of the liaison).

Tips

To reduce the fat content of a blanquette, a thickening paste made with equal quantities of cooking liquid and flour (a jaysee) can be used instead of a velouté.

If the sauce is too thin, strain it off into a second, clean saucepan. It can then be thickened without damaging or overcooking the main food item, either by being boiled rapidly to reduce it, or by having a thickening paste added to it. Strain the corrected sauce back over the food (which should have been kept hot).

When making a stew for large numbers it is easier to shallow fry the vegetables before the meat. Otherwise the juices released by the meat will make it difficult to brown the vegetables.

Comparison of four wet cooking processes

	Stewing	Braising	Shallow poaching	Deep poaching	Boiling
Cooking temperature (for main part of process)	100°C (212°F)	100°C (212°F) – higher when glazing the food	75-93°C (167-200°F)	75-93°C (167-200°F)	100°C (212°F)
Level of liquid	Covers food	Comes two thirds up height of food *but* small items covered	Comes one third up height of food	Covers food	Covers food
Final use of liquid	Part of dish	Made into sauce	Made into sauce	Not used	Not used
Size of food	Cut into small pieces	Whole items, but ox tail cut into pieces and liver sliced	Cuts and small whole items	Whole items and some cuts	Whole items
Method of covering pan during cooking	With lid	With lid	With grease-proof paper	With lid	Not always covered
Main cooking happens	In oven	In oven	In oven	On top of stove	On top of stove
Role of vegetables	Add flavour	Add flavour and provide protection for base of food	Add flavour (but used only in small quantities)	Give flavour to cooking liquid	Sometimes used for flavour

TEST YOURSELF

1. Name three cuts of beef and three of lamb/mutton you would choose for stewing, and say why they are suitable.

2. Name the two types of connective tissue in meat. Which one turns to gelatin when it is cooked?

3. Briefly describe two main differences between a blanquette and a fricassée.

4. What ingredient is used to thicken:
   a) brown stew
   b) blanquette
   c) fricassée
   d) curry
   e) Irish stew?

5. When is meat shallow fried before a stew is made? Give reasons for doing this.

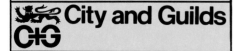
City and Guilds

Stews will keep their appearance reasonably well for some time, so are good for situations where service continues over an extended period – as in this self-service buffet.

The serving container should be refilled before the level of the food gets too low (or it will dry out) and the hot cupboard or bain-marie should be set above 63°C (145°F), but below a temperature at which the food could burn.

5 BRAISING

Braising is quite a lengthy process and requires a great deal of care and attention, but a successful braised dish can look really impressive and very appetising. A handsome joint of beef or a succulent goose gleaming with the glaze that this process produces and surrounded by carefully prepared, same-sized mushrooms and pieces of carrot and onion would make a good main course for a formal lunch or dinner.

Braised food has to be served as soon as it is completed because if there is any delay both its taste and appearance will deteriorate. Because of this, and the fact that braising takes a long time, it is best suited to set menus or as the dish-of-the-day on an à la carte menu in a restaurant or hotel. It is not often used in situations like canteens or self-service restaurants where the food has to look good over quite a long service period.

Although meat is the most usual food item to be braised, vegetables can also be cooked in this way, especially stuffed vegetable dishes, e.g. marrow with mushroom stuffing, pimentoes with rice pilaff or cabbage with sausage meat. Although vegetable dishes are at their best if they are served as soon as cooking is completed, they keep their appearance better than braised meat and so are more likely to be served in, say, a cafeteria.

The secret of creating the delicious flavours and textures of a really good braised dish has to do with careful and often time-consuming preparation and the use of the best ingredients. Stocks, for example, need to be of high quality, and the base of chopped vegetables – usually onions, celery, carrots and leeks in the case of meat dishes – needs to be well balanced.

Cooking temperatures and timing have to be well judged and carefully controlled. The impressive sheen that meat surfaces are given in braising comes from getting the right balance of gelatin-rich stocks and flour thickeners, as well as from frequent basting during the final cooking stages.

▶▶▶ TO DO

Are braised dishes ever put on the menu in your workplace or in restaurants near where you live or work? If so, make a note of what they are, and of any descriptions used to tempt the customer to order them. Against your list, describe what steps you think might be taken to ensure that the dishes look their best when served. If possible, discuss them with the chef or your tutor. If no braised dishes have recently been offered, try to find out why.

5 BRAISING

What happens

In braising, the food is partially covered with some kind of liquid which is kept at, or close to, boiling point. The cooking container is usually kept firmly closed for most, if not all, of the cooking time. When cooked, the food should have become very tender and there will almost always be a sauce from the cooking liquor.

Many braised dishes rely for at least part of their taste on the flavours caused by browning. But as the temperatures reached in braising are not high enough for browning to happen, the food needs to be browned first. It can either be shallow-fried in hot fat or, especially if it is too large to be handled safely in a frying pan, it can be flash roasted – this means roasting it for a very short time in a hot oven at 230°-250°C (450°-485°F).

In braising, the food is cooked in a moist environment: most of it (usually two-thirds) is actually immersed in the liquid, and the rest is surrounded by steam trapped in the container that comes both from the liquid and from the food.

Usually the liquid is first heated to boiling point on top of the stove. In most cases the container is then transferred to the oven, which has the advantage of providing a much more even heat all round. The cooking temperature is kept at a level which will keep the liquid simmering but avoid it drying out or burning.

See: Videos 4 and 5

Browning or searing the outside of meats, poultry and game that are to be braised gives them colour and brings out flavour. The duck shown in this picture has been placed in a roasting tray in a hot oven for 20 minutes to achieve this browning which has cooked only the surface. The inside does not even begin to cook. The same effect can be achieved by shallow frying.

Braising meat and vegetables

Braising is an ideal method for cooking meat that is too tough to roast but does not need to be cut into small pieces and stewed. When meat is braised, the tough connective tissue will have turned to gelatin by about the same time that the protein is thoroughly cooked – so there is less risk of the joint drying out and becoming tough.

Braising can also be used to tenderise vegetables, especially those which contain tough cellulose, e.g. celery, and, like meat, they will take in flavour from the liquid or sauce in which they are cooked. This flavouring effect is in fact the main reason why vegetables would be braised, as there is a serious loss of vitamins which does not happen to the same extent in boiling or steaming.

This picture shows three key features of braising: a base of chopped vegetables, e.g. carrots, onions, leeks and garlic (sometimes known as mirepoix or 'bed of roots'), a pan with a close-fitting lid, and the practice of browning or searing the food before the main cooking takes place. Once this duck has been placed in the braising pan, liquid (stock, demi-glace, wine, etc., according to the recipe) will be added to about two-thirds its height.

Even tough meat will eventually begin to fall apart if it is braised for too long, as this photograph shows.

> **Braised rice**
> When rice is braised, the cooking liquid and its flavours are completely absorbed, and no sauce is made. *See* recipe, Poaching/Practical Examples 3.

Helping the cooking process

Marinading

Meats, game and poultry are often soaked before braising in a liquid made up of oil, red or white wine, herbs, seasonings, and sometimes vegetables such as carrots or onions. This is called marinading and is a process which adds flavour to the finished dish. It may sometimes cause colour changes, depending on the ingredients in the marinade, for example, an acidic ingredient will turn red meat a browny-grey. Marinading can tenderise meat, but this effect is not very great, as the acids in the liquid (which act on the toughness) can only get at the surface of the food. It is possible to help the process by pricking holes in the food so that the liquid can penetrate, but the disadvantage of this is that it will lead to fluid loss during cooking.

Blanching

Vegetables are usually partly cooked in boiling water (blanched) before braising. There are several reasons for this:

- to keep their colour during cooking. (Blanching stops the process that causes discoloration.)

- to make rigid and/or brittle vegetables flexible. They can then be attractively shaped for cooking without ripping, bruising or snapping. (After blanching they are cooled under cold running water so that they can be easily handled.)

- to remove the bitter taste of vegetables like fennel, cabbage and celery.

Sweetbreads are blanched before braising to make it easier to remove the tough tissue that surrounds them.

Adding fat

Many of the meats suitable for braising do not contain much fat and will easily dry out during the long cooking process. To overcome this they usually have thin strips of fat threaded through the centre (this is called larding). A layer of fat is also sometimes placed on top of the meat (this is called barding) to help keep it moist. (*See* photograph in Method.)

Glazing the surface

Glazing gives a very attractive appearance to joints of meat and makes them look really appetising when they are shown to, or seen by, customers before carving or slicing. A good quality, very concentrated stock must form the basis of the cooking liquid. As soon as the meat is cooked it is removed from the cooking pan, placed on a shallow dish or deep tray with some of the cooking liquid, returned to the oven and basted frequently (a little of the liquid is spooned over the meat at short intervals). Soon the meat will have developed an attractive sheen or gloss – this effect is created partly by the gelatin from the bones used in the stock.

Adding flavours

The cooking liquid can include stock, wine, demi-glace or jus lié (*see* Introduction/Stocks), vegetables, tomato purée, bacon, herbs and, seasonings. These all add flavour to the food while it is cooking, and form the basis of the sauce that will be served with it.

▸▸▸ TO DO

Look at the braised celery recipe in Practical Examples 2. Take five heads of celery and cook them in separate saucepans, making one change to the recipe in each case, as shown in the following list:
1. Leave out step 4 (blanching)
2. Leave out base vegetables.

3. Use water and a stock cube instead of stock.
4. Leave out the bacon covering.
5. Follow recipe, including bacon covering.

Note down how the overall cooking time, the taste and the texture have been affected.

5 BRAISING

The key questions to ask when deciding whether or not to braise a food are:
– will it benefit from moist, slow cooking?
– will it be enjoyed cooked whole?
– will it benefit from being served with a sauce?

Meat

Braising is ideal for joints and cuts which are not tender enough to be roasted but are of higher quality than you need for stewing. It also offers an alternative to grilling and shallow frying for smaller cuts such as rump steak and chump chops. As a general guide, the following cuts are suitable:

Beef: topside, thick flank, rump, middle ribs, chuck rib
Veal: shoulder, shin, cushion, loin, best end
Lamb: shoulder
Mutton: chump chops
Pork: leg (cured as ham)

Poultry

Among poultry, it is usually only whole ducks or geese that are braised. Preliminary browning in a hot oven is particularly important since duck and geese contain a lot of fat and much of this fat is released during browning and can be drained off before cooking continues.

Whole chickens or individual chicken legs are sometimes braised, usually after being boned and stuffed, with finely minced pork, for example. Other meat can be braised in this style, called ballotine, including shoulder of lamb and pork, duck, turkey and guinea-fowl.

Game

Venison, hare, wild duck, teal, pigeon are all kinds of game that can be successfully braised. Pheasant, partridge, and quail are more suited to roasting, although older, tougher birds can benefit from braising.

Fish

Certain fish dishes, for example, salmon, halibut, trout, pike and squid are sometimes described on menus and in recipe books as 'braised', although it could be argued that they are in fact poached because the cooking temperature is kept below boiling point to avoid damaging the delicate fish flesh (the key feature in poaching).

The fish is sometimes larded or barded with bacon or pork fat. Or it may have strips of vegetables such as gherkins or carrots inserted into it before cooking. Some recipe instructions involve basting the fish frequently during cooking to produce a glaze.

Vegetables

When vegetables are braised, their flavours are added to by whatever cooking liquid is used, for example stock, demi-glace or jus lié. The vegetables shown in the photograph have an important feature in common: they will not turn to mush when cooked for a long time. They all contain a strong, rather inflexible substance called cellulose, which is (partly) broken down in the long braising process.

Clockwise from top left: Savoy cabbage, red, green and yellow peppers, lettuce, celery, fennel, chicory, onions and leeks. Other vegetables suitable for braising are red cabbage and artichoke hearts.

Rice

Types of rice that can be boiled to form the main part of a savoury dish (*see* Boiling/Food Selection 4), can also be braised. When rice is braised there is less rice in relation to the cooking liquid than if it were being boiled. This is because the aim is that the liquid (a good stock, for example) will be fully absorbed by the rice during cooking (*see* Poaching/Practical Examples 3).

✳ NUTRITION

Vegetables lose a lot of their nutritional value if braised. But boiled or steamed vegetables can increase the vitamin content and improve the appearance of braised meat dishes. They should be cooked immediately before the meat is to be garnished and served.

Offal: what it is and how to select and prepare it

This information will help you gain the Caterbase module, *Preparing Offal*.

Offal is a term used to cover internal organs, such as brain, heart, tongue, sweetbreads (the pancreas or the thymus glands), liver, kidneys and tripe, as well as the parts of an animal that are left after the meat on the carcase has been removed, e.g. the feet and tail.

Offal should always be of good quality, whether it is selected for braising, shallow frying, grilling or boiling. The smell and colour should not be unusual or unpleasant (green or yellow staining is never a good sign) and the surface should be moist but not sticky.

It is very important when preparing offal to:
– wash off any visible blood.
– remove any tough outer skin, membrane or sinew.

Liver (ox, calf, pork)
Cut away any tubes or sinew, and remove the membrane.

Kidney (ox, calf, lamb, pork)
Cut away any tubes and fat and remove the skin.

Tongue (ox, lamb, pork)
Soak in cold water: for 24 hours if fresh, 4 to 6 hours if pickled. Any bone or gristle on the back of the tongue should be removed.

Brains (ox, calf, lamb, pork)
Soak in cold, salty water for 4 to 6 hours to remove any blood. Remove all the membrane, then re-wash.

Heart (ox, calf, lamb)
Trim off excess fat and tubes, remove any clots of blood from the inside (heart is either sliced or if cooked whole, cut almost in half so it can be opened up, but not split).

Sweetbreads (calf, lamb)
To remove any visible blood soak in cold, salty water for an hour at least, then wash thoroughly. (*See also* Practical Examples 2.)

Tripe (ox)
Usually bought cleaned, trimmed and partly cooked (*see also* Boiling/Food Selection 5). Raw tripe must be boiled for 3 to 4 hours in salted water.

Stomach (lamb, pork)
Specialised use only: e.g. for haggis and sausages.

Tail (ox, pork)
Excess fat must be removed. Oxtail is usually skinned (and bought in this form) for soup and stews. If it is to be boned and stuffed it should be left unskinned. Pig's tail is singed and usually pressed after boiling to straighten.

Ears (calf, pork)
Singed and thoroughly cleaned.

Trotters (calf, lamb, pork)
Blanched, boned and singed, any tufts of hair removed. Hooves removed.

Head (calf)
Soaked for several hours in water and blanched.

Lungs (calf)
Beaten vigorously to expel air, cut into cubes and blanched.

Tender cuts of offal are highly suitable for braising. Shown here are: veal sweetbreads (*lower centre*) and ox liver (*right*) both of which benefit in flavour from being braised. Tougher cuts can be tenderised by the process: oxtail (*left*), sheep's heart (*top centre*) and ox tongue (*middle centre*).

▶▶▶ TO DO

Often the weight of prepared and cooked meat is quite different from the weight it was when it was bought. For example, a thick flank of beef on the bone weighing 6 kg may lose 1 kg once the bone has been removed and 1½ kg during cooking. If a standard portion of cooked meat is 150 g, how many portions will you be able to get out of the meat?

Terms

Braising is cooking whole food or quite large cuts in a closed container, so trapping the steam given off by the food and the cooking liquid (that partly covers the food). The cooking liquid is used as the basis for a sauce to accompany the dish.

Glazing is the process that gives an attractive, shiny appearance to the surface of braised meats – it involves frequent basting with the cooking liquid.

Flash roasting refers to the brief preliminary roasting of a joint of meat in a hot oven to brown its surface, before it is thoroughly cooked by braising.

Larding is the practice of threading lardons (in other words, strips of fat) through pieces of meat or fish.

Barding is placing a thin layer of fat over the surface of a piece of meat.

Marinading is soaking food before cooking in a flavoured, usually slightly acidic liquid. In braising it is used to add extra flavours to meat, game and poultry, and to partially tenderise the food.

Brown braising is the type of braising in which the food item and its vegetable base are browned before braising and dark-coloured ingredients such as brown stocks, red wine, demi-glace or jus lié are used.

White braising has two meanings. Traditionally it was a way of cooking white meats with a gelatin-rich stock to produce a glazed coating. This method was believed to seal in the meat juices, while avoiding the browning that would happen if the meat were seared.

White braising now more usually refers to dishes in which the cooking liquid is thickened after the meat is cooked.

Dry braising is not true braising. It is actually roasting in a closed container with a little butter. It is also known, more accurately, as pot roasting (*see* Book 1, Roasting/Terms and Equipment). No liquid is used, but the steam given off by the food is trapped in the container, creating a moister heat than is usual in roasting.

Clear braise refers to the use of a white stock, thickened with cornflour or arrowroot at the start of the cooking process, for braising dark-coloured meats or vegetables.

Mirepoix is the name given to the bed of roughly chopped vegetables (also known as base vegetables or bed of roots).

Equipment

The pans shown in the photograph on this page are made from aluminium. Tin-lined copper, stainless steel, enamelled and cast-iron pans are also suitable for braising, especially for dishes like braised red cabbage (in which vinegar is used) which would discolour aluminium.

As well as the earthenware dishes shown, Pyrex-type and porcelain dishes are suitable, providing they are oven-proof and have close-fitting lids. The fact that these materials conduct heat very slowly is a definite advantage in braising.

A *daubière* is a special earthenware, stoneware or tin-lined copper casserole, traditionally used for cooking 'en daube' (braising with wine, stock and herbs).

Bratt pans, sometimes called *tilting braising pans*, have the same disadvantages as ordinary pans used on top of a stove. Cooking is less even than it would be in an oven because the heat comes only from below and this also means that it is not possible to achieve a good glaze.

Although specially designed braising pans are available (the large oval pan in the centre of the photograph is an example), any pan or oven-proof dish can be used for braising as long as it has a tight-fitting lid and can stand the heat of an oven. It is also important to choose the right-sized pan for the food. The pan should be just big enough for the food to fit in without touching the lid, so that not too much cooking liquid has to be used for the food to be partially covered. If too much liquid is used the flavour will be diluted.

▶▶▶ TO DO

List the equipment in your workplace which would be suitable or which would have to be bought to braise:
a) a duck
b) enough leeks for 30 people
c) a large ham.

Include equipment used for any initial browning as well as the main cooking. Note after each item why you think your choice would be suitable.

5 BRAISING

Essential points

If you are being assessed for a Caterbase certificate in the combined module, *Braising/Stewing*, make sure you are familiar with the points in this section.

1. The work area should be clean, with the equipment and ingredients required for the dish ready to hand.

Successful braising requires thorough preparation and planning in advance to make sure that, for example, good quality stocks are available, or in brown braising, demi-glace or jus lié are to hand (*see* Introduction/Stocks). These key ingredients cannot be produced in an hour or so: for example, stock with a good gelatinous base is likely to require 6 to 8 hours' boiling. Other time-consuming activities you may have to do before braising can start include larding or marinading meats and soaking offal (*see* boxes).

Finally, as many braised foods are served or presented whole, you will need to take special care with their appearance, for example, vegetables need to be trimmed to an even shape, or tied with string if they are likely to lose their shape during cooking. Large joints of meat should be tied with string for the same reason.

2. Set the oven temperature and if necessary preheat the top of the stove.

The initial browning of the food must be done with hot fat on top of the stove or in a hot oven, where the temperature should be around 230°-250°C (450°-485°F). This stage will take anything from 10 to 40 minutes. For braising, the oven temperature should be enough to keep the liquid simmering: about 180°C (360°F) is a good starting point.

> **Soaking offal**
> Sweetbreads usually need to be soaked for about 1 hour. Pickled tongue should be soaked for several hours. Both require blanching before braising.

This picture shows (from top to bottom): blanched, pressed and sliced sweetbreads.

Before sweetbreads are braised, they should be left between plates under a heavy weight for 30 to 60 minutes. This will slightly flatten them, improving the appearance of the finished dish.

If sweetbreads are to be shallow fried, they are flattened and then sliced.

Marinading meats

The time required depends on how far the meat needs tenderising or how much its flavour and/or colour should develop, although if it is left too long in the marinade, the surface of the food will become mushy even though the inside is hardly affected. Some meat needs only 20 minutes marinading (e.g. lamb chops), but 2 to 3 hours or overnight is more usual. There is even a case where 7 days are suggested: venison being prepared in wintry conditions!

Some ingredients used in braising marinades

Liquids: red and white wine, brandy, beer, oil, orange and lemon juice.
Vegetables: carrots, onions, shallots, celery, garlic.
Herbs: bay leaves, thyme, parsley stalks, cloves, black or white peppercorns, coriander seeds, juniper berries.

Suitable containers

Glass, china and stainless steel bowls or dishes are suitable, providing they are big enough to allow the food to be covered completely. Aluminium should not be used as it reacts to the acids in the marinade, causing discoloration.

White braising is a way of cooking white meats, like veal, chicken and turkey, so that they keep their whiteness. Not surprisingly, the meat is not browned or coloured before braising and marinades are not used because they would tend to overwhelm the delicate taste of the meat.

A variation of white braising is still used for cushion of veal, sweetbreads, tongue and ham. A vegetable base is used with a white stock – which is thickened with arrowroot after the meat is cooked or reduced with the addition of a jus lié made from white stock.

Sweetbreads, tongue and ham are first blanched (placed in a saucepan covered with cold water, brought to the boil and simmered for a short time) and then refreshed (washed in fresh, cold water to remove any impurities).

One white meat that some chefs prefer to brown lightly before braising (by shallow frying) is veal, which would then be braised in a brown stock (like the cushion of veal in the top right corner of the photograph).

In *brown braising*, when only dark meats are used, the meat may have some fat added, as with the topside shown in the picture, to help the flavour and texture (which would otherwise be dry in spite of the cooking liquid). This has to be done by larding (inserting strips of fat) and/or barding (covering with a thin layer of fat).

The meat is often marinaded to improve flavour and is then browned or seared, as are the base vegetables.

Unlike white braising liquid, brown braising liquid is thickened at the start of cooking, traditionally by using demi-glace, jus lié or a brown sauce as well as stock, or by starting with a roux base.

🍴 CHEF'S TIP

When larding meats, make sure larding fat has been kept in a refrigerator: it is easiest to handle when very cold. For some recipes, the fat has to be marinaded before use.

3. Prepare the base vegetables.

The base vegetables are:
- used raw for some white braised dishes, or for a braised vegetable dish (when the cooking utensil should be buttered) or
- sweated without colouring if the colour of the final dish is to be as pale as possible or
- shallow fried (for brown braising) in the same pan that will be used to brown the meat.

If vegetables have been marinaded, they are strained, dried, browned and then used as base vegetables, and the marinading liquid forms part of the braising liquid.

4. Add the main food item, then add seasoning, stock, wine, etc., according to the recipe, making sure there is enough liquid to reach two-thirds up the height of the food.

In brown braising the recipe liquid will include a thickened sauce such as demi-glace or jus lié. Some chefs start by browning the base vegetables in the fat left after browning the meat, and then make a roux, mixing flour through the vegetables and cooking it for 8 to 10 minutes. Stock is then added, a little at a time to start with, and stirred in well.

In white braising the recipe liquid is not thickened until after the meat is cooked.

5. Bring the cooking liquid to the boil, skim off any impurities or fat that rise to the surface, then cover the pan with a tight-fitting lid and transfer it to the oven.

Vegetables and sweetbreads should be covered with a buttered piece of greaseproof paper, cut to fit neatly in the pan, before the lid is put on.

6. Check the food from time to time during cooking and baste it thoroughly.

You need to keep an eye on:

- the quantity of liquid. If it has reduced too much and there is a danger of the food drying out, add fresh stock or sauce (at boiling temperature).
- the temperature. The liquid should simmer gently. If you find it is boiling vigorously, reduce the oven temperature.
- the appearance of excess fat or impurities. These should be skimmed off and thrown away.

One of the advantages of using a layer of base vegetables is that they help to stop the underside of the meat sticking to the bottom of the dish and burning.

Base vegetables for braising are chosen both for their flavour, which will be taken into the cooking liquid, and for their structure, as they need more or less to keep their shape during cooking. So onions, carrots, celery and leeks are all suitable, unlike turnips and parsnips, which will fall apart during cooking.

▶▶▶ TO DO

The preparation of a braised dish can be very time-consuming. How long does it take, for example, to prepare Braised Duckling? Look at the recipe in Practical Examples 1 and calculate the time needed for each stage in the recipe. Then, working backwards from the serving time, calculate when you would need to start preparing the dish.

Glazing meat
For glazed dishes, the meat is removed from the oven as soon as it is cooked, then placed in a shallow dish (or deep tray) with enough of the reduced cooking liquid to allow effective basting. It is then returned to an oven heated to about 200°C (395°F) and basted frequently until a shiny surface develops.

Thickening the sauce

To thicken a sauce without colouring it, add a thickener such as cornflour, arrowroot or waxy maize starch. This method is usually used in white braising but is also useful in a brown braise if the sauce is still too thin when it is about to be served.

Adding a mixture of flour and water has the same effect as a roux-based thickener but avoids the need to add extra fat. This method should be used with great care because it easily turns lumpy, but is suitable for brown or white braising.

Adding beurre manié (roughly equal quantities of flour and butter mixed together to form a smooth paste), is a method suitable for both brown and white braising.

▶▶▶ TO DO

Measure out 30 g (1½ oz) of arrowroot and the same amount of a waxy maize starch. Dilute each with about 50 ml (2 fl oz) of cold water.

Pour ½ litre (1 pint) of water into each of two saucepans. Bring both to the boil, add the diluted arrowroot to one, the diluted waxy maize starch to the other. Reboil them both for one minute and then take them off the heat.

Make notes about the consistency and colour of each. Cool both solutions and then look at their consistency and colour again. Discuss the differences with your supervisor, and then decide which thickener you would use for braised sweetbreads and which for a clear raspberry sauce.

7. When the food is cooked, remove it from the oven, and set it aside on a tray in a warm oven or hot cupboard.

When cooked, vegetables should feel tender and give slightly when gently pressed. Meat can be tested with a trussing needle (a cocktail stick can be used for small items) – the juices released should be clear with no sign of blood. Very tender meats, such as a joint of veal, can be tested with a meat thermometer – the temperature at the centre should reach 80°C (176°F). (This test is not suitable for tougher meats, because they will need long cooking after the right temperature has been reached to make them tender.)

8. Strain off the cooking liquid, discard the herbs and vegetables used as the base, and skim off any impurities or grease that have risen to the surface.

This is the point when white braising liquid is thickened to make a sauce, and brown braising liquid can be reduced or thickened if it is not thick enough already.

The sauce should be neither so thin that it runs off the food straight away, nor so thick that it clings to the surface. A good sauce will flow easily and evenly over the food, coating it thinly.

9. Arrange the food in a warm serving dish. If the meat is to be served sliced, carve it separately and then arrange the slices on a serving dish.

Meat should be carved across the grain to produce a short-fibred, tender cut which is easy to chew. As braised meat has a softer texture than a roasted joint, fairly thick slices, of about 5 mm (¼ in.) are usually carved. A knife with a very sharp blade is absolutely essential, and a proper carving knife is best (see Introduction/ Knife Skills).

Braised meat tends to dry out very quickly once carved, so it should be lightly coated with stock or the sauce.

Vegetable garnishes are usually cooked separately.

Sauces should not be added to braised vegetables until immediately before service, otherwise the vegetables will discolour and the liquid that drains out of the vegetables while they are standing will dilute the sauce.

Braised duckling

See: Video 4

INGREDIENTS   SERVES 4

1 × 2 kg	duckling	1 × 4½ lb
5 g	white margarine or oil	¼ oz
100 g	onions	4 oz
100 g	carrots	4 oz
50 g	celery	2 oz
50 g	leeks	2 oz
1 l	thin demi-glace or jus lié	2 pt

(see *Introduction/Stocks*)
sprig of thyme, bay leaf and parsley stalks
salt and pepper to taste

1. Remove all loose fat from around the neck, from the base of the tail and from the body cavity of the duckling. Cut off the winglets through the middle of the first joint away from the body. Truss the bird.

2. Place the duckling on a roasting tray breast upwards, and dab or pour the lard or oil over the breast and over the top of the legs.

3. Place in a hot oven, 230°-250°C (450°-485°F) and leave until it has browned. This will take 30 to 40 minutes in a convection oven, 20 to 30 minutes in a forced air convection oven.

4. Remove the duck from the tray and drain well. This helps remove excess fat.

5. Wash, peel and roughly chop the vegetables.

6. Place a little of the hot duck fat, about 20 ml (¾ fl oz), in the braising pan and put the pan on the heat.

7. Add the vegetables and fry in the fat until lightly browned.

8. Drain off any excess fat and place the duckling breast upwards on the bed of vegetables.

9. Add the demi-glace or jus lié so that it comes two-thirds up the height of the duckling.

10. Bring to the boil and skim off any fat that has risen to the surface.

11. Cover with the lid and place in a moderate oven 175°C (350°F) to cook for 1 to 1½ hours. Baste the duckling with the sauce from time to time during cooking.

12. To test that the duckling is cooked, prick the top of the bird and the centre of the leg joints with a trussing needle. The juices that are released should show no signs of blood.

13. When the duckling is cooked remove it from the oven, drain it well, place it on a tray and keep it warm in a hot cupboard.

14. Strain the sauce into a clean pan, bring to the boil and skim off any fat that rises to the surface. If the sauce is too thin, keep boiling it until it has reached the right consistency. Check the seasoning.

15. Remove the string from the duckling, then cut into portions:

a) First, remove the legs, then cut each leg in half through the joint.

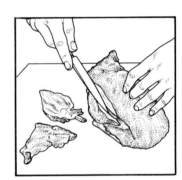

b) Remove the knuckles.

c) Cut off each wing parallel to the breast bone and down through the wing joints. Ensure that four similar-sized portions will be produced from the wings and breast.

d) Trim off the knuckle end from each wing.

e) Hold the bird upright (parson's nose upwards) and chop down between the breast and the carcase.

f) Cut any excess rib cage off the breast piece.

g) Cut the breast in half.

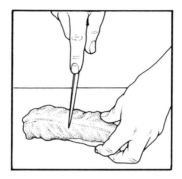

CHEF'S TIP

There are many different braised duckling dishes. Wine, a spirit, liqueur or fruit juice may be added to the sauce during cooking (or at step 14) to produce a distinctive flavour. A variety of garnishes may also be used, e.g. cooked vegetables, pasta or fruit.

Alternatively, the legs can be prepared as already described, but the wing and breast meat can be carved in thin slices, parallel to the length of the bird, as in the photograph.

16. Arrange the pieces of duckling in the warm serving dish allowing one piece of leg meat and one piece of breast meat (or two or three slices) per portion.

　Coat with some of the sauce. Serve the remaining sauce in a sauceboat.

Trussing poultry

See Poaching/Practical Examples 2 for how to pluck, draw and gut poultry.

1. Thread the trussing needle with string.

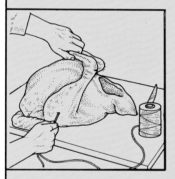

2. With the bird resting on its back, breast up, raise the legs then press them both down firmly towards the front.

3. Insert the needle through the middle of the leg at the joint between the drumstick and thigh bone, and push it through so that it comes out at the same point on the other leg.

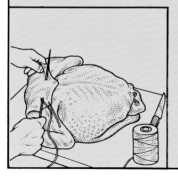

4. Turn the bird over and pierce through the centre of the wing joint.
　Large birds, such as the turkey in the illustration, are left with the winglet untrimmed. The string should go through the same place, whether the winglet is trimmed off or not.

5. Sew down the neck flap to the carcase, then pass the needle out through the opposite wing joint, so that the string ends up close to the point where it first went in.

6. Unthread the needle, and pull the string taut so that the bird is forced into a neat shape. Knot the two ends of string together and trim off any spare.

7. Thread the trussing needle with a second length of string, for tying down the ends of the legs. Push the legs down. Insert the string through the bottom of the carcase at the point where the leg knuckle touches.

8. Pull the string firmly through the body and then back over the tops of the legs. Tighten the string, knot the ends together and trim off any excess string.

Braised sweetbreads
Ris de veau braisé
or Ris d'agneau braisé

INGREDIENTS   SERVES 10

1.5 kg	veal or lamb sweetbreads	3 lb 5 oz
150 g	onions	6 oz
150 g	carrots	6 oz
75 g	leeks	2 oz
50 g	butter	2 oz
1 l	brown veal stock	2 pt

sprig of thyme, bay leaf and parsley stalks

Thickening

25 g	arrowroot	1 oz
100 ml	cold water	4 fl oz

1. Wash the sweetbreads in cold water. If they show any sign of blood, soak in salted water for about an hour.

2. Place the sweetbreads into a saucepan, cover with cold water and bring to the boil. Allow to simmer for about 15 minutes. (Blanching makes sweetbreads firmer and much easier to handle.)

3. Remove the pan from the stove, and place it under cold running water until all the scum and impurities have been washed off and the sweetbreads are no longer hot.

4. Drain. Trim off any fat and tough tissue surrounding the sweetbreads.

5. Wash, peel and roughly chop the vegetables.

6. Gently shallow fry the vegetables in the butter, taking care that they do not colour. (This step can be omitted to make the final result slightly less rich.)

7. Place the vegetables into a braising pan or casserole, then arrange the sweetbreads on top.

8. Add the brown stock so that it just covers the sweetbreads. (If the sweetbreads are only partly covered – as with many braised dishes – they will tend to cook unevenly.)

9. Cover the liquid and sweetbreads with a piece of buttered greaseproof paper and lid and bring the liquid almost to the boil on top of the stove.

10. Transfer to a moderate oven at 175°C (350°F) and cook for approximately 1 hour. Inspect the sweetbreads during cooking and skim off any fat. Also top up with extra stock if required.

11. When cooked, the sweetbreads should feel firm. Remove them from the braising pan, place them in a dish, cover with the cooking paper, and keep the dish hot in a warm oven or hot cupboard.

12. Strain the cooking liquor into a clean pan and reboil.

13. Dilute the arrowroot with cold water.

14. Whisk enough diluted arrowroot into the cooking liquor to lightly thicken it, then allow to simmer for 1 to 2 minutes.

15. Transfer the hot sweetbreads into a suitable, warm serving dish and coat with the sauce.

Braised celery
Céleri braisé

INGREDIENTS   SERVES 10

5	small heads of celery	5
750 ml	brown stock (see Introduction/Stocks)	1½ pt
250 ml	jus lié (see Introduction/Stocks)	½ pt
5	thin slices of fat bacon	5

sprig of thyme, 1 bay leaf and parsley stalks
chopped parsley

Base vegetables

100 g	onions	4 oz
100 g	carrots	4 oz
50 g	leeks	2 oz

1. Wash the celery and remove any damaged stalks.

2. Trim the root end and remove any blemishes with a peeler or small knife.

3. Cut each head to a length of about 150 mm (6 in.), and secure it neatly with string.

4. Submerge the celery heads in a saucepan of boiling water, simmer for 10 to 20 minutes, then drain them.

5. Peel and roughly chop the base vegetables, then arrange them in a small braising pan, saucepan with lid or casserole. Place the blanched celery on top.

6. Cover each celery head with a slice of bacon (if used).

7. Add the brown stock up to two-thirds the height of the celery.

8. Cover with a piece of buttered greaseproof paper and lid, then bring almost to the boil.

9. Place into a moderate oven at 175°C (350°F), and allow to cook until tender – about 2 hours.

10. When the celery is cooked, the point of a small knife should be able to penetrate the root end easily. Remove the celery (and bacon, if used), drain and place in a dish. Cover with the cooking paper. Keep hot in a warm oven or hot cupboard.

11. Boil the cooking liquor until it has reduced to half then add the jus lié.

12. Reboil, simmer for 2 to 3 minutes, then strain into a clean pan.

13. Skim off any fat on the surface and check seasoning.

14. Remove the string from the celery and cut each head in half length-ways. Neatly fold each head across its length.

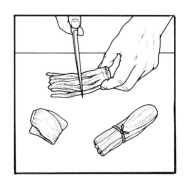

15. Place the celery in a warm serving dish, check that it is still hot, then coat with the sauce. If required, sprinkle with the chopped parsley.

See Video 5 for stuffed cabbage.

Braised stuffed cabbage
Chou farci braisé

INGREDIENTS		SERVES 10
1½ kg	cabbage (1 large cabbage)	3 lb 5 oz
250 g	sausagemeat	10 oz

The rest of the ingredients are the same as for braised celery, adding 50 g (2 oz) celery to the base vegetables and using 10 slices of fat bacon.

1. Wash the cabbage and remove any wilted leaves.

2. Carefully remove the largest outside leaves. Cut out their thick centre stalks.

3. Halve the cabbage, then cut each half into five wedge-shaped portions. Do not remove the centre stalks holding the wedges together.

4. Submerge the wedges and large outer leaves in boiling salted water and simmer until the cabbage ribs have gone limp – about 10 to 20 minutes.

5. Wash under cold running water until the cabbage is cold, then drain thoroughly.

6. Divide the sausagemeat into 10 small balls.

7. Remove the centre stalk from each wedge of cabbage and place a ball of sausagemeat in the centre.

8. Fold up the wedge of cabbage to enclose the sausagemeat. Place in the centre of one of the blanched outer leaves. Fold up the leaf so a ball is formed.

9. Squeeze one at a time in a clean cloth to neaten the shape of the balls and remove excess moisture.

10. From this point the steps are identical to step 5 onwards in the braised celery recipe. The cooking time is about 1½ hours.

Daube de boeuf

INGREDIENTS   SERVES 10

1.4 kg	lean beef	3 lb 2 oz
	(topside or thick flank)	
150 g	rindless pork fat	6 oz
200 g	piece of lean bacon	8 oz
200 g	onions	8 oz
150 g	carrots	6 oz
100 g	button mushrooms	4 oz
400 g	tomatoes	1 lb
2	cloves of garlic	2

bouquet garni – sprig of thyme, 1 bay leaf,
parsley stalks and the zest of an orange in a muslin bag
or tied up in a length of celery or leek

10 ml	oil	½ fl oz
750 ml	jus lié (see Introduction/Stocks)	1½ pt

salt and freshly milled black pepper to taste

Marinade

500 ml	white wine	1 pt
75 ml	brandy	3 fl oz
25 ml	olive oil	1 fl oz
	juice of 1 lemon	

Paste to seal container

100 g	flour	4 oz
75 ml	water	3 fl oz

1. Trim any fat or gristle off the beef and cut it into cubes of about 30 mm (1¼ in.).

2. Cut the pork fat into thin strips approximately 40 mm long and 3 mm thick (1½ in. × ⅛ in.). You will need one strip of fat for each cube of meat.

3. Peel the garlic cloves, roughly chop them, then sprinkle them with salt and crush them under the blade of a large knife. Roll the strips of fat (which should be ice cold) through the garlic.

4. Insert one strip of fat through the centre of each cube of beef (in the same direction as the grain of the meat) using a larding needle.

5. Wash, peel and roughly chop the onions and carrots. Wash the mushrooms. Place the vegetables into a porcelain or stainless steel bowl with the ingredients for the marinade and mix together.

CHEF'S TIP

In some recipes the meat and base vegetables are not browned, but put straight into the casserole dish after marinading.

6. Add the beef and mix again thoroughly.

7. Cover and leave for 4 to 5 hours in a cool place – a room where the temperature is less than 10°C (50°F) – or a refrigerator. Stir the marinade mixture 2 or 3 times during this period.

8. Remove the stalks from the tomatoes and plunge them into boiling water for 10 to 20 seconds to loosen the skin. Cool them immediately under cold running water. Remove the skins, cut each tomato in half, scoop out the pips and roughly dice the flesh.

9. Cut the bacon into cubes of about 15mm (⅝ in.).

10. Drain the meat and vegetables, but keep the liquid that was used for the marinade. Dry the meat in a clean cloth.

11. Shallow fry the vegetables in the oil, and then the meat, browning them. Drain off the fat.

12. Place the vegetables in the base of a daubière or an oven-proof casserole with a lid. Add the meat, bacon, tomato, herbs, seasoning and marinade liquid.

13. Add enough jus lié to almost cover the ingredients.

14. For the water paste blend together the flour and water to form a soft dough.

15. Shape a thin layer of the paste around the lip of the casserole. Press the lid firmly down on to the paste, so that the casserole is well sealed.

16. Place the casserole in the centre of a moderate oven, at 180°C (350°F), and cook for 2 hours.

17. At the end of this time, take the casserole out of the oven, carefully cut through the seal and remove the lid. Check that the meat is cooked (if not replace the lid and return it to the oven).

18. Remove the bouquet garni. Skim off any fat present on the surface. Check the seasoning.

19. If a casserole dish is being used, try to present it with the pastry that formed the seal left in place. But if the pastry seal has broken up and looks untidy, remove it completely and clean the lip of the dish and lid. Replace the lid so that it can be removed when the dish is served to the customer.

20. If a daubière or saucepan is being used, transfer the meat, vegetables and sauce to a warm serving dish, taking care not to include bits of the pastry seal.

21. Serve at once.

Spiced courgette and pasta pot

INGREDIENTS	SERVES 10 (main course portions)	
250 g	wholemeal macaroni	10 oz
10 ml	polyunsaturated oil	½ fl oz
500 g	onions	1 lb 4 oz
4	cloves garlic	4
1 kg	courgettes	2½ lb
150 g	green peppers	6 oz
150 g	red peppers	6 oz
500 g	button mushrooms	1 lb 4 oz
5 g	chilli pepper	¼ oz
	(the amount can be increased or decreased according to taste)	
10 g	ground cumin	½ oz
10 g	paprika	½ oz
250 g	cooked haricot beans	10 oz
7	eggs	7
400 ml	low-fat natural yogurt	16 fl oz
600 ml	skimmed milk	24 fl oz
	salt and milled black pepper to taste	
	chopped parsley	

1. Place the macaroni into boiling salted water. Return the macaroni to the boil, then simmer it for 12 to 15 minutes until it is cooked, stirring it from time to time.

2. Cool the macaroni immediately under cold running water, and then drain it thoroughly.

3. Prepare the vegetables, cutting the onions, courgettes and peppers into 3 mm (⅛ in.) slices:
   a) Peel the onions, then slice them.
   b) Wash but do not peel the courgettes, then slice them into rounds.
   c) Wash the green and red peppers, cut them in half through the stem and top, remove the pips and then cut the halves into slices.
   d) Wash the mushrooms, and strip off any untidy stalks.
   e) Peel the garlic cloves, roughly chop them, then sprinkle them with salt and crush them under the blade of a large knife.

4. Heat the oil in a large plat à sauter or frying pan, add the onions and garlic and cook for 4 to 5 minutes, without allowing to colour.

5. Add the courgettes, peppers, mushrooms and spices and fry until the vegetables are lightly cooked. Stir frequently to avoid burning.

6. Stir in the cooked haricot beans and macaroni very carefully to avoid damaging them. Allow to heat through.

7. Butter 10 individual oven-proof dishes or porcelain containers – capacity about 350 ml (12½ fl oz). Arrange the vegetable mixture in these.

8. Whisk together the eggs, yogurt, milk and seasoning until well combined.

9. Pour this mixture into the porcelain pots, so as to barely cover the vegetables. Make sure that the mixture has thoroughly soaked through the vegetables.

10. Place into a moderate oven, at 200°C (395°F), and cook until lightly set – about 20 minutes.

11. Clean round the tops of the cooking pots if required, sprinkle with chopped parsley, and serve immediately.

This is an example of a dish which combines several cooking processes. Like many other braised dishes it starts off with shallow frying, after which the food is cooked in a sauce. But as eggs are used to set the sauce, and a brown surface is required, the dish is not covered. So it could also be described as a baked dish.

🧑‍🍳 CHEF'S TIP

Accompany this dish with wholemeal bread (without butter, if possible) for an excellent and healthy vegetarian meal.

Haricot beans

INGREDIENTS		
250 g	haricot beans	10 oz
1	small carrot	1
1	small onion	1

1. Soak the haricot beans in cold water for 4 to 12 hours.

2. Drain the beans, wash them in cold water, then place them in a saucepan and cover with cold water.

3. Peel the carrot and onion and add them to the water. Bring to the boil, and boil vigorously for 15 minutes, then allow to simmer until cooked, when the beans should be slightly firm. (This will take from 30 to 90 minutes depending on their quality and how long they have been soaked.)

4. Discard the carrot and onion. Drain the beans, then cool them quickly by running cold water over them. Drain.

What went wrong

Severe loss of liquid or over-thickening during braising.

1. Oven temperature too high so that the liquid boils too fiercely and is lost through evaporation.
2. Pan lid too loose or not fitted properly.

The food should be checked during cooking:
– the temperature can be adjusted
– more liquid can be added
– the lid can be made to fit properly. If you find yourself using a very poorly fitting lid, you can improve the seal by covering the pot with tin foil before the lid is put on.

Meat has shrunk too much.

1. The fat or the oven was too hot when the joint was being browned.
2. The oven was too hot during braising.
3. The meat has been cooked for too long.

Use just enough heat to brown the joint. Check oven temperatures during cooking and reduce them if the liquid begins to boil fiercely. Towards the end of the cooking time test the meat to see if it is cooked and if so stop cooking immediately.

Meat is dry and stringy.

1. The meat has been overcooked.
2. The meat was too tender for the length of time needed in a braising recipe.
3. Too much delay between cooking and service.

Marinade turns grey.

The basin used to hold the marinading food was made of aluminium.

The sauce is too thin.

1. It was not reduced enough.
2. Too little demi-glace, jus lié or thickening was added.
3. Too much cooking liquid was used to begin with.

More thickening can be added.

The sauce is too thick.

1. It was reduced too much.
2. Too much demi-glace, jus lié or thickening was added.
3. Too little cooking liquid was used to begin with.

More stock can be added.

The sauce is too dark or too pale in colour.

The meat and base vegetables were either burnt or not browned sufficiently.

Gravy browning can be added if the colour is too pale.

Marinated meat is an uneven colour.

1. The marinade had not entirely covered the meat.
2. The meat was not turned regularly in the marinade.

Meat will not glaze.

1. Oven temperature set too low.
2. The meat was not basted often enough.
3. The original stock did not contain enough bones, or was not reduced enough to achieve the necessary concentration of gelatin.

Vegetables have a dry or shrivelled appearance.

1. The cooking pot was not covered with buttered greaseproof paper as well as a lid.
2. The vegetables were not basted during cooking.
3. They were left for too long between cooking and service.

Vegetables taste bitter.

Not blanched thoroughly enough.

⚠ SAFETY

Aluminium containers with lids tend to look as if they are cold, even if they have been in a hot oven. As a reminder not to lift them without using a cloth, sprinkle the handles with a little flour. It will brown with the heat.

Tips

If you are braising meats that have been marinaded, remove the meat from the marinade half an hour before cooking. Allow the meat to drain, then dry it thoroughly with absorbent kitchen paper or a clean cloth before browning. Damp meat will not brown properly.

A combination of flour and *fromage frais* (a soft French cheese) has similar thickening properties to beurre manié. It gives a more tangy flavour and has a much lower fat content (only 1%-8%).

If the braised dish is to be presented to the customer in the dish in which it was cooked, but the dish has got stained during cooking, rub the stains with a dampened cloth which has been dipped in salt.

The strips of fat used to lard meat can give more flavour to the meat if they are first marinaded for about two hours in a little brandy with the addition of a small amount of freshly milled black pepper, nutmeg and chopped parsley.

Don't braise rolled meat joints prepared by a butcher (unless they have been specially made for braising). They are often made up of pieces of meat, which will fall apart when the string is cut and the meat is carved

If you are preparing a base of vegetables for braising one particular vegetable, do not use the main vegetable in the base.

These braised leeks are being lightly coated with the sauce just before they are served. Also shown is celery (*top left*), fennel (*bottom left*) and onions (*right*). If the sauce is added too long before service, or an attempt is made to reheat the vegetables in the sauce, the colour, taste and texture of the finished dish will be badly affected.

These braised sweetbreads with Madeira sauce have been prepared with brown stock and demi-glace to complement the flavour of the Madeira. Alternatively a white wine, for example a Sauternes or Moselle, and white stock thickened with arrowroot after braising might be preferred – to present as a white braise.

TEST YOURSELF

1. Give three reasons why a marinade is used in the preparation of joints of meat for braising.

2. Give two ways in which braising is different from a) stewing and b) poaching.

3. Name four types of offal that can be braised. Describe how to prepare one of them for cooking.

4. Name three products suitable for thickening liquids. Describe how one of them is used to make a sauce for a finished item.

5. Name three vegetables which can be used to form a base for the main braised food.

6. Give one way in which braised rice is different from other braised dishes.

7. Give one method of testing whether a meat or vegetable is cooked or not. Name one sign which should be present.

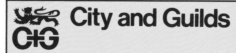 City and Guilds

6 STEAMING

Dark, rich Christmas pudding, satisfying jam sponge and tender steak and kidney pudding are among many people's favourite dishes. The moist heat of steam is used in dishes like these to cook the ingredients slowly, trapping the flavours so that they combine.

Caterers have made use of some of the advantages of steaming. Sophisticated equipment operating at high temperatures means that steaming can be an extremely fast method of cooking, and so vitamins and other nutrients are retained more effectively than in other cooking processes. At one end of the scale it is a fast and efficient way of cooking quantities of vegetables so that within minutes frozen vegetables can be ready for serving, at the other it is used to cook traditional dishes like Steak, Oyster and Mushroom Pudding. So steaming is useful in a wide range of catering situations from hospitals and the armed forces to *à la carte* restaurants, large-scale banqueting and conference centres.

History of puddings

The pudding was originally a number of ingredients boiled in a bag made from the stomach of an animal. (In the 15th and 16th century entrails were commonly referred to as puddings.) Later, cloths were used to hold the ingredients together, then basins and suet crusts, and steaming became the preferred method of cooking for puddings.

Many traditional recipes for both steamed and boiled sweet pudding have survived, especially from the 19th century, and are often named after a particular town or district: Chester Pudding, Huntingdon Pudding and Helston Pudding, for example.

These days, however, even the better known Spotted Dick and Plum Duff are giving way to sweet courses with no animal fats, less starch and less sugar, as a result of changing eating habits, and in particular the interest in healthy, low fat food.

The development of pressure cookers, which are in effect heavy saucepans with rubber washers and special catches to seal the lid and keep in the steam, has enabled the home cook to eliminate steamy kitchens and greatly reduce cooking time. Pressure cookers are frequently used to 'boil' potatoes and green vegetables, and to 'stew' meat although in fact these items are being steamed under pressure at a higher temperature than is achieved in either stewing or boiling. Because steam does not carry flavours from one piece of food to another as boiling water would, two or three different vegetables kept apart in wire baskets can be cooked together at the same time.

For customers on a low fat diet, or for people who enjoy eating food which is as close to its natural state as possible, steaming offers a healthy and attractive method of cookery.

▸▸▸ TO DO

Look at the menus at your workplace or in local restaurants and list three dishes that could be boiled or steamed, and two dishes that can only be steamed. Write down why you think steaming is the only possible method for the last two.

6 STEAMING

What happens

See: Video 5

Steaming is cooking food by steam. Heat is transferred to the food in two ways:

1. Convection. The steam carries heat from the gas burner or electric element to the food. The movement of the steam may be natural, or it may be forced either by a fan or through jets by a pump. Natural convection is the least efficient process because a thick layer of barely moving air (a 'boundary layer of air') forms over the food's surface, and before the heat reaches the food it has to get through this layer. If the steam is injected at high speed through jets, as in high-pressure steamers, there is no boundary layer to slow down heat penetration. If there is a fan in the cooking compartment, the faster movement of the steam will keep the boundary layer thin. The problem is that if the food has an uneven surface, any hollows will have thicker layers of air keeping the heat away, while the edges of the food will have no layer at all, so the food may not be cooked evenly.

2. Condensation. It takes a lot of energy (heat) to turn water to steam. When the steam touches the food it condenses (changes back to water) and the energy (sometimes called latent heat) is released again and heats the food.

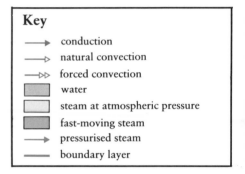

Key

→ conduction
↪ natural convection
↪↪ forced convection
▨ water
▢ steam at atmospheric pressure
▨ fast-moving steam
→ pressurised steam
— boundary layer

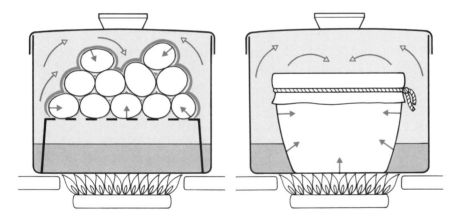

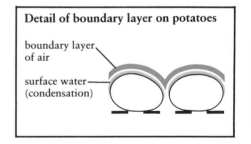

Detail of boundary layer on potatoes

boundary layer of air

surface water (condensation)

When the steam condenses (turns to water), heat is transferred from the steam to the surface of the food. The problem is that once the layer of water has formed, it insulates the food to some extent against further heat from the steam. The layer of slowly moving air above the food (sometimes called the boundary layer) also acts as a barrier to efficient heat transfer.

There are various ways of reducing the surface water problem. In the left-hand diagram, the potatoes have been placed on a perforated rack to allow as much of the surface water as possible to drain off. The pudding in the right-hand diagram is enclosed in a sealed container to protect it from too much moisture.

Although so-called steamed puddings are frequently cooked in the way illustrated here, this is not true steaming because the part of the basin submerged in boiling water is not getting heat from the steam. In this diagram the basin has been placed directly on the bottom of the saucepan and the food inside it could easily burn. Ideally the basin should be put on a rack.

Methods of steaming

In a saucepan

A small amount of water is put into a saucepan. The food is placed in a wire basket or on a trivet above the boiling water, and the steam circulates around the food and cooks it. So that as much steam as possible can surround the food, the container is kept closed.

In an atmospheric steamer

This type of steamer is specially designed with a water bath at the bottom of the cooking compartment to create steam and then a system of trays to hold the food in the steam. The boiling temperature of the water is raised a few degrees because of the slight pressure that builds up in the cooking compartment (sealed except for a small vent).

Atmospheric steamers work in much the same way as saucepans used for steaming and the same limitations apply: a layer of surface water forms on the food and a boundary layer of air just above it, both preventing the food from properly taking in the heat energy available.

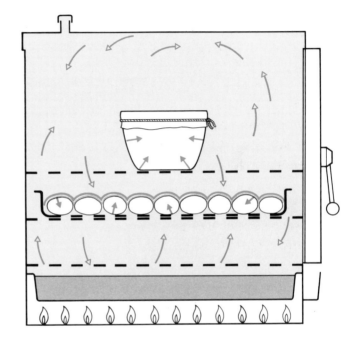

In a pressureless convection steamer

The most recent development in steaming equipment, these steamers use rapidly moving steam to force out any air from the cooking compartment. Experiments have shown that as little as 0.5% of air in the steam environment will halve the efficiency of the heat transfer. An external steam generator continually replaces the steam as it cools, but because the steam is allowed out of the compartment at the same rate that it enters, no pressure builds up and the temperature remains at around 100°C (212°F).

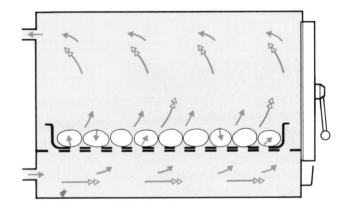

⑥ STEAMING

In a high pressure steamer

High pressures are generated in these steamers. This means that the boiling temperature of the water is raised and a much hotter cooking chamber is created. So cooking times are greatly reduced. As the steam pressure builds up, most of the air is forced out of the cooking compartment.

The model in the top illustration still has the disadvantage that a boundary layer of air can form around the food, but this can be solved – as in the lower illustration – by using equipment in which the steam is injected on to the food through fine jets.

An even more sophisticated version of this equipment uses high temperature steam. In an external steam generator, purified water is fed through tubes heated to around 315°C (600°F). The water immediately turns to steam, and this is fed directly into the cooking compartment.

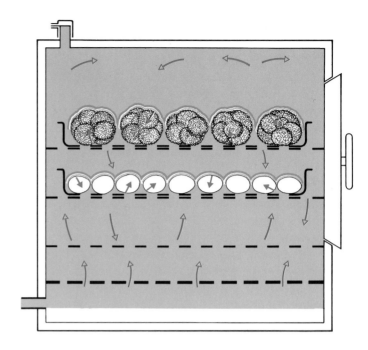

♟ CHEF'S TIP

Steamed puddings and sponges that use baking powder (to make the mixture light) are unsuitable for high-pressure steaming, because the pressure will stop the baking powder working.

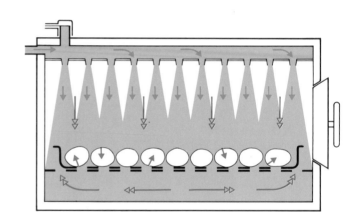

⧊⧊⧊ TO DO

Using a saucepan with a wire basket to hold the food above the boiling water and a tight-fitting lid, steam a potato or carrot until it is cooked. Time how long it takes from when the water is boiling and the vegetable is added, to when it is cooked.

In a second saucepan, bring to the boil enough water to cover a potato or carrot when it is put in. Add the vegetable, keep the water at boiling point, and time how long it takes to cook.

Compare the timings and the textures and flavours of the steamed vegetable and the boiled vegetable.

Steam pressures and temperature

	Steam pressure		Temperature (approx)	
	kN/m²	lb/sq. in.	°C	°F
Boiling water in a saucepan	atmospheric		100	212
Atmospheric steamer	17	2½	103	218
High pressure steamer				
minimum	70	10	115	239
maximum	105	15	121	248

Pressure is measured in force per unit area, that is, thousand Newtons per square metre (kN/m²) or pounds per square inch (lb/ sq. in.).

Advantages of steaming

Steaming creates a moist heat, so there is no risk of the food drying out or burning, as there is in roasting or grilling, for example. As a very plain method, it allows the food to cook without other flavours, like the ones that result from browning, being added. The other cooking method this is true of is boiling, but steaming has a number of important advantages over boiling:

- There is no cross flavouring (transfer of flavours) between two food items cooked in the same container.

- As the food is still and does not roll around as it does in a boiling liquid, it is less likely to break up.

- Providing cooking times are accurate, steamed food is less likely to over-cook than boiled food.

- Fewer of the water-soluble vitamins B and C are lost, particularly in equipment which reduces or prevents the formation of surface water.

- The loss of vitamins through contact with air is also reduced, especially in pressureless convection and high-pressure steamers.

- Pressureless convection steamers allow any gases formed by the food as it cooks to escape.

All this makes steaming an ideal method for cooking most vegetables.

Steaming can be convenient because:

- food requires very little attention while in the steamer

- the timer on most cooking equipment makes it unnecessary to keep checking how the food is doing, and the cooking then stops automatically at the required time

- vegetables do not require straining

- loading and unloading is easy

- the rapid speed of cooking means vegetables can be cooked immediately before they are served, even from a frozen state.

Cooking smells
Most vegetables in the cabbage family (which includes cauliflower, broccoli, turnips, Brussels sprouts and mustard) have sulphur-containing compounds in their cells. During cooking, these can cause various unpleasant smelling compounds to be produced including hydrogen sulphide (typical of rotten eggs) and ammonia, which may react together to form even more smelly compounds. The longer the vegetable is cooked, the more of these compounds are produced, and the stronger the flavour gets. So it is important to avoid overcooking.

Steaming as a way of tenderising meat
For some traditional steamed meat dishes, e.g. steak and kidney pudding, tough meat can be used. The long cooking time in moist conditions enables the connective tissue, collagen (which is partly responsible for toughness) to be changed into gelatin, which dissolves in the cooking liquid. These changes make the meat tender.

6 STEAMING

Vegetables

In general, all the vegetables that can be boiled in water can also be steamed. High-pressure steaming is ideally suited to vegetables because it is so fast that they can be cooked immediately before service, in large quantities if required, so avoiding the need for prolonged holding (when vitamin loss will be considerable, and there will be some discoloration). The small amount of water in contact with the food in high-pressure steaming also means that very few vitamins are lost through dissolving in water.

A disadvantage of steaming as a method of cooking vegetables is that acids are retained. Unlike boiling, there is no water to dilute them and even the acids that could escape into the air are trapped by the saucepan lid or steamer. In green vegetables, these acids turn the colour a dull, olive green, which looks unattractive. Fortunately change of colour stops at boiling point, but it does mean that in low-pressure steaming, the colour of the vegetables has already changed by the time they have reached boiling point. In high-pressure steaming, on the other hand, there is very little time for this to happen and the slight change in colour is more than compensated for by the fact that important vitamins have been retained.

▸▸▸ TO DO

Look at catalogues or manuals produced by manufacturers of steaming equipment, and work out the different times required for cooking four kinds of vegetables using at least two different types of equipment.

A wide range of vegetables can be cooked rapidly in steamers:
1) Cauliflower 2) Swede 3) Potato 4) Carrots 5) Turnips 6) New potatoes 7) Mange-tout 8) Runner beans 9) French beans 10) Savoy cabbage 11) Broccoli.

Potatoes respond equally well to both low and high-pressure steaming. Steaming is a useful first step for many potato dishes like sauté and duchesse, where the quality of the end product is spoiled if the potato has absorbed too much water (which may happen with boiling). Beetroot is frequently steamed before being cooled for use in salads. Unlike green vegetables, beetroot does not suffer from colour loss as a result of steaming.

Overcooked vegetables lose some of their nutritional value, and become flabby and wilted, or break up, so careful timing is most important. As it is difficult with low-pressure steaming to check on the degree of cooking without releasing some of the steam around the food, and impossible with high-pressure steaming, take care to follow any guidelines on timing given in recipe books or supplied by the manufacturers of the steamers.

> **▸▸▸ TO DO**
>
> Steam two portions of the same green vegetable using two different steaming methods. Steam one portion in a saucepan and the other in a high pressure steamer. Note any differences in colour, taste and texture.

Frozen vegetables

This information will help you with the Caterbase module, *Preparing Frozen Foods*.

Quality control is very important in the use of frozen vegetables:
- The date stamp on the packet should be checked and if the 'use by' date has passed, the contents should be thrown away.
- Packets should be checked before use. If the package has split open, or has been crushed or torn and the contents are damaged, report the problem to your supervisor and do not use the contents.
- Rotate stock. New deliveries of frozen food should be stored so that they are used after current stocks have been exhausted.
- Follow instructions on the packet. Pay particular attention to the storage time. For frozen vegetables stored at -18°C (0°F) or below this varies between 3 and 12 months.
- Frozen vegetables should not be defrosted before cooking. This will avoid loss of water-soluble vitamins and colour and possible damage to the texture that can happen during thawing.

Some of the frozen vegetables available to caterers: 1) Diced mixed peppers 2) Brussels sprouts 3) Sliced green beans 4) Broccoli 5) Cauliflower 6) Leaf spinach 7) Corn on the cob 8) Peas 9) Sweetcorn.

> **♈ CHEF'S TIP**
>
> When making lemon or orange sponge puddings, add some grated orange or lemon skin to the marmalade or lemon curd in the bottom of the pudding basin to strengthen the fruit flavour.

Fruit

The use of fruit in steaming is usually restricted to steamed puddings. Suet puddings can be filled with all forms of fruit – fresh, tinned or dried. Steamed sponge puddings can be made with dried fruits like currants or sultanas mixed through the sponge.

Frozen fruit has to be defrosted before use. As the freezing process often causes the fruit to become over moist, some liquid may need to be drained off. If fresh, tinned or (defrosted) frozen fruits are used, they should be put into the base of the pudding basin to form a cap on the finished sponge when it is tipped out. Fruit jam, curd or marmalade may be used in the same way.

6 STEAMING

Meat

The use of meat in steaming is usually restricted to steamed puddings. Meat which might otherwise be recommended for stewing can be used for this purpose: it should be cut into small chunks, placed in a pudding basin which has been lined with suet pastry and then steamed. Other ingredients are usually added to improve the flavour, as in a steak and mushroom pudding where chopped onion, mushrooms, chopped parsley, stock and seasoning would be included.

Steaming is sometimes suggested as an alternative method of cooking meats that can be boiled, but it is unlikely that most joints would actually benefit from this. Atmospheric steaming would certainly not be suitable: there is no opportunity to improve the flavour of the meat by adding vegetables and herbs during the cooking process, and any cooking juices that are produced are lost. High-pressure steaming has the same disadvantages but there may be a small gain in terms of speed of cooking, and the food may shrink a little less than it would if it were boiled.

The prepared ingredients for steak and kidney pudding – one of the most popular steamed meat dishes.

Suet

Suet is the layer of fat that forms around the kidneys of the ox. In its unprepared state it is hard and solid. The papery skin and connective tissue should be removed and the suet chopped finely or shredded in a mincer. A little flour is usually added to prevent the fragments sticking together.

Suet helps to give cooked pastry a crumbly texture. This is because the solid fragments melt during the cooking, and the steam that is left causes expansion. The more suet, the lighter the mixture. Suet has a characteristic flavour and because it melts at a temperature only slightly higher than normal body temperature, it causes a slight clinging sensation in the mouth.

Left, unprepared suet, and *right*, suet after preparation and shredding.

🄵 CHEF'S TIP

Be careful when you are making suet dough: if it is kneaded too much and becomes rubbery, the suet breaks up into even smaller pieces causing a heavier, tighter end product.

Fish and shellfish

As a very plain method of cooking, steaming is sometimes appropriate for fish such as whiting and cod. Cooking times need to be carefully controlled, because the delicate structure of the fish will start to break up if it is overcooked.

A number of crustaceans (a category of shellfish) are suitable for rapid cooking by steaming. These include prawns, king prawns and scampi.

1) Prawns 2) Whiting fillets 3) Cod fillet 4) King prawns
5) Scampi (Dublin Bay prawns).

6 STEAMING

Terms

Steaming is cooking food by steam. This can be done under varying degrees of pressure. Heat is transferred to the food by convection and conduction. The greater the pressure, the higher the temperature of the steam and the shorter the cooking time.

Atmospheric steaming is steaming food roughly at atmospheric pressure, so the pressure inside the cooking container is broadly the same as the pressure outside it. The container is kept firmly sealed and the pressure in it may increase very slightly, taking the boiling temperature up by a small amount.

Low-pressure steaming is an alternative term for atmospheric steaming.

High-pressure steaming is cooking food by steam at pressures four to six times greater than the pressure outside the oven. This raises the temperatures by as much as 21° or 22°C (36° or 37°F).

The *boiling point* of a liquid is reached when the energy (in other words, heat from the gas or electric burner) begins to turn the liquid into gas (vapour). It takes a lot of energy (heat) to turn water to steam. In normal conditions this happens at 100°C (212°F). Bubbles of gas or vapour form at the hot bottom of the saucepan, for example, and rise to the surface. Once the water has got to 100°C, it will begin to turn to steam until all the water has gone, but it will never get hotter.

Atmospheric pressure is the pressure produced by the weight of air at any one point on the earth's surface. There are fewer molecules in a column of air over a mountain top so the pressure is lower than at sea level, where there are many more molecules. The boiling point of a liquid is lower on a mountain top, because with the lower atmospheric pressure the molecules need less energy to turn to steam.

Equipment

Atmospheric or *low-pressure steamers* are the most common in catering establishments. They operate at a pressure of not more than 17 kN/m² (1½lb per square inch). Models are available which operate by:
- electricity, when an immersion element heats a bath of water in the oven (rather like a water immersion heater)
- gas, when gas burners heat the water bath from underneath
- direct connection to an external steam supply.

In electric and gas models the water bath is located inside the oven, at the bottom. The water level is kept constant by an automatic cold water feed tank outside the oven, either at the back or on one side.

The oven is fitted with a vent or valve so that when the heat source is turned on and the oven filled with steam the cold air is pushed out. The vent also stops the pressure rising too high. The water temperature is kept automatically at boiling point.

A drip trough in front of the door catches any condensation that drips down when the door is opened, and the door is fitted with a special seal and shutting mechanism.

The inside of the oven is designed to hold trays, racks or wire baskets for ease of loading. The trays are usually slotted or perforated so that the steam can reach as much of the food surface as possible.

High-pressure steamers are designed to allow the steam pressure to build up to between 70 and 105 kN/m^2 (10-15 lb per square inch). At 105 kN/m^2, the boiling point of water is about 121°C (248°F) and food cooks at two or three times the speed it takes at normal pressures. Gas or electrically operated models are available. As with atmospheric steamers, some versions have the steam generated inside the oven, and others have a steam supply from an external generator.

A pressure safety valve allows steam to escape once the right pressure has been reached. The door-shutting mechanism prevents the oven being opened when it is in operation.

In some models the steam is sprayed at very high speed from jets at the top of the oven and this enables heat to be transferred to the food much more rapidly.

Many models have timers and alarms which indicate when cooking is complete.

Some high-pressure steamers can be operated at atmospheric pressure if necessary by adjusting a simple control.

Pressureless convection steamers use steam generated outside the compartment (gas or electric models are available). The steam is forced into the cooking compartment and then allowed to leave freely. This means that no pressure builds up (which is said to help prevent damage to the structure of vegetables). As the steam is circulated very rapidly through the cooking compartment, the heat is transferred more efficiently to the food. Condensation on the food's surface is also avoided, and so is the formation of an air barrier (or boundary layer) over the food, another factor that could slow down cooking.

Steaming equipment: 1) Combi oven 2) High-pressure steamer 3) Aluminium steamer (for use on top of cooker) 4) Atmospheric steamer. Containers for steaming: 5) Stainless steel trays (with solid and perforated bases) 6) Basins with lids 7) Selection of basins 8) Pudding sleeve. *Small picture*: Pressureless convection steamer.

Combi-ovens combine the benefits of a steamer with some of the features of a convection oven. They are forced-air convection ovens which can be converted to steam injection. While cooking is in progress, low-pressure steam is injected into the oven compartment. The hot air and the steam are carried around the oven helped by a fan (*see* Book 1, Roasting/Terms & Equipment). This allows the food to stay moist, as well as becoming tenderised by the steaming process, and the hot air browns the surface and helps the cooking.

Cleaning and maintenance
Steamers must be kept clean. When they are not in use they can be ideal breeding grounds for harmful bacteria. Leave the door open slightly after use so that air can circulate inside and cool the equipment.

The inside should be cleaned regularly with a mild solution of hot water and detergent and then rinsed thoroughly. Take special care to clean the tray runners properly and remove any food deposits, especially in the drip channels.

The outside should also be scrubbed regularly, with particular attention being paid to the water tanks, the back and the legs. Grease traps should be cleaned using a special solution.

Make regular checks on the safety valves, the door-shutting mechanism and the seals around the door. Report any problems to your supervisor immediately.

 **STEAMING**

Essential points

If your work is being judged for the Caterbase module, *Steaming*, your supervisor or assessor will look at how well you carry out the essential activities connected with this process.

These points are of course important whenever you are steaming food, and will help ensure that your customer enjoys steamed food at its best.

1. Check that the steam supply is operating efficiently.

It is important to make sure that there is enough water to produce the continuous amount of steam required throughout the cooking time. If there is too little steam, the drop in temperature may result in food being spoiled. If you are not sure how the steam supply works, check with your supervisor or consult the manufacturer's instructions.

2. Ensure that the steam pressure is at the right level before attempting to cook the food.

There are several types of equipment in which food can be steamed (*see* previous spread), but whichever type is used, it is essential to ensure that you have selected the correct steam pressure for the particular food to be cooked, before this item is put into the steamer.

3. Select the appropriate container.

Most foods are placed on perforated trays or containers to allow condensation and surface water to drain away. Non-perforated containers are used for delicate foods, such as fish, where some liquid in the tray will help with handling after cooking.

Sweet and savoury steamed puddings should be placed in a greased pudding basin.

4. Some foods should not come into direct contact with the steam or condensation and need to be covered.

Items such as vegetables, meat and fish do not require any protective covering; but dishes which contain flour, e.g. steamed sponge puddings and steak and kidney puddings, should be protected by a cover of greased greaseproof paper and/or pudding cloth or tin foil, otherwise the texture, flavour and appearance of the food will be spoiled. The cover should be pleated across the middle to allow for expansion as the mixture rises. String is then tied around the rim of the basin to keep the covering in place.

▶▶▶ TO DO

Prepare the sponge mixture in Practical Examples 2 (or use an alternative recipe). Divide the mixture into two containers. Cover one correctly but leave the other uncovered. Place both containers in a steamer. Steam the sponges for the same length of time. Compare the results.

This picture shows a combi-oven with a tray of plain steamed potatoes just ready for service. Note how the operator is using the door as a protection from the escaping steam.

5. Once the steamer is ready for use and you are ready to place the food in the cooking vessel or chamber, open the door (or lid) slowly and carefully so that you don't get scalded by the rush of hot steam.

Use the door to protect yourself from the escaping steam, where possible, for example, stand behind the door as you open it.

6. After the food is safely in, make sure that lids/doors are sealed firmly so that the pressure will stay at the right level. Check that the steam pressure stays the same during cooking.

If the equipment has a pressure gauge, check from time to time that the level is correct. If the level drops for no apparent reason and stays down, turn the equipment off and report the problem to your supervisor. If the pressure is not restored very quickly it may be necessary to throw the food away.

For steamers without gauges, you should check that steam is coming out through the vent, can be seen through the glass doors, or, if you are using a saucepan, that it is escaping from under the lid. If you are steaming a pudding for a long time in a saucepan, check the water level regularly and top up when necessary with boiling water.

7. Follow cooking timings carefully.

It is very easy to overcook small items, especially in a high-pressure steamer. As the cooking time will depend on the exact pressure used by the equipment, follow the manufacturer's guidelines for your machine.

For low-pressure steaming (in an atmospheric steamer or saucepan), it is important to find out the exact cooking time required for a specific item. Sponge and suet puddings will need a long time to allow raising agents to act, and also for the meat to be thoroughly cooked. For example a 4-portion sponge or suet pudding takes between 1 and 1½ hours, a steak and kidney pudding 3 to 3½ hours, and a Christmas pudding 5 hours.

8. Serve the food attractively.

Steamed savoury pastry items are served in the container in which they have been cooked: the paper foil or cloth is removed, the sides of the basin cleaned and then wrapped in a napkin and placed on an oval flat. A paper dishmat is placed between the basin and the oval flat for presentation purposes. Sweet pastry and sponge items are carefully removed whole from the basin or cloth in which they have been cooked and placed on a dish with a suitable accompanying sauce.

Steak and kidney pudding

INGREDIENTS		SERVES 10
1 kg	beef (topside or thick flank)	2½ lb
250 g	ox kidney	10 oz
250 g	chopped onions	10 oz
25 g	flour	1 oz
15 ml	Worcester sauce	3 tsp
400 ml	brown stock	16 fl oz
800 g	suet pastry (see box)	2 lb
	chopped parsley	
	pinch of salt and pepper	
	white fat for greasing basin	

1. Remove any fat or gristle from the beef and cut the meat into cubes of about 20 mm (¾ in.).

2. Trim the kidney and cut it into cubes of about 10 mm (⅜ in.)

3. Place the beef, kidney, onions, parsley, seasoning and flour into a bowl and mix together until combined.

4. Add the Worcester sauce and enough stock to cover the ingredients and mix together.

5. Cover and keep chilled until required for use.

6. Lightly grease two pudding basins, each with a capacity of 800 ml (about 32 fl oz).

7. Roll out three-quarters of the pastry and line the basins with it.

8. Fill the basins with the mixture leaving a small gap, about 15 mm (½ in.), between the filling and the top of the pastry.

9. Dampen the edges of the pastry with a little stock or water.

10. Roll out the remaining pastry and use it to cover the puddings.

11. Seal the edges and trim off any excess pastry.

12. Cover each pudding with a circle of lightly greased greaseproof paper, pleating the paper in the middle to allow for expansion during cooking, and then a pudding cloth. Secure with string and tie the ends of the pudding cloth together.

13. Place into an atmospheric or low-pressure steamer or over boiling water in a saucepan and steam for four hours. Check this timing with any instructions given by the equipment manufacturers.

14. At the end of this period remove the cloths and paper and clean around the sides of the bowls.

15. Wrap a folded napkin round each basin and serve on a salver lined with a dishpaper. Just before service a sprig of parsley can be placed in the centre of each pudding as decoration.

Suet pastry

INGREDIENTS		MAKES 800 g (about 2 lb)
400 g	plain flour	1 lb
20 g	baking powder	1 oz
200 g	chopped beef suet	½ lb
250 ml	cold water	½ pt
	pinch of salt	

1. Sieve the flour, baking powder and salt into a bowl.

2. Add the suet and thoroughly mix the ingredients together.

3. Add the water and lightly mix to form a paste.

✳ NUTRITION

For a healthier alternative to traditional suet pastry, use 100 ml (4 fl oz) polyunsaturated oil (e.g. sunflower, corn or soya) in place of the suet and reduce the water in the recipe to 140 ml (5¾ fl oz).

Steamed fish

INGREDIENTS   SERVES 20

$20 \times 150\,g$	*skinned fish fillets*	$20 \times 6\,oz$

(small whole fish or fish steaks could also be used)

500 ml	*fish stock, milk or water*	*1 pt*
	pinch of salt and white pepper	
20	*pieces of lemon*	*20*
	sprigs of parsley (optional)	

1. Fold the fillets in half across their length.

2. Lightly grease the base of a suitable cooking dish (with lid) or a non-perforated steamer tray (with cover) and place the fillets in it.

3. Season the fillets lightly and moisten them by dribbling a little of the fish stock, milk or water over them.

4. Cover with the lid and steam in an atmospheric or low-pressure steamer for 15 to 20 minutes (the exact timing will depend on the type of steamer and the size of fish). If adapting this technique for smaller quantities cooked on a domestic stove, the timing is the same.

5. When cooked, arrange the fish in a serving dish and pour a little of the cooking liquid over it to coat it.

6. Garnish with the pieces of lemon and, if required, parsley.

Steamed potatoes
Pommes vapeur

INGREDIENTS   SERVES 20

$2\frac{1}{2}\,kg$	*small new potatoes*	$5\frac{1}{2}\,lb$

1. Wash and scrub the potatoes. If the potatoes are different sizes, cut the larger potatoes to the same size as the smaller ones.

2. Place into a perforated steamer tray and steam in an atmospheric or low-pressure steamer until cooked: 15 to 20 minutes.

3. Place neatly in a service dish.

Steamed green beans

INGREDIENTS   SERVES 20

$2\frac{1}{2}\,kg$	*fine French beans*	$5\frac{1}{2}\,lb$

1. Wash the beans, then top and tail them, and remove any strings.

2. Place into a perforated steaming tray, and steam in a high-pressure steamer until cooked. *Important:* the cooking time will vary depending on the pressure used when cooking, so you will need to consult the manufacturer's instructions. Cooking time at 100 kN/m² (14 lb per square inch) is 1½-2 minutes.

3. Arrange the beans neatly in a serving dish.

The finished dish: steamed fillet of plaice and steamed halibut cutlet.

CHEF'S TIP

If you are steaming a pudding in a basin, tie a piece of string across the basin, attaching it at each side to the string under the rim. This will make it easier to lift the pudding in and out.

Breadcrumbs can be added to suet pastry in place of half of the flour to make a lighter textured pudding.

Steamed fruit sponge pudding

INGREDIENTS		SERVES 4
75 g	butter or margarine	3 oz
75 g	caster sugar	3 oz
1	large egg	1
125 g	self-raising flour (see Chef's Tip)	5 oz
25 ml	milk	1 fl oz
75 g	selected fruit	3 oz
	e.g. sultanas, currants and raisins	
250 ml	custard sauce (see box)	½ pt

1. Lightly grease the pudding basin ready for use.

2. Wash and thoroughly dry the fruit.

3. Place the butter or margarine and sugar into a mixing bowl and cream together until light and white in colour. Scrape down the bowl occasionally to achieve an even mixture.

4. Add the egg a little at a time, thoroughly beating into the mixture. While you are doing this scrape down the bowl as before.

5. Lightly fold the flour through the mixture until it is almost combined.

6. Add the milk and combine with the mixture.

7. Blend the fruit into the mixture.

8. Place the mixture into the pudding basin, cover the basin with a circle of greased greaseproof paper and secure round the rim with string, making sure that the paper is not pulled taut (to allow for expansion of air as it heats). To make quite sure there is room for this, the paper can be pleated in the middle.

9. Steam in an atmospheric or low-pressure steamer for 1½ hours.

10. Turn the pudding out on to a suitable serving dish and serve with the custard sauce.

Spotted dick

INGREDIENTS		SERVES 10
500 g	plain flour	1 lb 4 oz
25 g	baking powder	1¼ oz
125 g	caster sugar	5 oz
250 g	chopped suet	10 oz
100 g	currants	4 oz
75 g	sultanas	3 oz
300 ml	milk	12 fl oz
500 ml	custard sauce (see box)	1 pt

1. Lightly grease a pudding sleeve, and then line with greased greaseproof paper ready for cooking.

2. Sieve the flour, baking powder and sugar into a bowl.

3. Add the suet and fruit and thoroughly mix together.

4. Add the milk and mix until a fairly stiff paste is produced.

5. Place the mixture into the pudding sleeve.

6. Steam for 2 hours in an atmospheric or low-pressure steamer.

7. At the end of this time remove the pudding from the sleeve and the paper and cut it into slices.

8. Serve with the sauce. A redcurrant and raspberry sauce is an alternative to custard.

🍴 CHEF'S TIP

Self-raising flour can be made by sieving together plain flour and baking powder, 50 g baking powder for 1 kg flour (1 oz baking powder for 1 lb flour).

Custard sauce

INGREDIENTS		MAKES 500 ml (1 pt)
500 ml	*milk*	*1 pt*
20 g	*custard powder*	*1 oz*
50 g	*sugar*	*2 oz*

1. Place a little of the cold milk into a bowl, add the custard powder and blend together until you have a creamy paste.

2. Bring the remaining milk to the boil in a saucepan.

3. Whisk the custard mixture quickly into the boiling milk.

4. Stir constantly until a smooth sauce is obtained and bring back to the boil.

5. Simmer for about 2 minutes. Stir occasionally to avoid burning.

6. Mix in the sugar. It should dissolve quite quickly.

7. Pour the custard into a sauceboat and serve immediately.

For brandy sauce, replace the custard powder with cornflour and when the mixture is cooked, flavour it with brandy.

Christmas pudding

INGREDIENTS		SERVES 20
		Makes two 1 kg (2½ lb) puddings
200 g	*plain flour*	*8 oz*
10g	*mixed spice*	*½ oz*
¼ tsp	*ground nutmeg*	*¼ tsp*
½ tsp	*ground ginger*	*½ tsp*
200 g	*soft brown sugar*	*8 oz*
150 g	*white breadcrumbs*	*6 oz*
50 g	*ground almonds*	*2 oz*
200 g	*chopped suet*	*8 oz*
150 g	*sultanas*	*6 oz*
250 g	*currants*	*10 oz*
200 g	*raisins*	*8 oz*
100 g	*mixed peel*	*4 oz*
1	*carrot*	*1*
1	*lemon*	*1*
1	*orange*	*1*
50 ml	*brandy*	*2 fl oz*
50 ml	*sherry*	*2 fl oz*
100 ml	*stout*	*4 fl oz*
4	*eggs (size 2)*	*4*

Steps 1 to 5 should be done one or two days
in advance of cooking.

1. Wash, peel and grate the carrot: you should end up with 50 g (2 oz) grated carrot.

2. Grate the zest off the orange and lemon and set aside with the other dry ingredients. Cut each fruit in half,

squeeze out the juice, strain it and keep with the wet ingredients.

3. Thoroughly mix together in a large mixing bowl all the dry ingredients, including the fruit zest and carrot.

4. Make a hollow in the centre of the dry ingredients then pour into it the wet ingredients (fruit juice, brandy, sherry, stout and eggs). Thoroughly mix everything together (by machine or by hand). In some kitchens it is traditional practice for all the staff to give the pudding mixture a stir for good luck.

5. Cover the mixture and leave it in a cool place for 1 to 2 days.

6. Lightly grease two large pudding basins with margarine or butter and fill them with the mixture. The basins should be filled to within 25 mm (1 in.) of the top. If you are using tin or plastic basins with their own lids, make sure that the lid seals firmly. If the basin does not have its own lid, cover the top with a circle of greased greaseproof paper cut so that it will fold over the edge with a margin of about 50 mm (2 in.). Tie the paper in place with string drawn tightly around the outside. It is a good idea to use a pudding cloth as well as paper, tying the ends together over the top of the basin (*see* photograph in Practical Examples 1).

7. Steam for 6 hours in an atmospheric or low pressure steamer.

8. When cooking is completed, take the puddings out and store them in a cool dry place until required for service. Paper and cloth covers should be replaced with a new covering as soon as the puddings have cooled. Note: Christmas puddings improve in flavour if left to mature for two to three months.

For service

1. Steam the puddings for 2½ hours in an atmospheric or low pressure steamer.

2. Carefully turn the puddings on to warm serving dishes.

3. Place a small quantity of the icing sugar in a fine sieve and shake over the top of the puddings or use a dredger. Decorate the puddings with sprigs of holly. If required, the puddings can be flamed at service time with brandy or rum. Warm the spirit first, then light it and pour it over the pudding. Accompany with a sauceboat of brandy sauce (*see* Custard sauce box) or brandy cream (whipped cream lightly sweetened with caster sugar, then flavoured with brandy).

What went wrong

Steamed fish is unpleasantly flavoured.

> The steamer has not been thoroughly cleaned after being used to cook strong-flavoured items.

Steamed puddings have a solid heavy texture.

> 1. They have been cooked in a high-pressure steamer which has made it impossible for the baking powder or self-raising flour to work.
> 2. The wrong proportions of ingredients were used: too little raising agent or too much liquid.
> 3. Some of the flour should have been replaced by breadcrumbs.

Pastry is dark.

> 1. The pudding has been overcooked.
> 2. It has been held too long before serving.

Green vegetables are tasteless and have lost their crispness.

> They have been overcooked.
> It is very easy to overcook green vegetables, so careful timing is essential to ensure that they stay crisp.

Vegetables are not all equally cooked.

> Vegetables were uneven in size.
> For best results, use similar sized vegetables or pieces.

Puddings are soggy (after being cooked in a low-pressure steamer).

> 1. Steam has reached the pudding as a result of a damaged lid.
> 2. The dish or pan has not being properly covered.

TEST YOURSELF

1. Give two reasons why a high-pressure steamer is more suitable for cooking green vegetables than an atmospheric steamer.

2. What are the effects of different pressures of steam on cooking times?

3. Name two vegetables which should not be steamed in a low-pressure steamer and give reasons.

4. Give the reason why slow steaming is suitable for tough meats. What changes take place during cooking to make the meat more tender?

5. Name four safety precautions that should be taken when using a steamer.

6. What sort of container would you use for steaming:
   a) jam roly poly
   b) steak and mushroom pudding
   c) potatoes
   d) fish
   e) green beans?

City and Guilds

Tips

Sometimes a pudding cloth is used instead of a pudding sleeve. In this case, before using the cloth, dip it into boiling water, wring it out, spread it out on the work surface and then sprinkle it with flour. Then it is ready to have the pudding placed on it and should not stick.

Bicarbonate of soda can be used in place of some or all of the baking powder in a recipe for a rich fruit or treacle pudding, for example, to give the pudding a darker colour. You should use only half as much bicarbonate of soda as you would have used baking powder, e.g. substitute 15 g (½ oz) of bicarbonate of soda for 30 g (1 oz) baking powder.

   Don't use bicarbonate of soda in a delicately flavoured pudding because it leaves an unpleasant-tasting residue after cooking.

Steamed potatoes

7 MICROWAVE

Meals and snacks can be provided in just a few minutes with very little effort using microwave cooking. As well as being fast, energy-saving and versatile, microwave ovens are easy to operate, and often have a whole range of pre-set programs so that the user does not even have to time the process.

With these advantages it is not surprising that microwave ovens are being used in more and more catering kitchens. High-class restaurants may well use microwaving as part of the cooking process, cafés and take-away outlets use them to heat up anything from pre-prepared sausage rolls to baked jacket potatoes that have been cooked in advance and then kept in chilled storage.

Microwave ovens were developed as a result of experimental work with radar technology. Engineers noticed that when the radar waves were passed through certain substances, they had a heating effect.

The first commercial microwave oven was shown to caterers at the Hotelympia trade fair in 1960. Since the 1970s both catering and domestic models have been widely available and are now fitted with an increasingly wide range of sophisticated controls.

Because so many people now have microwave ovens at home, they are likely to understand the advantages this piece of equipment has for a pub or a snack bar, and to be quite happy for their food to be prepared in one. They will probably also realise that the choice of food can be wider and service faster than it would be if conventional cooking were used.

Many establishments actually have the microwave oven in the service area rather than hidden in the kitchen. This can in fact reassure the customer, who can often see exactly what is happening to the meal chosen from the chilled display, and know that it will be served freshly heated and piping hot.

▶▶▶ TO DO

Pay a visit to either your college refectory, works canteen or a local snack bar (serving hot food) and make a list of the dishes that either already are or could be microwaved. Against this list, indicate what equipment has been used for the initial cooking or the reheating of pre-cooked (and chilled) foods. Say which stage has been performed, or could be replaced by microwaving and explain why you think this is so.

7 MICROWAVE

What happens

In microwave cooking energy (not heat in the ordinary sense of the word) is transferred to the food by electro-magnetic radiation. Microwaves pass into the food and make the water molecules vibrate causing them to heat up very quickly. But the microwaves can penetrate only about 4 cm (1½ in.) into food, so if the food is thicker than this the rest of the cooking (towards the centre) happens by conduction of heat from the outer layer.

Microwaving cooks with radiation, but it is very different from the infra-red radiation used in grilling. The inside of a microwave oven does not get hot as a grill does and the heating/cooking happens right through the food instead of being concentrated at its surface.

Microwaves make very effective use of energy. They travel through the air and the cooking container to the food, and it is only when they penetrate the food (that is, come into contact with the water in it) that they are used up, so no energy is used in heating the oven space or the cooking container.

▶▶▶ TO DO

If you are not already using a microwave oven in your workplace, look at some sales leaflets produced by manufacturers of microwave ovens (you may need to send off for them) and, working from these, list at least ten food items that can be microwaved along with the times they are supposed to take to cook. Take a note of any comparisons in cooking times with conventional cooking equipment and details about the output wattage (or power) of the equipment. On the basis of this information would you recommend using a microwave in your workplace? If so for what purpose?

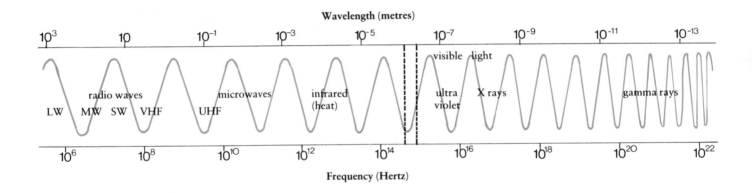

What happens to the water molecules
The microwaves heat the food by agitating the water molecules in it. Each water molecule is slightly positive at one end and slightly negative at the other. When an electromagnetic field is created, the molecule lines itself up with the direction of the field. As soon as the field is reversed, the molecule turns round. This happens 5 billion times per second. The energy produced from the movement of water molecules is transmitted to other molecules of protein, fat, etc., and the temperature of the food quickly rises.

When the microwave cooker is turned off, the water molecules take a moment to slow down and stop, giving a short extension to the cooking process (known as carry-over cooking).

Electro-magnetic radiation has many uses. Gamma rays – used in military weapons – are one very destructive use. X-ray machines also use electro-magnetic rays, which, although they are very useful, have to be treated with great care because they can be damaging – you may have noticed that staff operating X-ray machines in hospitals and dental surgeries take certain precautions because they could be exposed to the radiation so often. Ultraviolet rays in sunlight can cause nasty sunburn.

Electro-magnetic waves can be classified according to frequency (the number of waves per second), e.g. gamma rays are very high frequency, while radio waves are quite low. The higher the frequency, the greater the danger.

There are strict safety standards that microwave ovens have to be made to because of the risk of leakage of microwave energy. But they can become dangerous if they are badly maintained or treated carelessly so that the door seals and/or fittings are damaged. A microwave oven in bad condition can cause burns, and there is even a possibility that using leaky appliances over a long period can contribute to the development of eye cataracts.

Container materials

Microwaves react in different ways to different materials. Broadly speaking there are two sorts of material:

1. those that *reflect* microwaves

2. those that *transmit* microwaves – this can either be very efficient (when no energy is lost) or inefficient when a lot of energy is lost because the material itself heats up.

Metal

If microwaves hit metal, they cannot pass through it, but are reflected by it. So metal cooking containers should never be used: the microwaves will simply not be able to get through to the food.

China and glass

When microwaves come into contact with china and glass they are transmitted, that is, they pass through the material. Glass and china are very good transmitters so the microwaves do not lose any of their energy and pass straight through to the food.

Plastic and paper or cardboard

Some specially made plastics and paper or cardboard are as good at transmitting microwaves as china and glass.

Air transmits microwaves without heating up, which is why the inside of a microwave oven does not feel warm to the touch when the food is cooking.

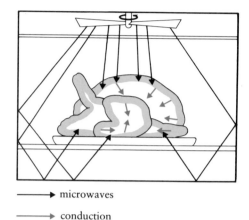

→ microwaves

→ conduction

Most microwave ovens operate at a frequency of exactly 2,450,000,000 cycles per second, or 2,450 MHz (a Megahertz is a million cycles per second). This frequency was chosen so that radar communications, which use the same band as microwaves, would not be disrupted.

At this frequency the microwaves can penetrate to a depth of about 4 cm (1½ in.). This can vary slightly, for example, food with a very low water content will have marginally less penetration than food with a high water content. The rest of the cooking (beyond about 4 cm) works by conduction of heat in the food.

A. *Metal surfaces* reflect microwaves. So metal saucepans and tin foil containers are not suitable for use in microwaving.

B. *Glass* and *ceramic* materials allow microwaves to pass through them without heating up, so they are good for use in microwave cooking.

C. All food contains some *water*. Microwaving moves the water molecules about very rapidly causing them to heat up through the food.

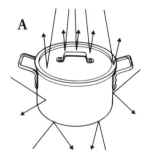 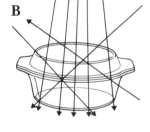 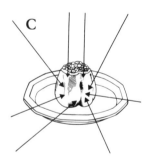

The difference between conventional and microwave ovens

Microwaves generate heat only once they have penetrated the food, so the oven itself stays cool. This is completely different from the way a grill or oven works. A grill generates *radiant heat* and an oven produces *convected heat*. In both cases the inside of the equipment heats up and the air around the food gets very hot – much hotter than the 100°C (212°F), the boiling point of water, that is the maximum temperature of food in a microwave oven. So grills and ovens are good for browning food and creating a crisp texture – something microwave ovens cannot be used for.

Which food microwaving is best for

Microwaving is most suitable for food which:

– is usually cooked quite fast anyhow

– is usually cooked at a fixed temperature

– is no more than 4 cm thick and needs even cooking

– does not need browning to enhance its flavour or change its surface texture.

Food that benefits from being cooked quickly

Microwave energy cooks food rapidly, generally much faster than any of the conventional methods of cookery, but it tends to cause a greater fluid loss. So it is not suitable for those foods which need slow, moist cooking.

You cannot adjust the rate at which a microwave oven cooks in the way that you would normally adjust the temperature on conventional equipment, for example by turning the heat up or down under a frying pan. The only factors which will vary the time it takes to cook the food are:

– the overall output wattage (or power) of the microwave oven (different ovens have different levels of maximum output)

– how full the oven is (the more food there is in the oven, the less energy is available for activating each water molecule).

Although most models have adjustable output, with high, medium or low settings, you would still usually use the same setting for the whole cooking time (which is very short). Food that needs careful temperature variation during its cooking, for example, meat that needs a very high temperature at the start of cooking, but a lower temperature at a later stage, cannot be microwaved.

Food that benefits from being cooked evenly

Microwave cooking can penetrate 4 cm (1½ in.) into food, so food items that are up to this thickness will cook at the same speed throughout. The effect achieved in a grilled or shallow fried steak done medium or rare, cannot happen using microwave energy.

The gradual transfer of heat from the very outer layer of food to the inside that occurs in all other cooking processes does not happen in microwaving, although a similar heat transfer does take place in thick pieces of food from the point the microwaves reach inside through the rest of the food.

Food that does not need browning

The browning of the surfaces of, for example, steak, roast potatoes and cake, which is very important to their taste and appearance, can only happen at temperatures above 150°C (302°F). In microwaving, as it is the water molecules that do the heating, the temperature of the outer layer of food never gets higher than 100°C (212°F), the boiling point of water.

Food that does not need a crisp surface texture

What turns the surface of a bread roll crisp in a conventional oven is the fact that the air temperature in the oven is higher than the temperature of the food. In a microwave oven the air is cooler than the food, so a crisp surface cannot be created.

In addition to this, some of the water in the food (heated by the microwaves) produces steam which condenses (turns to water again) on the cooler outer surfaces of the food that are in contact with the cool air, so pastries, cakes and similar foods tend to go soggy.

Reheating cook chill foods

As microwaving heats food up to 4 cm (1½ in.) thick evenly and thoroughly, it is a very good method of reheating food cooked by other processes that have already given it the desired flavour and texture. Food that has been promptly chilled and stored at a low temperature until required for service can be reheated in a microwave oven:

– very quickly

– with little risk of drying out

– without danger of burning.

▸▸▸ TO DO

Obtain three small potatoes about the size of tangerines. Wash them and then prick them with a skewer. Put one of the potatoes in the microwave oven on full power for approximately four minutes, or until cooked. Remove it and cut it open. Note the appearance, texture and flavour.

Now put the other two potatoes into the microwave oven together, also on full power. Record the time it takes to cook them and if it is different from the time required for the first potato, work out why.

How a microwave oven works

The part of a microwave oven that creates microwaves is called a magnetron. It uses the mains electricity supply to produce microwaves, which make the water molecules in food vibrate at a rate of about 5 billion times a second, and it is this action which makes the water heat up and cook the food. At the moment, domestic microwave ovens are made with output powers ranging from 400 to 800 watts. Commercial models tend to have outputs of 1,000 watts (1 Kw) to 2,000 watts (2 Kw). The higher the wattage, the more microwave energy is generated, so cooking times vary between models.

The microwaves are passed through a tube from the magnetron into the oven. Metal reflects microwaves and there is a circulating fan (sometimes called a wave stirrer) just inside the oven with metal blades for the microwaves to bounce off. Some of the microwaves then hit the metal walls and floor of the oven and are bounced back again. The combined effect of all this is an even distribution of microwaves round the food.

The food rests on a ceramic or glass shelf so that the microwaves can penetrate it from all angles.

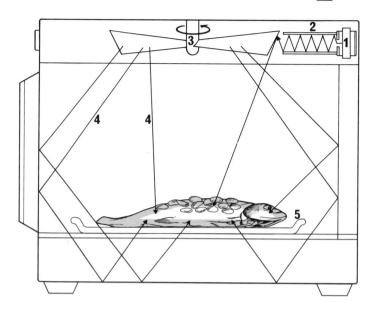

The picture shows: 1) Magnetron 2) Wave guide 3) Circulating fan (stirrer) 4) Reflected and direct microwaves hitting food (all reflected off the stirrer) 5) Dish that microwaves can pass through.

Problems in microwaving frozen food

The problem with putting frozen food directly into a microwave oven is that it is unlikely to thaw and reheat evenly.

Microwaves have very little effect on the water molecules of food frozen to -18°C (0°F) and below, because they pass through ice at these low temperatures without doing much heating. Eventually the ice on and near the surface of the food begins to thaw. This means that as it turns to water it absorbs the microwaves more and more successfully and so the microwaves do not have enough energy left to thaw the ice at the centre of the food. Food which looks as though it has been successfully reheated may well still have frozen portions in the centre. If it is then put back in the microwave there is a danger that the already hot portions will over-cook and dry out before the centre portions have been thoroughly heated.

One way of overcoming the uneven heating effect in frozen food is to use the microwave oven to defrost it first. This has to be done by a process of turning the microwave energy on and off intermittently (there is an automatic programme for this on many models). The off periods give the heat generated by defrosting water molecules time to warm the still frozen ones.

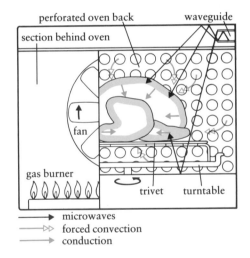

Combination microwave oven
As microwave ovens never heat the food to a temperature higher than boiling point, they cannot brown the food or create a crisp texture, as grills or ovens can.

To overcome this disadvantage, some microwave ovens also incorporate a conventional heat source. In some models this is radiation from an infra-red grill. Others have an external gas burner or electrical element, and the convected heat is circulated into and around the oven by a fan (as in the diagram above).

A wide variety of commodities can be successfully cooked by microwave energy. Some have to have water added, others need a protective coating.

Vegetables

Many vegetables are good for microwaving, because of their high water content and fragile structure (but vegetables with skins need special treatment – *see* box). Green vegetables keep their colour because they are cooked for such a short time. But some fibrous vegetables, like cauliflower and cabbage, are not really suitable. Potatoes can be cooked either peeled or in their skins, but if a crisp skin is required as in baked potatoes, or a browned, crisp surface as in roast potatoes, this can only be achieved by doing most of the cooking in the microwave and then finishing them off in a conventional oven. Of course, a combined microwave/convection oven is the ideal solution.

Whereas vegetables cooked by traditional methods often suffer vitamin loss, microwaving uses very little water and cooks fast, so retains most of the vitamins.

Fruit

As fruit contains a lot of water it is ideal for microwaving. It is best to switch off the microwave just before the fruit is fully cooked because the high water content means that there will be some carry-over cooking after it has been removed from the oven.

Herbs

Herbs can be dried in a microwave oven.

Fish and shellfish

With their high water content and delicate structure which benefits from rapid cooking, fish and shellfish are ideal for microwaving.

Eggs and cheese

Both eggs and cheese require special care. They can be overcooked very easily, and then they become rubbery. On the whole it is better to undercook and let the carry-over cooking complete the process. Scrambled eggs are easy to cook in a microwave and will develop a light and fluffy texture. Cheese melts very quickly and makes an ideal topping for jacket potatoes.

Eggs in their shells should never be cooked in a microwave – *see* box on opposite page.

Pasta and rice

Pasta and rice contain very little water. To cook them a lot of water has to be absorbed, and microwaving cannot do this any faster than normal boiling or braising. But if the pasta or rice has been pre-cooked, microwaving is a very good method for reheating.

Pastries and baked goods

Pastries and baked goods will tend to come out soggy when cooked in a microwave, so it is better to use conventional cooking methods for these.

Breadcrumbs can be dried in a microwave oven. The moisture in them is turned to steam and escapes.

A few examples of foods that can be cooked in a microwave: 1) Tronçon of turbot 2) Paupiette of lemon sole 3) Salmon steak 4) Halibut steak 5) Suprême of haddock 6) Trout 7) Délice of lemon sole 8) Chicken 9) Dover sole with the ingredients for 'bonne femme' (chopped parsley and sliced white mushrooms) 10) Flageolets 11) Potatoes 12) Broccoli 13) Chicken (suprême, drumstick and thigh) 14) Duck suprême 15) Pork fillet (sliced).

A small selection of pre-cooked frozen vegetarian dishes that can be reheated in a microwave: 1) Spicy beans 2) Vegetable strogonoff 3) Vegetable lasagne 4) Asparagus and tomato quiche 5) Sweet and sour almonds.

Meat and poultry

Many meat dishes have to be browned at some stage. As this cannot be done in a microwave oven, you will need to choose a conventional cooking process to combine with microwaving:
- meat and vegetables for a brown stew can be briefly shallow fried before the cooking is finished off in a microwave oven
- a 'roast' chicken can be started off in a hot oven.

Microwaving is most efficient for small pieces of meat or poultry, because the microwaves penetrate all or most of the food and therefore cook it very fast.

With large pieces of meat, particularly those that are an uneven shape, e.g. a chicken, the microwave energy will tend to penetrate the outer 4 cm (1½ in.) rather unevenly. The position of the meat in the oven should be changed several times during cooking to compensate for this. Some microwave ovens have a mechanically rotating base for just this purpose.

Whenever meat is cooked, no matter which method is used, several important considerations need to influence how this is done:
- the tenderising process (converting the connective tissue to gelatin, which microwaving is effective at doing)
- getting the muscle protein to set or firm up
- not allowing the muscle protein to dry out and fall apart (which will start to happen as soon as it has become firm).

Because microwaving happens so fast, careful selection of meats is very important.

Tender, relatively large joints, such as sirloin of beef or leg of lamb are not suitable, because while the meat beyond the reach of the microwaves – more than 4 cm (1½ in.) towards the centre – is being cooked by conduction of heat, the outer layer will overcook and dry out.

For tougher cuts of meat, the fast cooking time tips the balance in favour of microwaving, as long as you also use a conventional cooking process for browning, or browning is not important to the particular dish.

The tough connective tissue is converted faster than it would be in conventional cooking and happens at more or less the rate that it takes the muscle protein to set. The meat will be tender before it gets too dry.

Thawing frozen foods

If a microwave oven is used for thawing, this has to be done by switching the microwave energy on and off in short bursts. Otherwise the outside of the food thaws fast and may even begin to cook while the centre of the food stays frozen. You can control this process manually by using full power for about 30 seconds and then switching the power off for about 90 seconds – you will need to repeat this at least three times for a pork chop, for example, and six or eight times for a dish of lasagne. But many microwave ovens are now fitted with an automatic on-off defrost control. In general it is best not to defrost the food completely so that there is no risk of it beginning to cook and dry out. Instead, allow the food to stand and finish thawing of its own accord for a short time before cooking (about 10 minutes for minced meat or poultry portions, for example, and 30 to 45 minutes for a whole chicken).

Microwaving is not recommended for the large quantities of food that have to be thawed in a cook freeze system. A special rapid-thawing cabinet should be used before reheating in a microwave oven (as long as non-metallic containers are used).

△ SAFETY

Food which has a skin or shell, e.g. tomatoes, potatoes, apples, peaches, whole eggs, egg yolks and whole trout, should be pricked or pierced before microwaving. Unless this is done the build-up of pressure inside as the water molecules turn to steam will cause the skin or shell to burst or explode, and the food will splatter all over the inside of the oven. So never try to boil an egg in a microwave oven!

▸▸ TO DO

You will need a microwave oven with a thaw or defrost setting for this. Place a frozen fillet of white fish about 125 g (5 oz) in weight on a glass or china plate and put this in the centre of a microwave oven. Close the door and set to defrost for 2 minutes using the special setting. After this time, remove the fish from the oven and note down how it looks and what its texture is like. Leave it to stand for 1 minute and then note any changes in appearance and texture. If the fish has not defrosted completely, return it to the oven and repeat the defrost process for a little longer. Record how much longer it takes and discuss with your tutor or supervisor why more time has been needed.

Terms

Microwaving is cooking food using the energy of microwaves which makes the water molecules in the food vibrate and generate heat. Microwaving can also be used to defrost and reheat food.

Carry-over cooking is the cooking that occurs in the food after the source of microwave energy has been turned off. It takes a few moments for the molecules of water to pass their heat on to surrounding molecules. This period is also sometimes referred to as *standing time*.

The *output wattage* of a microwave oven is the measure in watts or kilowatts of its cooking power (or the energy used in thawing, cooking or reheating the food).

The *input wattage* is greater than the output because of the amount of electricity used in creating the microwave energy and operating the moving parts of the oven, such as the fan and turntable.

△ SAFETY

Microwave ovens do not have to be pre-heated and they should NEVER be switched on when empty. If this happens the magnetron will be damaged.

Never attempt to use a microwave oven if it is damaged or faulty, or you even suspect that there might be something wrong with it.

Safety standards

Microwave ovens are manufactured and designed to international safety standards. These cover electrical and mechanical safety, but also the containment of microwave energy. Most of Europe, Japan and the USA use the International Electrotechnical Commission (IEC) set of standards, IEC 335.

The British Standard Specification 5175, is based on this. One of the regulations is that the maximum amount of microwave leakage (microwaves escaping from the closed appliance) should be no more than 5 milliwatts per square centimetre (5mW/cm^2) at any point 5 cm or more from any part of the external surface of the appliance.

In Britain there is also health and safety legislation covering the installation and maintenance of microwave ovens. Many commercial models are guaranteed safe by the Electricity Council and when new will have an EC Safety label. All domestic models should have a similar British Electrotechnical Approvals Board (BEAB) label.

Equipment

Microwave ovens

There is now a very wide range of ovens available to caterers. An important factor to consider when choosing one is the size of the oven: will it be big enough to deal with the anticipated throughput?

Many of the ovens found in private homes or high street electrical shops are not suitable for the heavy use and rough handling they would be likely to receive in a catering establishment. They are also not powerful enough. The output of microwave ovens designed for commercial use is in the range 1,000 to 2,000 watts, whereas domestic models have an output range of 400 to 800 watts. Some commercial models also have two magnetrons which provide a better distribution of microwave energy.

Combination microwave ovens

To overcome the limitations of using pure microwave energy to cook food (not being able to brown foods or make the surface crisp), combination or dual-purpose ovens have been developed. These use infra-red and/or convected heat from electric elements or gas burners, either alternately with the microwave energy, or at the same time. A convection model has a fan to circulate the heat round the oven.

As dual-purpose ovens get hot inside, plastic containers cannot be used. Some models are specially designed to take metal containers (on the floor of the oven) – without lids, of course. The microwave energy reaches the food through the top surface only, but as long as the container has low sides and a large surface area, the food will still cook faster than it would in a conventional oven (though more slowly than in an ordinary microwave oven).

▶▶▶ TO DO

Have a look at a sales leaflet from a microwave oven manufacturer and pick out one particular model (or if there is one where you work, look at that). Note any particular design features and capabilities and decide which of these points would be important for a busy pub offering lunchtime snacks and pre-prepared dishes. Note any extra features you feel would be necessary and study manufacturers' leaflets to see which models would provide these. Compare the costs with your example model.

Three of the many models of microwave ovens available to caterers. The model at the bottom left uses convected heat in addition to microwave energy (in this case supplied by a gas burner). Note the fan at the rear of this oven. Note also that the doors of all three ovens open in a different way. The two ovens on the left have shelf fittings and revolving bases.

Design features of microwave ovens

The following features are usual in most catering microwave ovens.

— See-through window (in door) made of toughened glass. This will usually be covered with a perforated metal screen, so the energy is contained within the oven.
— Interior oven light, which usually lights up once the oven is switched on.
— Splash guard to protect the wave stirrer (fan).
— Dial timers to allow individual time settings.
— Push-button controls which can be programmed for particular types of food that are likely to be prepared frequently.
— Digital display showing the time, the output wattage of the oven and which program is in use.
— Defrost or pulse button, providing energy bursts followed by rest periods. On some models these energy bursts (or pulses) can vary in length according to the type of food being defrosted.
— Automatic shut-down (power switching off) at the end of the program.

— Variable power controls for different speeds of cooking.
— Rotating turntable or platform to make sure that the microwaves penetrate the food (especially large pieces) evenly and avoid the need to turn food manually.
— Special shelf fitting to allow two dishes of food to be cooked or reheated at the same time.
— Bell or buzzer that sounds when operation is complete.
— Sliding, hinged or drop-down door with a latch, push button or door handle to assist opening.
— Infra-red heat source for browning food.
— Convection heat source.
— Temperature probe to indicate when the centre of the food has defrosted or reached a certain cooking temperature. The required temperature can be programmed into the oven controls, so that when it has been reached a buzzer will sound or the power will be automatically turned off.

Cleaning microwave ovens

Always follow the manufacturer's cleaning instructions, but here are some general points.

Use a soft, soapy cloth to remove any spilt food inside the oven, then rinse the oven surfaces with a clean cloth and finally polish them with a soft cloth or duster. This cleaning routine should be followed regularly. If spills are not wiped up immediately after they have happened, the spilt food will absorb microwave energy and quickly burn. Take care to clean carefully around the door – a build-up of spilt food will prevent a tight seal and the effectiveness of the oven will then be reduced.

The air filter, which is at the back or bottom front of most ovens, should be taken out and washed regularly with water and a mild detergent, dried and replaced.

Shields, which protect parts such as the stirrer, should also be cleaned with a mild detergent and water.

Abrasive cleaners should never be used – they will scratch the surface and reduce the effectiveness of the microwaves. Aerosol cleaners should also be avoided as they will get into the internal parts of the oven.

Maintenance

The door alignment, locking mechanism and plug should be checked regularly. If any faults are found, the machine should be labelled 'out of order' and the fault reported so that a service engineer can be called.

The cooker door should always be closed gently, never banged shut. The vent on the top (or side) of the oven should never be covered – in fact nothing should be draped over the oven, not even a stray tea towel.

Microwave cookers must be serviced professionally according to how much and how often they are used, but usually every six to twelve months.

Containers

The best containers are non-porous (so they will not absorb liquid) and allow microwave energy to be transmitted through them, but will not melt or warp when holding hot foods. Metal reflects microwaves and so is not suitable for containers.

Not all plastics are suitable for microwave cooking. Those made from thermostet polyester, thermoplastic polyester and polysulfone are best. Many plastic containers are re-usable, dish-washer proof and dual-purpose – they can be used to store chilled food and later be placed straight into the cooker for regeneration.

Special cooking utensils are also available which can safely be left in the microwave oven during cooking (useful when an item requires regular stirring).

It is now possible to obtain special browning or searing dishes, though these are mainly for domestic use. Instead of transmitting all the microwave energy, these dishes actually absorb some of it and get hot, so that when food is placed on them, the food surface turns brown. The disadvantage is that these dishes have to be pre-heated, so it is usually quicker to use a grill (especially in a busy catering kitchen).

△ SAFETY

If metal containers or tin foil coverings are used in a microwave oven, there can be a sparking effect which, if it happens repeatedly, will begin to damage the walls of the oven and reduce the efficiency of the magnetron.

Any metal that touches the metal walls of the oven can cause an arcing or short-circuit effect.

If you use an ordinary kitchen thermometer to check whether, for example, a joint is cooked, never leave the thermometer in the oven or it may explode. Take the food out of the oven to test the temperature.

▶▶▶ TO DO

List a sample of six main course dishes from your workplace menu (or that of a local restaurant) which could be cooked in a microwave oven. Beside each one, note suitable containers for any pre-cooking required and for cooking the food in the microwave oven. Say why you have chosen each container.

The shape of containers

The most important consideration in choosing the shape of a container, is that the food must absorb microwave energy evenly. Rectangular dishes, for example, may tend to have less food in their corners and this food will absorb too much of the energy, overheat and dry out before the food in the middle is thoroughly cooked. Round dishes are good. The larger and flatter the dish, the more surface area of food there will be for the microwaves to penetrate. A liquid should be heated in a tall container such as a jug, rather than a low, shallow dish such as a soup plate. This makes handling easy and the liquid is less likely to spill over the top if it begins to boil.

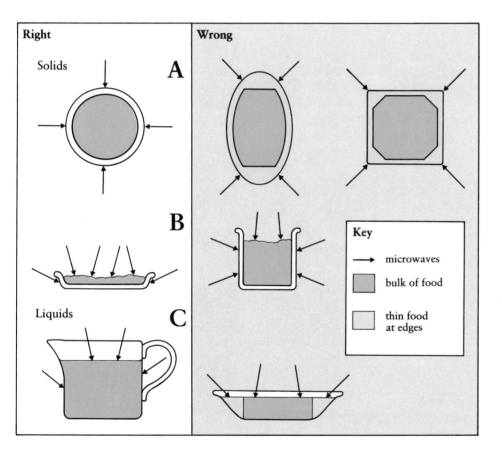

Suitable for microwaving

Containers
Thermoplastic – the label will indicate if it can withstand extreme temperatures, but double check if you are using a combination microwave oven.
Paper plates and cups (providing they are moisture-resistant and can stand high temperatures).
Oven-to-table glassware.
Boil-in-the-bag pouches (as long as a hole is made in them to allow steam to escape).
China (providing it has no metallic decoration, e.g. a gilt trim).
Earthenware.
Other containers clearly labelled as suitable for microwave ovens.

Underlinings (which are sometimes placed between food and plate or dish to absorb excess moisture).
Kitchen paper.
Paper, cotton or linen napkins.

Coverings
Greaseproof paper.
Kitchen paper.
Paper, cotton or linen napkins.
Plastic wrapping film labelled as suitable for microwave ovens.

BUT AVOID:
Any dishes partially or wholly made of metal or even trimmed with metal, including gilt decoration.
Ceramic that contains aluminium oxide – called pyroceramics.
Lead crystal.
Antique glass.
Containers with glued handles.
Waxed paper.
Some plastics such as Tupperware and melamine.
Polythene bags.
Ordinary plastic wrapping film (because at high temperatures it may release harmful substances into the food).

The illustration above shows which sorts of container are best for microwaving. So that microwaves can penetrate the food evenly:

A. A plate with a narrow rim is better than a deep dish and round shapes are better than oval or square.

B. A large shallow dish is better for solid foods than a small deep dish.

C. Containers for liquids should have straight sides (slopes set up thin edges of food which become overheated).

Essential points

There are a number of very important basic activities which should be carried out when using a microwave oven. If your work is to be judged for the Caterbase module, *Microwaving*, your supervisor or assessor will look at how well you have carried out these essential steps.

1. Make sure the inside of the oven and door are clean.

> If the oven walls or floor is dirty the microwaves will not be reflected properly around the oven, and the food will heat unevenly.

2. Collect together the cooking utensils and containers you will need for the job.

> Which utensils you choose will depend on whether you are using the microwave oven for defrosting, cooking or reheating, and whether you want to keep the food moist or to dry it out.

3. Work out how to set the microwave oven, taking into account how much food you are dealing with, its quality, thickness, how solid it is, and any manufacturer's instructions relating to its defrosting, cooking or reheating.

> The position of the food in the oven and the power setting will depend on the food itself and what is to be done to it.
> Make sure that large, dense pieces of food, in particular poultry, are thoroughly defrosted before cooking.
> If you have to deal with more than one type of food at a time, put in first the items which will take longest to defrost, cook or reheat.
> If you are cooking a dish with a stuffing or filling, e.g. stuffed peppers, remember that you will have to allow more time than you would for the peppers alone.

4. Consider whether the food will need protection or a covering to prevent splashing or drying out while it is in the oven.

> Some foods may need to be coated with oil or melted butter to prevent them sticking to the container while cooking.
> Cover any foods which need to stay moist during cooking. Also cover foods which might splash or splatter (kitchen paper is good for this).
> Most food should be covered during defrosting. The exceptions to this are frozen cakes and pastries.

5. Select the appropriate power setting and time.

> If there is no turntable in the oven, you should rotate and re-position large pieces of food so that you can be sure they have cooked evenly.
> Stir food such as a stew that is defrosting, or turn over/re-position if it is a solid item.

△ SAFETY

Always remember to follow a safe and logical work flow. For example, allow the steam to escape safely from covered foods by gently raising the lid or cover on the side furthest away from you. Remember that although the container itself will not be hot, the food inside can cause a nasty burn if handled incorrectly.

The pasta for this dish of lasagne has been boiled on a conventional stove, but microwaving has been used to boil the sauces (although the bolognaise sauce was started with shallow frying before being completed with boiling).

A microwave oven can now be used to reheat the lasagne, and it should then be briefly browned under a grill.

Right

Wrong

Before microwaving, food should be arranged evenly on the plate. Any slow heating foods and/or thicker items should be placed towards the outside edge of the plate so that they receive maximum exposure to microwaves. Thinly cut items or foods with a light structure should be put towards the centre of the plate. If thick and thinly cut items are being heated together, it is a good idea to arrange the thicker items so that they overlap or cover the edges of the thinner ones.

6. Ensure the food has been heated to the correct temperature without burning or drying out.

A probe can be used to check the temperature of large items. Smaller items are easier to check — you should be able to tell whether they are done or not by inserting a cocktail stick into the centre of the piece of food, this will test whether it is tender or if juices are the correct colour. If the food is not ready return it to the microwave oven and re-set as appropriate. Remember to allow for carry-over cooking.

Sauces need to be stirred regularly to prevent them over-thickening at the outer edges, and to allow the heat to penetrate to the middle of the container.

7. Transfer the food from the microwave oven and serve immediately, unless it needs to be browned under a grill or in a conventional oven before service.

Choose utensils that will allow you to handle the food without danger of it breaking up, as well as keeping you safe — it is easy to burn or scald yourself.

When food is microwaved on a plate, the plate does not heat up. So once it is out of the oven the food will lose its heat fairly quickly. It may be a good idea to pre-heat the service plates, for example, in a conventional oven at a low temperature, so that the microwaved food can be transferred on to this and stay warm longer.

▶▶▶ TO DO

Put together a list of instructions for a member of staff who has not had much catering experience and will need to use a microwave to heat up a range of dishes for a snack evening meal service in a bar. Base the menu on one offered in a local bar of your choice and choose at least three dishes.

You need to cover: a) what sort of containers should be used b) which food should or should not be covered c) approximate times for reheating d) final touches (possibly with conventional equipment) before service.

Cooking times

The cooking times and oven settings in these recipes have been marked with an asterisk (*) to remind you that they have been worked out for use with a microwave oven with a power output of 1,400 watts. If you are using an oven with a different power output, for example of 900 or 2,000 watts, the setting and cooking times will need to be adjusted as follows:

Output of oven	1,400	900	2,000
For Sausage and bacon hotpot and Moroccan lamb stew			
Setting	Medium	High	Low
Time	As recipe	As recipe	Increase time by a third
For Broccoli and Lasagne			
Setting	High	High	Medium
Time	As recipe	Increase time by half	As recipe

Suitable containers
Refer to Terms and Equipment 2 for the kinds of dishes you can use. The hotpot, broccoli and Moroccan lamb stew have to be cooked in dishes with lids.

Sausage and bacon hotpot

INGREDIENTS   SERVES 6

750 g	*beef sausages (12)*	1 lb 14 oz
350 g	*piece of lean bacon*	14 oz
200 g	*onions*	8 oz
1	*clove garlic*	1
100 g	*mushrooms*	4 oz
500 g	*potatoes*	1¼ lb
350 g	*tinned tomatoes*	14 oz
200 ml	*white stock*	8 fl oz
	(see Introduction/Stocks)	
2 tsp	*paprika*	2 tsp
1 tsp	*Worcester sauce*	1 tsp
	salt and pepper to taste	
	chopped parsley	

1. Wash and prepare the vegetables:
   a) Finely chop the onions and crush the garlic.
   b) Slice the mushrooms.
   c) Thinly slice the potatoes.

2. Remove any fat from the bacon and cut the bacon into small cubes.

3. Prick the sausages with a cocktail stick, place them with the other ingredients (except the parsley) in a suitable dish and cover with a lid and place into the microwave oven.

4. Set the oven to *medium and cook for four periods of *3 minutes, allowing a 1-minute gap between each period of cooking. Turn the sausages during each rest period.

5. Test that the sausages are cooked by pricking with a cocktail stick. They should feel tender and only clear juices should come out.

6. Add salt and pepper as required and serve sprinkled with chopped parsley.

Moroccan lamb stew

INGREDIENTS		SERVES 4
450 g	boned leg of lamb	1 lb 2 oz
200 g	onion	8 oz
2	cloves garlic	2
200 g	carrots	8 oz
300 g	tinned tomatoes	12 oz
100 ml	plain yogurt	4 fl oz
400 ml	beef stock (see Introduction/Stocks)	16 fl oz
200 g	courgettes	8 oz
200 g	leeks	8 oz
5 g	paprika	¼ oz
½ tsp	ground ginger	½ tsp
	bay leaf	
	salt and milled black pepper to taste	
	chilli powder to taste	

1. Remove the skin and any fat or sinew from the lamb, then cut it into 20 mm (¾ in.) cubes.

2. Wash and prepare the vegetables:
   a) Finely chop the onions and crush the garlic.
   b) Thinly slice the carrots into rounds.

3. Mix together the meat and spices (paprika, ginger, chilli powder) then place into a suitable dish.

4. Add the onions, garlic, carrots, tomatoes, yogurt, stock, bay leaf and seasoning and mix together.

5. Cover and place into the microwave oven at *medium setting.

6. Allow the stew to simmer until the meat is just tender – about *35 minutes. Stir occasionally during cooking, removing the dish briefly from the oven to do so.

7. Wash the courgettes and leeks. Trim the ends off the courgettes and then slice them into rounds 5 mm (¼ in.) thick. Wash the leeks, cutting them in half lengthwise to make sure all dirt is removed, then cut into half rounds 5 mm (¼ in.) thick.

8. Continue cooking the meat and vegetables until they are tender – about 6 minutes.

9. Check seasoning and serve on a bed of hot couscous. You can also serve a green salad with this dish.

Couscous

INGREDIENTS		
350 g	couscous	14 oz
500 ml	hot chicken stock (see Introduction/Stocks)	1 pt
15 ml	oil	½ fl oz
	salt and pepper to taste	

1. Place the couscous into a cooking bowl with half the stock and allow to soak for about 10 minutes. Stir occasionally to separate the grains.

2. Stir in the oil and the other half of the stock and season lightly.

3. Cover the dish and place it in the microwave at *medium setting.

4. Cook for *8 to 10 minutes, stirring occasionally. When ready, the couscous should be tender and light and fluffy.

If you prefer to make your own couscous:

Sieve 150 g (6 oz) of finely ground hard wheat into a large bowl. Add water, a drop at a time, and work the flour with your hands until a thick, creamy consistency is produced. Place this mixture in a fine sieve and steam it over a pan of boiling water for 15 minutes. Then put the couscous on to a deep tray and work with your hands until the grains are all separated.

Broccoli

INGREDIENTS		SERVES 4
450g	broccoli	1 lb 2 oz
	salt and pepper	

1. Wash then prepare the stalks, trimming off any thick bottom ends. If the broccoli is very thick, cut it in half lengthwise. Trim the stalks so that they are about 30-40 mm (1-1½ in.) long.

2. Place the trimmed broccoli into a suitable dish with the flower heads pointing towards the centre.

3. Pour water into the dish so that it just covers the base – about 100ml (4 fl oz).

4. Lightly season the broccoli with the salt and pepper, then cover the dish with a lid and place into the microwave oven at *high setting.

5. Cook until tender – about *5 minutes. Test after 3 and 4 minutes to avoid overcooking.

6. Take the broccoli out of the microwave oven, transfer it to a pre-heated serving dish and serve.

Lasagne verde

INGREDIENTS — SERVES 2 (main course portions)

100 g	green lasagne	4 oz
350 ml	bolognaise sauce (see box)	14 fl oz
175 ml	béchamel (see Introduction/Stocks)	7 fl oz
25 ml	cream	1 fl oz
40 g	grated Parmesan cheese	1¾ oz
5 g	butter for greasing the dish	¼ oz
	grated nutmeg to taste	
	salt and milled black pepper to taste	

1. Boil the lasagne fairly vigorously in plenty of salted water. Stir from time to time to prevent the leaves or sheets from sticking together.

2. When cooked (12-15 minutes), refresh the lasagne under cold running water and then drain thoroughly.

3. Mix the cream through the (cold) béchamel sauce and season with the nutmeg.

4. Butter two suitable earthenware dishes of a capacity of 400 ml (¾ pt).

5. Place a layer of the cooked lasagne in each dish.

6. Coat with a layer of (cold) bolognaise sauce and sprinkle this with Parmesan cheese.

7. Cover with a further layer of lasagne then coat with the cream sauce and sprinkle with Parmesan.

8. Repeat with alternate layers of lasagne, bolognaise sauce and Parmesan then cream sauce and more Parmesan until the dishes have been filled; finish with a top layer of lasagne, cream sauce and Parmesan.

9. Place into the microwave oven and thoroughly reheat – *4 minutes at the *high setting (the time will vary depending on whether the dishes are being reheated together as well as on the power output of the oven.) Note: reheat to a minimum internal temperature of 80°C (175°F). Test with a thermometer probe if you are not sure.

10. Place the dish under a hot grill or salamander until the top layer develops a good brown colour, then serve.

Bolognaise sauce

INGREDIENTS — Makes about 350 ml (14 fl oz)

10 g	butter or margarine	½ oz
50 g	onion	2 oz
4	cloves garlic	4
150 g	minced beef	6 oz
10 g	tomato purée	½ oz
200 ml	demi-glace (see Introduction/Stocks)	8 fl oz
100 ml	brown stock (see Introduction/Stocks)	4 fl oz

1. Finely chop the onion and crush the garlic.

2. Heat the butter or margarine in a saucepan, add the onion and garlic and shallow-fry for 2 to 3 minutes.

3. Add the minced beef and continue shallow-frying until lightly browned (for 8 to 12 minutes).

4. Add the tomato purée, demi-glace and stock and bring to the boil.

5. Skim off surface fat and simmer gently for about 45 minutes. During cooking, stir occasionally to prevent burning and top up with additional brown stock if the mixture gets too thick.

6. Adjust seasoning if necessary. If the mixture is too thin, continue to simmer. It should just reach a pouring consistency.

Cornish pasties

INGREDIENTS   SERVES 10

| 750 g | savoury short pastry (see box) | 1 lb 14 oz |

Filling

375 g	coarsely minced beef	15 oz
250 g	finely diced potatoes	10 oz
125 g	diced onions	5 oz
	salt and pepper to taste	

Egg wash

| 2-3 | eggs beaten lightly with a little water | 2-3 |

1. Prepare the filling: place all the ingredients into a bowl, then mix them thoroughly together.

2. Roll out the pastry to a thickness of 3 to 4 mm (³/₁₆ in.), then cut it into 10 rounds using a plain round pastry cutter 150 mm (6 in.) in diameter.

3. Place 75 g (3 oz) of filling on each pastry round then brush a band of egg wash 1½ cm (½ in.) wide round the edge: this will help to stick the edges of the pasty together.

4. Fold the round in half, bringing both edges of the pastry upwards so that they meet over the top of the filling, then press together to seal.

5. Make a series of pinches in the tops to create an attractive wavy edge (see illustration), then neatly place the pasties on a lightly greased and floured baking tray.

Savoury short pastry

INGREDIENTS   MAKES 750 g (l lb 14 oz)

450 g	soft flour	18 oz
225 g	butter or margarine	9 oz
90 ml	water	3½ fl oz
	pinch of salt	

1. Sieve the flour to make sure that it is free of lumps.

2. Chop the fat into small lumps and then rub it into the flour as lightly as possible to make a sandy texture.

3. Dissolve the salt in the water then add to the fat and flour.

4. Lightly mix together until a smooth dough is formed.

---

6. Brush the pasties with egg wash, then bake at 200°C (390°F) in a conventional oven until cooked and golden brown – about 40 minutes. Alternatively, the pasties can be baked in a combined microwave and convection oven at a temperature of 225°C (435°F) on *quarter microwave power (for a microwave oven with full output power of 1,400 watts). This will reduce the conventional cooking time to about *25 minutes.

7. When the pasties are cooked, take them out of the oven. Either serve them immediately or quickly cool them and store them chilled until they are required for service. They can then be thoroughly reheated in a microwave oven.

(When preparing food that is to be cooked and chilled later, always follow the DHSS Guidelines on Pre-Cooked Chilled Foods, see Cook Chill/Insight 2).

♟ CHEF'S TIP

Reheating short-pastry products in a microwave oven tends to result in a loss of crispness. If possible, use a combined microwave and convection oven at a high temperature of 250°C (480°F) with the microwave oven set at *half power.

What went wrong

Liquids start to spill over.

> Container is too small.
>   Open the microwave oven door and the problem will stop. Wipe up the spillage and transfer the food to a larger container.

Foods explode.

> The surface or skin has not been pierced enough or at all, or a sealed container has been used.

Food has dried out.

> 1. The food has been cooked for too long.
> 2. The wrong power setting has been used.
> 3. The food was not protected during cooking (sometimes necessary).
> 4. Food should have had moisture added during cooking (some foods require this).

Sauces and gravies have gone lumpy.

> They have probably not been stirred enough during the cooking process.

Food which should have turned golden brown has not.

> Microwaving on its own is not the right cooking process for getting this effect. The food should have been browned either before or after microwave cooking, using conventional equipment, e.g. an oven or grill. Ideally use a combined microwave and convection oven.

Condensation forms in the oven.

> The high moisture level in some foods causes this.
>   If the containers are covered, less condensation will form. But when it does happen, make sure you leave the door open for a few seconds after use and allow the condensation to disperse.

Cooking by microwave energy gives similar finished results to other cooking processes where heated water is important: steaming, boiling, poaching and stewing. This means it is ideal for cooking most vegetables, this broccoli, for example, but not successful for cooking foods that require the browning and/or drying out and colouring effects achieved in grilling, deep and shallow frying, roasting, braising and baking.

The Yorkshire pudding shown in this photograph had risen perfectly when it was in the oven and appeared to be cooked, even though it looked rather pale. But as soon as it was taken out of the oven it collapsed, because the surface or shell had not dried out enough to hold its shape.

Tips

For getting rid of persistent smells in a microwave oven, add about a teaspoon of lemon juice to a cup of water, then place the cup inside the oven and switch it on for a few minutes.

Kitchen paper is ideal for absorbing moisture from defrosted goods and prevents pastry items becoming soggy as the moisture builds up in the microwave oven on heating. Paper is also good for absorbing any excess fat or oil. But if you use a piece of paper or a similar thin material to cover or rest food on, take care that it does not get caught under the door. If it does, the door will probably still shut, but the seal may well be broken and leakage of radiation may occur.

If you are worried that the heating effect in a microwave oven is not even, test it by cooking a tray of scones, leaving the tray in the same position for the whole cooking time. All the scones should rise by the same amount.

If you open the microwave oven door to stir the food during defrosting or cooking, remember that you have to switch on the microwave energy again.

Sprinkle foods such as sweet pastries with sugar *after* microwaving. The sugar will caramelise and may even burn if it is microwaved.

The flavour of spices is intensified in microwaving. Use less than you would in ordinary cooking processes.

TEST YOURSELF

1. Give two reasons why fish is considered suitable for microwaving.

2. Give one reason why metal containers should not be used in a microwave.

3. Explain briefly why the door of the microwave oven should be kept clean.

4. Give two ways in which food could be prevented from splashing in a microwave oven.

5. Describe briefly how food is cooked in a microwave oven.

6. What shapes of container are recommended for use in a microwave oven and why?

7. Name three advantages for a caterer in using a microwave oven rather than conventional equipment.

City and Guilds

Dishes such as this lamb stew use the advantages of microwave cooking to the full: it is convenient to prepare (only one cooking container is used and one cooking process), quick (cooking time is less than half what it would be in conventional stewing), attractive in appearance and tastes delicious.

8 COOK CHILL

Cook chill is not a single cooking process, like baking, shallow frying or boiling, but a whole system of catering. Customers in catering establishments which use the cook chill method are unlikely to realise that the food they are eating was prepared some days in advance and that this may well have been done at a separate establishment. They should not be able to detect any difference in quality between cook chill food and freshly prepared dishes, although they may wonder how it is that such a range of food and such complex dishes are on offer.

Many customers will have come across cook chill foods in supermarkets, and if they have tried these products, will recognise and appreciate how useful they can be. The benefits of cook chill include:

— A greater variety of dishes available at a consistently higher standard than would be possible with conventional methods of cooking. As long as cook chill food is used within two or three days of preparation, it loses little of its quality and taste.

— Lower preparation costs: a centralised production system that has been planned efficiently results in savings on labour and materials, so it is cheaper to prepare the food. This cost saving can mean lower prices for customers.

— Standardisation. Because the food is produced on a large scale, customers should be able to rely on consistent standards as far as portion size and quality are concerned.

— More efficient service: pre-preparation of foods reduces the chance of any service delays and ensures that customers' requests are met promptly.

> **History of cook chill**
> The introduction of the cook chill system has been accredited to J. Lyons & Co, the caterers, who in the 1950s set up a centralised kitchen at Cadby Hall, Hammersmith, London, from where they delivered a wide selection of pre-prepared chilled food to many of their teashops spread across London. But the real breakthrough in cook chill techniques for the caterer happened in the early 1970s.

Almost any food can be cook chilled so long as the right methods are used in preparing it. This means that the cook chill system is very versatile and as a result it is widely used. It can be found anywhere that bulk catering is required, for example in schools, hospitals, catering run by social services departments, staff canteens and on airlines and trains. It is often used for banquets, in conference and exhibition catering, and vending operations, for example, for self-service cabinets dispensing light meals in factories.

Cook chill is also popular when customers expect a range of dishes to be prepared and ready to eat a short time after they have ordered them, whether they are in a high-class restaurant with elaborate dishes such as lobster in a rich and delicious sauce or in a snack bar serving vegetarian hot pot.

▶▶▶ TO DO

If possible, visit a unit which operates a cook chill system. Make a note of the equipment used, the number of staff employed and the number of meals served. How does the number of staff in relation to the number of meals produced compare with how many staff would be necessary in an ordinary kitchen? Write down your observations.

What is cook chill?

Cook chill is a complete catering system based on preparing food in bulk at one central point and then using rapid chilling techniques and refrigeration to store the cooked food until it is needed for service.

At a central unit the raw ingredients of the dishes are collected together, and the foods are prepared and cooked to a safe temperature to kill any bacteria present. The cooked food is then placed into suitable containers and chilled immediately.

After chilling, the food is stored at just above freezing point – between 0°C (32°F) and 3°C (37°F) for up to five days (including the day of cooking and the day of eating).

At the service area the food is reheated. This may be many miles away from the production unit – an aircraft might take the food aboard in London and serve it shortly before landing in Sydney! In many cases the food will be transported from the production unit to a number of different service units using specially equipped refrigerator vans.

So the difficulties in conventional cooking systems, where the food cannot always be cooked immediately before it is served and has to be kept warm, are overcome. This means that deterioration in the taste and nutritional quality of the food is significantly reduced.

Stages in cook chill

The diagram opposite shows the organisation of a typical cook chill system. The stages are:
1. Food cooked in bulk
2. Food portioned into containers
3. Containers sealed
4. Containers loaded on trolley
5. Fast chilling in blast chiller
6. Storage in cold room at 0°-3°C
7. Containers placed in insulated boxes
8. Boxes loaded into van
9. Boxes unloaded at destination
10. Containers loaded on trolley
11. Containers reheated
12. Hot food ready for service.

Advantages of cook chill

1. *Choice of time of production.* As the food can be kept for up to five days, batches of meals can be cooked together but served independently.

2. *Skilled staff can work together in a central kitchen.* This is much less costly than employing skilled staff at a number of smaller kitchens, and allows the staff in the central kitchen to concentrate on preparing the food to high standards in a more orderly and relaxed atmosphere than is possible in most ordinary kitchens which have peaks of activity at meal times.

3. *The best use can be made of equipment.* Expensive labour-saving equipment can often be afforded because it will produce such a large number of meals and can even be in use around the clock, if there is shift working.

4. *Fewer staff will be required but working conditions are likely to be better.* The production time is not geared to meal times so straight shifts at hours to suit a range of people can be operated.

5. *Less space is needed.* The space taken up by equipment and staff to prepare 1,000 meals in one kitchen all through the working day is much less than would be required at five kitchens each preparing 200 meals for specific meal times.

6. *Energy costs can be reduced.* Equipment can be used at full capacity and turned on only when it will actually be used.

7. *Food costs can be reduced and quality of food purchases controlled easily.* Bulk buying and lower prices are easiest to organise for large quantities to a single delivery point. Quality can be strictly checked.

8. *A greater range of dishes can be produced than is possible using the cook freeze system.* Foods with delicate cell structures that are easily damaged by freezing, such as soft fruits, can be used. Also, recipes do not need major modifications, as they do in cook freeze. The drawback of cook chill systems is that they are costly to install: the special chilling, handling and storage equipment is very expensive. In addition, the cook chill establishment needs a whole range of expensive conventional cooking equipment such as bratt pans, steam-jacketed kettles and automatic deep fryers arranged carefully in spacious premises to handle the necessary quantities hygienically and efficiently.

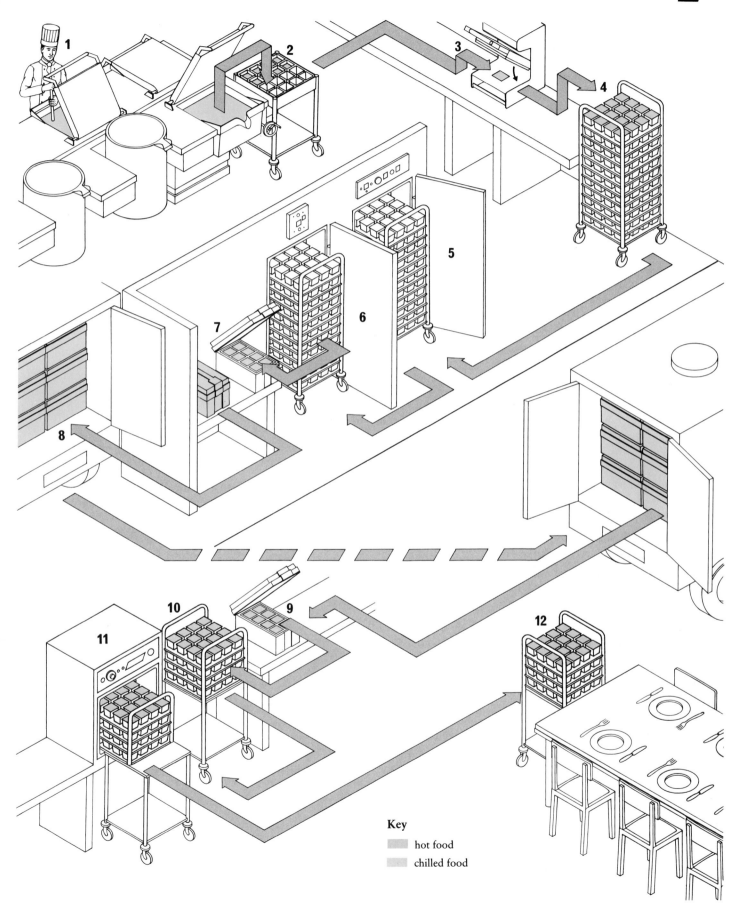

Key

hot food

chilled food

8 COOK CHILL

The dangers of cook chill

It is essential:

— to maintain correct temperatures

— to keep to the highest hygiene standards

— to use top-quality raw ingredients.

One of the reasons for cooking food, apart from making it more digestible and palatable, is to kill harmful micro-organisms which may be present in the food. If food is to be first cooked, and then stored and reheated, as in cook chill systems, control of micro-organisms, especially bacteria, is even more important than in normal cooking procedures, because the food goes through a critical temperature zone three times (*see* diagram).

The greatest danger is *food-poisoning bacteria*. There can be literally millions of these present on the food, but they are completely invisible. The food looks, smells and tastes perfectly normal. The way to make sure that these bacteria are kept harmless is strict temperature control. Food-poisoning bacteria are killed at temperatures above 63°C (145°F) and cannot grow at temperatures below 5°C (41°F).

> Micro-organisms are small living things (individually too small to be seen with the naked eye) which are present virtually everywhere. Not all micro-organisms are a problem but some can result in food spoilage and food poisoning given the right temperature and length of time to develop.
>
> *Food spoilage organisms* include: fungi (yeasts and moulds) and some bacteria.
>
> *Food poisoning organisms* include pathogenic (or harmful) bacteria.

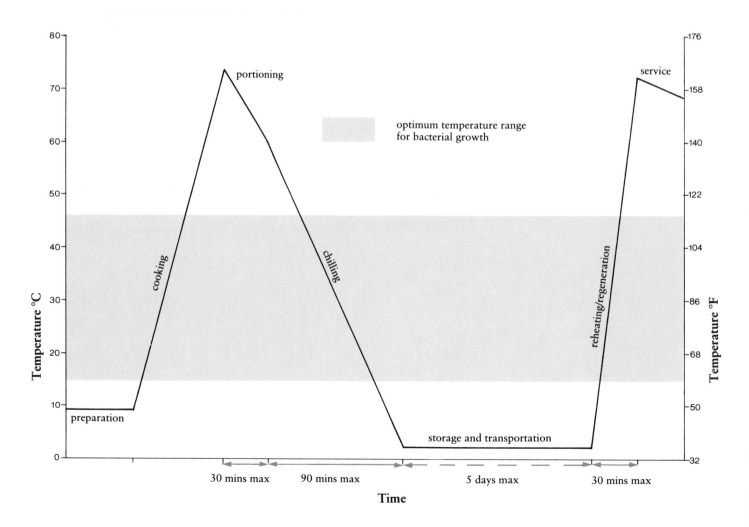

170

Reducing the dangers

There are a number of requirements laid down by the Department of Health and Social Security in a leaflet called *Guidelines on Pre-Cooked Chilled Foods*. Most cook chill establishments follow the DHSS recommendations.

At point of entry

The food purchased must be of prime quality. It must then be stored under strict conditions of hygiene.

Initial cooking

The centre or core of the food must reach a temperature of at least 70°C (158°F). Some experts recommend 75°C (167°F) as an even safer internal temperature.

Portioning

Portioning should be carried out quickly and hygienically whether the food is hot or cold. The size and shape of the container should be selected for fast chilling. The depth of the food in the container should be no more than 5 cm (2 in.). The containers must be clearly labelled with date of cooking, number of portions, and reheating instructions.

Chilling

Food must be chilled within 30 minutes of cooking and reduced to a temperature of 0-3°C (32-37°F) within a further period of 90 minutes.

Portioning after chilling

In some cook chill systems the food is chilled in multi-portion containers, then plated before reheating. The portioning process must then be carried out within 30 minutes of the food leaving chilled storage and before reheating starts, at temperatures under 10°C (50°F). It is then transported in a chilled state to the eating area, for example the hospital ward, and reheated to at least 70°C (158°F) on the plate on which it is served.

Storage

The chilled food must be stored in a special refrigeration area, and never next to other fresh or conventionally prepared products. The temperature must be monitored regularly and immediately adjusted if it varies.

Reheating

Cook chill food must be heated as quickly as possible to a minimum temperature of 70°C (158°F), but ideally to 75°C (167°F).

For foods to be chilled to under 3°C within 90 minutes, they have to be fairly thin. The whole chicken (*above*) has not reached a safe temperature, but the joint (*below*) has.

▶▶▶ TO DO

Visit your nearest large supermarket. Identify food that has been cook chilled (rather than cook frozen) and note the range of dishes available. If possible, buy a sample that will enable you to compare the taste and texture with a freshly cooked product. Note your findings, recording how the freshly cooked product was cooked, what the ingredients cost, and how long the dish took to prepare and cook. Compare the cost to that of the cook chill version and the preparation time to the reheating time.

Planning menus and production

Careful menu and production planning are important. Production must be accurately forecasted. If too much food is produced the excess will have to be destroyed after the five-day storage period. If too little is produced, customers' choice of dishes will be cut down or conventionally produced foods will have to be substituted.

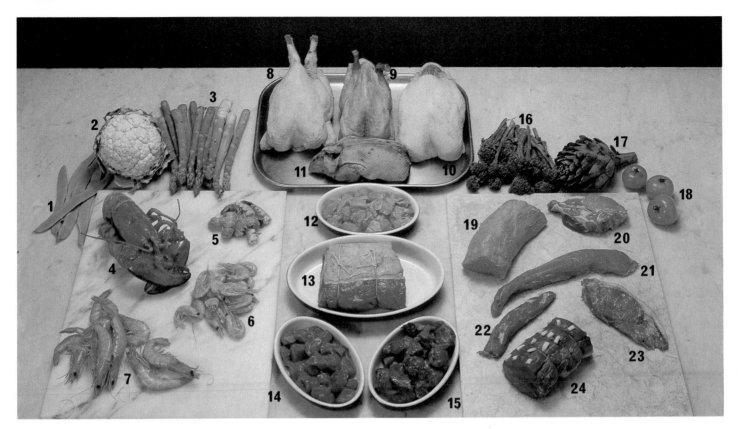

1) Runner beans 2) Cauliflower
3) Asparagus 4) Lobster 5) Scampi tails
6) Prawns 7) Mediterranean prawns
8) Chicken 9) Guinea fowl 10) Duckling
11) Wild duck 12) Diced veal
13) Contre-filet of beef 14) Diced
stewing beef 15) Diced venison
16) Broccoli 17) Globe artichoke
18) Tomatoes 19) Cushion of veal
20) Pork fillet 22) Fillet of lamb
23) Rump steak 24) Fillet of beef.

Almost all food items are suitable for the cook chill system. But some combinations of foods can withstand the changes in temperature better than others and look and taste better after reheating. As the food needs to stand up to chilling, storing and reheating, only the best quality raw foods and additional ingredients should be used. Food which is of doubtful quality or condition should be rejected.

Perhaps the most important thing about cook chill dishes is the way they are prepared and cooked. One of the few published investigations into the effects of chilling, storing and reheating food (carried out in Germany in the late 1970s) found the following problems that can arise:

— Dishes containing meat tend to develop a flat taste and if spices have been used these can overwhelm the flavour of the meat by the end of the maximum storage life (day 5).

— The flavour of veal and poultry dishes deteriorates after three days.

— Chilled meat dishes without sauces can develop acidic tastes.

— Fatty foods (including oily fish) tend to develop off-flavours as a result of the oil oxidising.

— Fish dishes deteriorate more rapidly than meat dishes generally.

— Vegetables in general may discolour and taste strong, although peas are relatively stable in taste.

— Dishes containing starch may taste stale.

▶▶▶ TO DO

Choose three of the food items shown in the picture, including one vegetable, one meat and one fish. Then find one recipe for each commodity that you feel would be suitable for cook chilling (using the Practical Examples in this book or recipes in other cookery books). Explain why you have chosen these particular recipes.

Keeping nutritional value

How much nutritional value cook chill meals have depends on two things: a) the nutrients in the raw food, and b) how the raw food was processed. Certain nutrients, especially vitamins from the B group and Vitamin C, are easily lost into cooking liquid or destroyed by heat.

In order to serve food of the maximum quality and nutritional value, certain guidelines should be followed:

– Purchase the freshest possible raw foods and use them immediately. A cook chill system should allow for careful planning and a minimum length of storage. Large operations may even be able to buy direct from farmers.

– Plan food preparation so that it is done immediately before cooking. This avoids the loss of vitamins that happens after food has been cut up.

– Cook vegetables in as little boiling water as possible or use a high-pressure steamer.

– Chill food as fast as possible after cooking. Some vitamin loss will happen during chilling and this loss will be reduced if the chilling time is shortened.

– Reheat and serve cook chill foods immediately. Never keep them standing at their reheated temperature.

✚ HYGIENE

Common food poisoning bacteria

Salmonella
Commonly found in the intestines of animals (and some humans). Raw poultry, meat and meat products are often contaminated with *Salmonella* on arrival in the kitchen. This is why they must be kept separate from other food and then cooked thoroughly. Salmonella poisoning accounts for over 70% of recorded cases of food poisoning and can be fatal to the very old, young or ill.

Staphylococcus aureus
Between 20% and 50% of the population have this bacterium present somewhere on their bodies. Cuts, boils, spots, etc. can harbour large numbers of these bacteria and must always be covered. Good personal hygiene is essential to ensure that this type of bacteria does not get transferred to food.

Clostridium
This bacterium is found in similar environments to *Salmonella*. Its spores can be found on raw poultry and meat and in the soil (so they can be on vegetables). An added problem is that these spores are heat-resistant, so normal cooking temperatures do not destroy them. In a cook chill system, if cooling happens slowly this can reactivate the bacteria. Strong growth of this bacterium occurs in oxygen-free conditions, for example, at the bottom of a stew or in a rolled joint of beef.

All these bacteria – known as pathogenic, that is harmful – grow and multiply well on moist, protein-containing foods, such as poultry, meat, fish and shellfish, eggs, dairy products, etc.

Essential precautions

It is very important to take all possible measures to prevent cross contamination between raw foods and cooked foods. Separate chopping boards and knives should be reserved for preparing meat, poultry, offal and fish, so that they are only ever used for one type of food.

During the period before preparation, raw food must be stored at the correct temperature and humidity. The temperature should be between 1° and 3°C (34° and 37°F) with fish at the lower end of this range. The humidity should be around 80% – this is very difficult to check accurately, unless the equipment has a humidity gauge. If it is too high (so there is too much moisture) the surface of food will become soft and mushy and moulds will grow; too low and the food will dry out and shrivel.

8 COOK CHILL

Terms

Cook chill is a complete catering system based on the bulk centralised preparation and production of food and the use of rapid chilling techniques and refrigeration to separate cooking from service.

Blast chilling is a term sometimes used to describe the rapid chilling of the food in special equipment. This often describes any type of fast chilling, but refers particularly to a kind of equipment which incorporates powerful fans so that cold air circulates rapidly within the chilling compartment.

Reheating (sometimes called regeneration) is the final stage in the cook chill system, when the chilled food is quickly heated to a safe temperature for service and eating.

CPU is an abbreviation sometimes used for the central production unit or kitchen.

Satellite kitchen or *satellite unit* are common names for the kitchens which do the final reheating and then send out the food to the customers.

Warm holding is keeping food warm over a period of time after it has been produced and before it is served. Cook chill systems are designed to eliminate the need for this practice, which is harmful to food texture and its nutritional value, but above all very dangerous because it can allow food-poisoning bacteria to grow.

Time buffer is the term sometimes used for the extra time between preparation and service that cook chill systems can provide.

Batch cooking describes splitting large quantities of a particular item into batches to cook because either the cooking equipment or the chilling equipment or both are not large enough to process the entire amount in one go.

This tilting steam kettle could be used in a cook chill CPU for boiling pasta or rice, for example, or bulk preparation of sauces and white stocks.

▸▸▸ TO DO

Suggest a cook chill meal suitable for serving in a works canteen. Describe the various stages that the food needs to go through, from delivery of the raw ingredients to serving the meal.

In purpose-built cook chill kitchens such as this one, all the equipment is on a large scale. The capacity of the cooking equipment is designed to match that of the chilling equipment.

Cooking equipment

Cook chill systems use standard equipment for the initial cooking of the food. With the emphasis on bulk preparation, equipment with a high output and large capacity is usually used, such as:

– forced air convection ovens for baking, roasting and braising

– combi-ovens or convection/steamers for baking, roasting, steaming and braising

– bratt pans for boiling, shallow frying, stewing and poaching

– steam-jacketed kettles or boilers for boiling and stewing

– atmospheric and high pressure steamers for steaming

– pressure and automatic fryers for deep frying.

Portioning equipment

Assembly line production with conveyor belts is used in many large cook chill systems for the portioning and packing of the foods. Automatic equipment is available to pack some foods, particularly liquids such as soups, and to seal containers.

All equipment should be easy to clean.

Containers

The container used should protect the quality of the food at all stages, so that it can be chilled rapidly, stored safely and reheated effectively. It must:

– be sturdy so that it can withstand chilling, handling and reheating without getting damaged

– be made of a substance that will neither cause poisonous or harmful substances to develop in the food nor react with foods to cause discolouring or spoilage

– have a lid that is easy to remove without damaging the contents or causing spillage

– be attractive, if it is to be seen by the customer

– be as airtight and watertight as possible so that moisture, flavours or odours do not penetrate or escape during storage and transportation.

Single-portion containers are made from:

– cardboard laminated with plastic. These containers can be handled when the food inside is hot with no risk of burning.

– tin foil which has good heat-transfer abilities but cannot be used for reheating in a microwave oven; also the lids cannot be fully sealed.

– plastic compounds which can withstand high temperatures. These containers usually seal tightly enough for the container to be reheated in boiling water.

– stainless steel and ceramic materials, which are durable and reusable, but may create storage and distribution problems. Stainless steel containers are not suitable for reheating in microwave ovens.

Multi-portion containers are usually made of strong plastic compounds, stainless steel or ceramic materials. Cardboard, plastic laminates, tin foil or other flexible or semi-rigid containers are not suitable because they cannot hold the weight of food – they usually only take up to ½ kg (1 lb).

Gastronorm containers are containers usually made of stainless steel to a standard international size, based on a module 530 × 325 × 50 mm. They usually hold about 3.5 kg (8 lb) of food. Various sizes based on this module are available. Many refrigerators, storage racks and trolleys are designed to take these containers.

A different container size of 530 × 220 × 50 mm, which holds about 2.3 kg (5½ lb) called *Euronorm* is used in some parts of Europe. At the moment, though, it is not compatible with most cook chill equipment in Britain.

When cook chill containers should be sealed

During chilling
Whether lids are kept on or off containers at this stage depends on the equipment. Ideally the lid should be on because otherwise the food may become dehydrated. But it is essential that chilling happens rapidly and as having the lid on slows down this process some equipment may not be able to cool the food fast enough. Check what your particular establishment does.

During storage and transport
Containers should always be sealed.

During reheating
Whether the lid is kept on or off for reheating is decided by the type of dish. For food that should have a crisp surface, for example, the lid should be left off.

---

8 COOK CHILL

Transport equipment

Trolleys and *mobile cabinets* are important pieces of equipment in cook chill catering, which often involves moving heavy, bulky food from one place to another for each stage of preparation. Large-scale chilling, storage and reheating equipment is usually designed to take trolley-loads of food. Trolleys should always be loaded so that there is enough space around the containers to allow the free flow of air. This is important to all the stages: chilling, storage and reheating.

Stacking baskets can give more choice over quantity and types of container than trolleys, since the number of baskets stacked on the mobile base can vary, and baskets are able to hold containers in a variety of shapes, if necessary.

✚ HYGIENE
Trolleys and baskets should be washed down regularly with a pressure hose.

Trolleys play an important role in helping to move large and heavy quantities of food quickly and with minimum handling.

▶▶▶ TO DO
Design a label giving the information you feel would be necessary on a food container delivered to a restaurant using a cook chill system.

The temperature probes and fans for circulating the nitrogen gas in this cryogenic chiller can clearly be seen. Note also the controls at the top: on the right a preprogrammed control panel with a choice of programmes (specific lengths of time for particular food items), on the left, a digital temperature display, and lights to indicate when the fan, power and gas injection are on, and an alarm that indicates the end of the cycle.

Chilling equipment

Only purpose-designed chilling equipment can take the temperature of cooked food down to safe levels fast enough.

Blast chillers or *air blast chillers* use rapidly moving cold air to chill the food evenly and rapidly. They are the most commonly used equipment at present and are available in a wide range of capacities. Chillers which take trolley loads of food are specially designed so that the cold air is channelled along the trolley's shelves and does not by-pass any of the food or disturb the food which might spoil its appearance. Some models have temperature probes so that the temperature of the chilling food can be checked without opening the door.

In *cryogenic batch chillers* liquid nitrogen at a temperature of -196°C (-321°F) is sprayed into a chilling cabinet containing the warm food. In the warmer temperature of the cabinet, the liquid nitrogen turns to super-cold gas absorbing a massive amount of heat as it does so. Fans move the cold gas over and around the food, and once the gas has become warm it is let out of the cabinet. The amount of liquid nitrogen fed into the cabinet is regulated automatically according to the amount of heat inside the cabinet. A temperature probe placed in the food inside the cabinet measures the drop in temperature, which is then shown on the outside of the equipment.

Some equipment uses carbon dioxide instead of nitrogen. A layer of partially frozen carbon dioxide (dry ice) is deposited on the food. As carbon dioxide is expensive this equipment is not used much in the catering industry.

In *water chilling equipment* the food is put into a sealed bag which is then placed in cold water. Water is four times more efficient as a chilling medium than cold gas or air.

Tunnel chillers or *roll-through chillers* use a conveyor belt system to move the food through the chilling equipment. By the time the food comes out it is chilled to the correct temperature.

Labelling

Labels must stick securely to the containers used and be easy to apply. Many cook chill caterers have automatic labelling equipment.

Colour coding is sometimes used to help identification, with particular coloured labels used, for example, to indicate different parts of a meal.

Combined equipment

In the most modern cook chill equipment, the food is handled by machines at every stage in the process: cooking, chilling and packaging.

Liquids, semi-liquids and small foods such as stews, pastas and rice, are cooked in a special kettle which has automatic stirrers and temperature control – often hundreds of litres are cooked at a time. The food is then pumped directly from the kettle into special plastic bags. These are sealed and loaded into a drum which is revolved in a bath of water kept just above freezing point. The drum is perforated to allow the water to flow between the tumbling containers of food.

In some systems, the food is vacuum-sealed into strong plastic bags which are then also heated. This is a form of pasteurisation that makes the food 'long-life' so that it will last quite some time longer than food prepared in ordinary cook chill systems.

Solid food is actually cooked by steaming in the sealed container (although it is sometimes browned first using conventional equipment if a rich colour is wanted, e.g. for meat). This process is described in detail in Book 1, Vacuum Cooking.

Chilled storage equipment

Special refrigerated cabinets or cold rooms are used for storing cook chill foods until they are reheated. Maintaining the temperature at under 3°C (37°F) is critical, so all equipment has a temperature monitor and some kinds have an alarm system to warn of any change in temperature.

Distribution

Refrigerated vans are used for long journeys between chilled storage and the reheating and service point. For shorter journeys (of two to three hours) insulated boxes are available which will keep the food at a low enough temperature. If the food is not being transported by road but is still being taken some distance, for example, within a large hospital, refrigerated trolleys should always be used.

Distribution problems

Perhaps the most serious overall problem in distributing cook chill food is the risk of delay. This can happen for all sorts of reasons – anything from delivery vans breaking down to key staff being absent at the arrival point.

To safeguard against this sort of difficulty, most cook chill catering companies have special procedures, for example:

– thorough maintenance of delivery vehicles (careful checking of fuel, oil, water, tyre pressure)

– carefully worked-out service schedules

– driver reporting in by radio or telephone if there are traffic delays, accidents, breakdown

– logging of staff at arrival point and strict reporting of absences

– checklists to ensure that trolleys are always available where they are needed at despatch and delivery points.

Reheating equipment

The choice of equipment depends on the quantity of food to be reheated.

Microwave ovens are suitable for reheating small amounts of food rapidly (*see* Microwave/Terms & Equipment).

Infra-red ovens are also suitable for small quantities of food and have the advantage that metal containers can be used. High-intensity infra-red heat is radiated from elements at the top and bottom of the oven, and in some models there is a fan to circulate the hot air.

Steamers are good for reheating bulk quantities.

Combi-ovens, which can be used with steam are also useful for large amounts of food.

There is also another type of cook chill reheating equipment that works on the same principle as forced-air convection ovens. The heating compartment is designed to take a trolley load of food, and fans at the back circulate heated air over the food so that it is all raised to a uniform temperature. Automatic thermostatic and timing controls make this process easy and efficient.

▶▶▶ TO DO

Obtain two examples of the same cook chill dish. Reheat each one using different types of equipment (for example a steamer and a microwave cooker) and appropriate containers. Compare the results – flavour, texture, smell, appearance, time taken, ease of operation.

Some establishments have *combined chilled storage/reheating equipment.* This is a trolley (or movable cabinet) that stores the food at the correct chilled temperature, and then, at the touch of a switch, turns into a heating compartment.

Some models are designed with a number of individually controlled compartments so that different types of food can be heated for different lengths of time. Cold air circulated from a compressor unit keeps the temperature of the food below 3°C (38°F). At the right time before service, the compartment containing food that needs the longest reheating time turns into a heating chamber. The compartment containing food needing a shorter reheating time remains chilled until a later stage. A third compartment with food items such as salads and sweets to be served cold, remains chilled. In this way a complete meal can be served to a customer with all the items reheated for the correct period and served at the right temperature.

Reheating equipment using forced air convection.

How long should food be chilled or reheated for?

Various factors affect how long food will take to chill and reheat:

1. the amount of food placed in the container
2. the shape and thickness of the container and what it is made of
3. whether the container is sealed or not
4. the density of the food and how fast it conducts heat.

Reheating times are always clearly stated on the labels on food packages or in workplace instructions and will take account of the type of reheating equipment to be used. For example a microwave oven will take less time than a reheating trolley, or forced air convection oven.

Here, to give an idea of the variations in chilling times between different foods, are some examples of how long it would take to chill them in a cryogenic chiller.

Under 15 minutes

Sliced roast meat
Cauliflower
Jam tart

16 to 45 minutes

Rice
Stew
Curry
Peas
Carrots

45 to 60 minutes

Spaghetti
Chicken portions
Cheese sauce
Rice pudding
Apple crumble

60 to 90 minutes

Mashed potato
Custard

Essential points

The steps in this section on portioning, labelling, chilling and storage will help you with the Caterbase module, *Cook Chilling*.

Preparation of foods for cooking

1. Ensure that the area of preparation is ready, and that the equipment needed is to hand and spotlessly clean.

The food preparation area should be separate from the cooking and portioning/packaging areas to avoid any possibility of cross contamination (germs on uncooked food being transferred to cooked food).

Equipment used for cook chill food preparation should be used solely for this purpose. Make sure that movable items that could come in useful in other areas, such as knives and chopping boards, are kept separate – a good way of identifying them is to use colour coding.

In addition, equipment used to prepare meat, poultry, fish, vegetables and fruit should all be kept separate and used only for that particular commodity.

Staff dealing with raw materials should not handle equipment or food in the cooking/packaging/chilling areas unless they have changed their uniform and washed their hands thoroughly.

2. The appropriate ingredients and foods should be collected together before preparation, whether they are fresh, frozen or dried.

See box for information about storage and preparation.

3. After preparation, foods should be kept refrigerated at below 10°C (50°F) until required in the cooking area.

Prepared foods must be stored separately in containers and refrigerators kept for each type of food. The period between preparation and cooking should be as short as possible so that loss of nutrients is kept to a minimum.

Cooking foods

1. The equipment used to cook the food should match the capacity of the chilling equipment, so that the food can pass easily from one stage to the next.

Delivery and storage

All raw materials must be checked on delivery to see that they meet the quality requirements specified by the establishment. These are likely to cover such aspects as grade (which will usually be the highest available), weight (a small margin either side of the requested overall weight or weight per item, for example per chicken, may be allowed), packaging (in good condition), fat content (usually the minimum), country of origin (to safeguard quality) and temperature on arrival, -18°C (4°F) for frozen foods.

Food which is of doubtful quality or condition should be returned to the supplier immediately.

Foods must be stored in areas especially set aside for them:
- fresh fish should be kept in a fish refrigerator at just above freezing point
- fresh meat should be kept apart from other chilled products at a temperature just above freezing
- fresh fruit and vegetables should be kept in a cool and well-ventilated area; high humidity is important for salad items, low humidity for most vegetables; many vegetables and fruits can be stored at temperatures just above freezing, but 4°-7°C (40°-45°F) is more suitable for apples and citrus fruit and just above 10°C (50°F) for tropical fruits, raspberries and strawberries, and for aubergines, peppers, tomatoes and cucumbers
- frozen foods should be kept frozen at below -22°C (-8°F) until required for use, when they should be defrosted, usually in their original containers, at temperatures between 4°-7°C (30-45°F).
- canned and dried foods must be kept in cool conditions.
- proper stock rotation must always be followed so that the first food delivered is the first to be used and 'Use by' dates kept to. Storage temperatures should be checked regularly.

2. It is important to select a method of cooking that will preserve the maximum nutritional value and produce the most acceptable flavour and textures in the final product.

The cooking process for any food must enable it to withstand the chilling process, prolonged storage and reheating without suffering in quality. Some processes are better than others, for example, plainly grilled food tends to work less well than shallow fried food served in a sauce; deep fried foods tend to become soggy, and the fat absorbed by the food develops 'off' flavours. If there is a choice between boiling and steaming green vegetables, choose steaming (a method more likely to preserve vitamins). Roasts require special care (*see* box).

3. Temperature probes should be used to check that the temperature at the centre of the food has reached the safety level before cooking is completed.

> Test food in more than one place. The temperature should be at 70°-75°C (158°-167°F) for at least four minutes to ensure thorough cooking.
>
> Temperature probes should be checked regularly to test that they are accurate, and sterilised before each use.

Portioning

1. The work area should be prepared so that it is ready for operation, with a supply of the correct containers to hand. The portioning area should ideally be separate from the cooking area and the room temperature not more than 10°C (50°F).

> The containers must be of the right depth and portion size and checked to ensure they are clean and undamaged. If stainless steel, ceramic or similar re-usable containers are being used, they must be sterilised before use.

> **Roasting for cook chill**
> It is usually recommended that cuts of meat are no more than 3 kg (6½ lb) in weight and poultry not more than 1.2 kg (2 lb 10 oz) – larger carcases should be cut into smaller pieces for cooking. This is because of the danger that a large piece of meat will cool down so slowly after cooking that bacteria could multiply, and the risk that when reheating takes place the centre of the meat does not get hot enough – another health hazard. A joint should be small enough to allow the centre to reach a safe temperature of 70-75°C (158-167°F) without drying out or burning on the outside.

2. Collect the pieces of equipment required for the task, ensuring that they are clean and sterile.

> These will include gloves (preferably disposable) of the correct size for the operator, and small equipment for portioning such as: knives, ladles, scoops, etc.

3. Portion the food into the containers following the establishment's requirements for weight and portion size.

> Handling of food at this stage should be kept to the absolute minimum to avoid contamination and damage to the appearance of the food.
>
> The portioning process should be completed as quickly as possible and should not take longer than 30 minutes for any product. This means that special attention must be paid to meats and poultry which need carving or slicing. Food that needs slicing is left for 10 minutes after cooking and covered with greaseproof paper. Slicing machines should be sterilised before use.

4. The containers must be filled evenly, and the food should be no more than 5 cm (2 in.) deep at any point.

5. If possible the edges of the containers should be kept free of food.

6. The containers should be covered (sealed if necessary) and placed aside ready for chilling. The temperature of the food must be checked and recorded at this point.

7. A sample of the food should be taken from each batch, labelled and appropriately stored.

> This sample is kept for at least two days after all the batch has been consumed (or discarded), so that if there is any complaint about the food, the catering establishment can analyse the sample.

Labelling

1. The containers must be labelled with information about: the contents, reheating instructions (which may be colour-coded), production date, and storage life/eat-by date.

2. The label should be firmly attached and in a position where it can be easily read during subsequent handling and storage.

⑧ COOK CHILL

Chilling

1. Chilling must start within 30 minutes of the food being cooked. The chiller should be clean, empty and at the correct temperature.

2. The food should be chilled to between 0° and 3°C (32°-37°F) within 90 minutes from start of chilling.

3. The temperature of the food should be checked with a sterilised temperature probe and recorded.

4. The time taken to chill the food should be recorded.

> It will depend on:
> – the size, shape and construction material of the container
> – the density of the food and its moisture content
> – how well the food conducts heat and can therefore lose its heat
> – the thickness of the container and how much food is in it
> – the temperature of the food when it is put in the chiller
> – whether the food is covered or not. Chilling with lids prevents the food drying out, but increases the chilling time by 10 to 15%. If this means that the chilling time would be longer than the permitted 90 minutes, the lid should be left off.

5. The containers must be correctly stacked so that the air can circulate all round them.

> The use of trolleys designed to take a specific range of containers will ensure correct stacking. Basket carriers, which can hold containers of a variety of shapes, need to be filled carefully so that air can circulate round them easily.

> **Monitoring chilling temperature with probes**
> In equipment with built-in probes it is possible to monitor the chilling and to stop the process once the correct temperature has been reached. The door of the chiller should not be opened until the process is complete.
>
> If you are using equipment without built-in probes, wait until the time by which the food should be chilled to the correct temperature and only then open the door to check the temperature with a sterilised probe. Allow to chill further if necessary.

6. Immediately after chilling is completed, the containers should be transported to the chilled store. The labels should still be firmly in place.

Storing

1. The food should be kept in a chilled storage compartment or cold room at 0°-3°C (32°-37°F).

> If for any reason the temperature should vary by up to 2°C either side of this band and the situation is promptly spotted and corrected straight away, then this is just about acceptable. But this kind of variation should not happen more than twice in the period before reheating. If the temperature rises above 5°C (41°F), but remains below 10°C (50°F), the food must be consumed within 12 hours. If any other temperature variations occur, the food must be discarded.

2. The containers (covered or sealed, as appropriate) should be stored so that air can circulate.

> Containers kept chilled in a cold room should be above floor level and away from the door, to keep them out of draughts which might cause temperature variation.

3. Stock rotation procedures must be maintained, with appropriate records. Food that has been stored longest should be used first on a first-in, first-out principle.

4. Chilled storage facilities should not be used for storing other food items.

5. No foods should be stored beyond the date of expiry (which will be no longer than five days from the day of cooking).

> Foods which have passed the date of expiry should be destroyed.

Distribution

This information is essential for the Caterbase module, *Distributing Cook Chill Foods*.

1. The correct temperature should be maintained at all times during transportation.

> This temperature should be the same as for storage (a similar tolerance is usually allowed).

2. Handling times – when transferring the food from storage to the transporting vehicle or to insulated boxes, or from the vehicle or boxes to the final storage area and/or reheating point – should be kept as short as possible.

> The distribution of chilled foods is the most difficult part of the process to control effectively in terms of temperature fluctuations. If during this stage the food is exposed to room or outdoor temperatures for more than ten minutes, its temperature must be checked and recorded. Any deviation from the 0°-3°F (32°-37°F) range should be dealt with as described in step 1 of *Storing*.

3. The temperatures of the food should be checked and recorded before and during transportation, and immediately on arrival at the distribution point. Any variations should be reported.

4. The loading of the containers should be planned so that if several deliveries are being made during the journey, the first containers to be delivered are the easiest to get at.

> Careful checks must be made to ensure the correct order is being despatched – the right food, the required number of portions and that the destination of the consignment is clearly marked.

5. Containers with damaged packaging, or which do not look clean, or which have the wrong date or contents should not be used but noted, kept to one side and reported.

6. Documentation should be completed correctly, including any delivery notes.

7. On arrival the containers should be transferred to a chilled holding cabinet if they are not going to be reheated immediately.

Reheating or regenerating
The information in this section is essential for the Caterbase module, *Regenerating Cook Freeze or Cook Chill Foods*.

1. Ensure that the reheating equipment is absolutely clean and is working correctly – check thermostats, pressure and timing controls. Any other equipment for serving the food should be assembled and ready for use.

2. The food to be reheated should be checked to ensure it is the right type, quality and quantity and that it has not reached the end of its storage life. Remove the lid for certain foods: follow the instructions on the label. Moist food is heated with the lid on so that it does not dry out, food which should have a crisp surface is re-heated with the lid off.

3. The equipment being used for reheating should be prepared for use.

> Ovens should be pre-heated to the temperature required (stated on the container label or in standard establishment instructions).

4. Place the food without delay in the reheating oven for the stated time.

> Microwave cookers and steamers will have to be set to the required temperature/pressure.

5. Ensure that the internal temperature of the food is reheated to at least 70°C (158°F), or preferably to 75°C (167°F). Use a sterilised probe to check that this temperature has been reached.

> Some containers will become very hot to the touch after this reheating, so insulated gloves or some other protection should be used when handling them.
>   The reheating process should be as short as possible, lasting no longer than 30 minutes. It should take place as soon as possible after the food has been removed from chilled storage and certainly no more than two hours later. (If this period is exceeded the food should be destroyed.)
>   If the food has to be portioned further or plated after reheating this process should be as quick as possible otherwise the taste and nutritional value will be badly affected.

6. The reheated food should be eaten as soon as possible.

> If there is any delay at this final stage in the system, all the benefits of the cook chill method will be undone. One of the main aims of this system is to avoid food being kept warm for prolonged periods.
>   Food which is not eaten shortly after reheating should be destroyed. It should never be re-chilled, frozen or reheated again.

8 COOK CHILL

What went wrong

Food has not been put in the chiller within 30 minutes of being cooked.

1. Portioning took too long.
2. The right equipment was not available.
3. The chiller was in use.
4. Too much food was cooked in relation to the capacity of the chiller.
5. Not enough staff were available to portion the food.

There will be reporting and control systems and procedures to avoid problems like this: get to know them and follow them.

At the end of its chilling time the food has not reached 3°C (38°F).

1. Food may have been packed too deep in the containers – some foods will not chill even if they are less than 5 cm (2 in.) thick.
2. A lid may have been put on when it should not have been.
3. Although you are unlikely to come across this, there could have been a malfunction in the equipment.

Supervisors should be informed at once. If the chilling time was less than 90 minutes, then the food can probably be given some more time in the chiller. But if it has already been in the chiller for 90 minutes then the food will have to be discarded.

Food in the chilled storage area is uncovered.

This should never happen. If lids are not used when food is chilled, there should still be a supply of lids/coverings available when the food is removed from the chiller and transferred to the storage area.

Food which has passed its 'eat by' date is found (for example in the chilled storage area or on delivery).

The control system has not been followed carefully.
Food which has not been used on the fifth day after it was cooked should have been discarded and a record kept so that it could not be used.

Temperature of food rises above 3°C (38°F) during transportation.

1. The journey has taken too long.
2. The refrigerated van/trolley was not working correctly.
3. The insulated box (if used) was not pre-cooled or its lid was not properly fitted.

Whatever the cause proper reports must be completed and your supervisors should be told what has happened. If the temperature has not risen above 10°C (50°F), and the food is going to be served within 12 hours, then the problem is not disastrous and your supervisor might allow the food through. Outside these limits it should always be discarded.

Food is overcooked after reheating.

1. Heating has lasted too long.
2. Temperature was too high.
3. The equipment is out of condition and uneven heat distribution has caused hot spots.

Food does not reach 70°C (158°F) within the 30 minutes allowed for reheating.

1. Reheating instructions have not been followed properly.
2. The label information was incorrect.
3. The lid should have been taken off and was left on.
4. Equipment malfunction. This is unlikely, but if you suspect a problem, report it immediately.

Whatever the reason for the food not getting hot enough it will be unsafe and so must be thrown away.

Containers are damaged.

1. Mishandling during transport or washing up (this can even apply to stainless steel containers).
2. Tin foil containers easily get bent or split if they are stacked rather than distributed in a basket system.
3. Lids that are not attached to equipment easily get lost.
4. Identification labels can be difficult to remove if the glue is not water soluble.
5. Labels can go missing or become illegible through damage during handling or some operational fault – all unidentifiable containers of food must be destroyed.

Tips

To check that temperature probes are working properly, dip them into boiling water. They should record 100°C (212°F).

If food has been chilled without a cover, it should always be covered immediately after chilling to prevent it drying out during storage.

To chill liquid products in a blast chiller or a cryogenic chiller, place the liquid into special plastic bags, then seal the bags and lay them flat on the shelves. These should be relatively small amounts as large volumes of liquid cannot be chilled to the required temperature within 90 minutes.

In this cook chill production unit, staff working in the portioning and chilling area wear grey coats and trousers. Staff in the food preparation area wear traditional white uniforms with blue hats. This makes it immediately apparent to supervisors if a member of staff is in the wrong area.

Personal hygiene

The highest standards of personal hygiene are essential whenever food is being handled. Cook chill systems demand extra precautions:

- working clothes should be changed daily and never worn outside the kitchen area
- working clothes should also be changed when moving from raw food preparation areas to cooking/portioning and packaging areas
- working shoes should be clean, safe and comfortable and never worn outside the kitchen
- disposable gloves should be worn when portioning and packaging food
- regular medical screening for all staff is advisable.

✚ HYGIENE

The *Guidelines on Pre-Cooked Chilled Foods*, published in 1980 by the Department of Health and Social Security, form the basis of most cook chill systems. The Caterbase performance criteria and information in this book are based closely on the *Guidelines* (available from HMSO, 51 Nine Elms Lane, London SW8).

▶▶▶ TO DO

The driver of a cook chill vehicle does a job which, if it is done badly, can undermine the whole cook chill system and ruin the food or even make it unsafe. Make a list of the problems the driver might have to deal with and say how these could have been avoided.

TEST YOURSELF

1. Name two advantages and two disadvantages of a cook chill system in comparison to a conventional kitchen?

2. What is the temperature food should reach or be held at in a cook chill system during:
a) initial cooking
b) chilling
c) storage
d) transportation
e) reheating or regeneration.

3. Briefly describe the meaning of cross contamination. Name one way in which it can be avoided in preparing foods for cooking.

4. What is the maximum permitted depth of food in a container or tray to be chilled within 90 minutes?

5. How quickly should cook chilled food be used after initial cooking?

6. Name one piece of equipment in each case which might be used for the initial cooking of:
a) soup
b) poached fish
c) fish in batter
d) roast chicken
e) green beans
f) fruit flan.

7. Is it safe to eat cook chill food if it has reached a temperature of 5° C during distribution? Give two reasons why or why not.

 City and Guilds

9 COOK FREEZE

Frozen food is now generally accepted as part of modern living. Many homes have a freezer and an increasing number now also have a micro-wave cooker. With this equipment families can enjoy a meal of good quality after only a few minutes of preparation and within a short time of deciding to eat. Frozen food is widely available and is a useful convenience food, with only a little effort required before it is ready to be eaten.

If frozen food is home-prepared, the initial preparation and cooking may have been done days or several weeks in advance, when there were fresh ingredients to hand and time to prepare them. Alternatively the frozen pack of prepared food may have been bought from a super-market or specialist frozen food shop.

Food items that have been carefully prepared and deep frozen so that they can then be served on demand have many advantages for the caterer supplying food to a wide range of customers, as well as for the customers eating the food (*see* box on opposite page).

How freezing was discovered
As long ago as 1100 BC the Chinese built ice houses to store foods during warm weather, using blocks of ice cut from frozen lakes during winter months. During the 17th and 18th centuries, the same technique was used in Europe: many grand houses had an ice house in their grounds. Large-scale freezing of meat was started as early as 1880, but the American Clarence Birdseye, often thought of as the father of deep freezing, built his first automatic quick-freezing machine in 1924. While living in Labrador between 1912 and 1916 he had noticed that at temperatures of -45°C (-50°F) fish froze as soon as it was caught, and he then started experimenting with fish, seal, caribou meat and even a special shipment of cabbages that he had sent out to him.

Frozen food production systems are operated by large-scale operators like hospitals, the school meals services, industrial catering (whether it is feeding the employees of a factory or providing meals for head office) and the Services, e.g. at depots for the Army, Air Force or Navy. There are also specialised caterers who supply in-flight meals to airlines, and those that deliver to hotel and restaurant chains. It is quite possible to produce an entire meal of several courses, from the starter to the sweet, from frozen foods. Alternatively only the main course might be frozen, or the vegetables or the sweet. Each establishment can decide what use it will make of frozen foods in its operation either by buying in from specialist supply firms, or by setting up a cook freeze operation in its own premises, although these systems are expensive to install and the running costs can also be very high.

▶▶▶ TO DO

Look at the deep-freeze cabinets at your local supermarket and make a list of the pre-cooked frozen foods suited for a main course, with their weight and portion size. Note your comments on how the portion size and cost would suit either a building labourer or an elderly administrative clerk.

Special advantages of cook freeze

1. The preparation and cooking stages can be separated from the peaks and troughs of demand and the frenzied activity that often leads up to meal service periods. This should produce better quality food and service for customers.

2. Food can be produced on a larger scale than would otherwise be required for immediate consumption. Batches of similar items needed for several meal services in the coming weeks can be prepared and cooked at the same time, making the best use of the capacity of equipment. Costs can often be reduced as a result, with benefit to customers.

3. The choice of dishes available to customers does not have to depend on seasonal availability or suffer from the delivery problems of producers or markets.

4. Food can be bought in season when it is at its best and relatively cheap.

5. If the methods of buying and taking delivery of fresh food are organised efficiently, there should be very little delay between arrival and cooking, so nutritional value will be protected and eating quality improved.

6. Food wastage at the point of service can be reduced, because only the food that customers actually choose needs to be reheated. As a result, greater variety can be offered.

7. There is no need to keep food warm over an extended period of meal service, which can cause a deterioration in quality and nutritional value (and increase the risk of food poisoning).

8. It is easier to provide for special diets and eating requirements, as there is no need to rely on the availability of the necessary fresh ingredients at the time of demand.

9. Control systems can be more precise with accurate portion and stock control and good quality control. This means savings to the caterer and lower costs to customers.

10. Providing the recipes used and the cooking and reheating equipment and procedures are appropriate to the foods being processed, the taste, appearance, colour and nutritional value of the finished product should be as good as it would be if freshly cooked.

9 COOK FREEZE

What happens

Cook freeze is a specialised food production and distribution system that allows caterers to take advantage of the longer life that the freezing process and low temperature storage can give cooked foods before they are served to customers.

The system has eight separate stages:

1. The best quality raw foods are purchased, often in bulk. Delivery should happen as close to the scheduled preparation time as possible to avoid any deterioration. Storage should always be in the correct conditions of temperature and humidity.

2. The food is prepared in the same way as in conventional catering kitchens, except that the preparation area is usually quite separate from the cooking areas. Because the quantities of food are usually very large, mechanised peeling, chopping and slicing equipment is often used. Special attention is paid to good hygiene practices, for example separate sets of equipment are always used for different foods.

3. Cooking is done in batches using large-scale conventional equipment or the food is fed through to a special cooking chamber on a conveyor belt. Each dish is usually prepared in large quantities. Certain recipes have to be specially adapted so that they are not spoilt by the freezing process.

4. The food is then quickly portioned and packaged in suitable containers. Guidelines published by the Department of Health and Social Security state that this stage should take no longer than 15 minutes. (The exception is cooked meat which has to be sliced, when a longer period is acceptable – *see* Method pages for details.)

5. The cooked food is then frozen in special fast freezers. This process should be as fast as possible, but it should never take longer than 90 minutes for the temperature of the food to drop to at least -5°C (23°F). It should then drop again to -18°C (0°F).

6. Next, the food is stored in freezers at between -20°C and -30°C (-4°F and -22°F) but never above -18°C (0°F), as recommended in DHSS guidelines. Most food can be stored in this way for about two to six months. If it is kept for longer than this, the nutritional content may be seriously affected. Also, foods with a high fat content tend to go rancid, which makes them smell and taste unpleasant (*see* Food Selection section). On the other hand, there are certain foods that will keep satisfactorily for much longer periods.

7. The food is then distributed in its solid, frozen state under temperature-controlled conditions.

8. At the service point or adjacent kitchen, the food is then regenerated (or reheated) for service to customers. This reheating may either be done from frozen or, as in some systems, the food is thawed first (under carefully controlled conditions). The regeneration stage should happen as fast as possible.

How freezing stops food spoiling

The processes that cause food to spoil or deteriorate are linked to temperature, exposure to air (which can result in oxidisation) or exposure to moisture (which is often present in the air surrounding food). Freezing makes food last longer by stopping or at least slowing down the processes, and the lower the temperature, the more effective this is.

Freezer damage

The structure of the food can be quite badly damaged during the critical period when the ice crystals are forming. The thing to remember is that the slower the freezing, the more damage is likely to happen. This is why fast freezers should be used. Storage freezers (and home freezers) take much longer to do the job and so are not as good.

But not all goods respond well to freezing – it can cause permanent changes in flavour, texture and colour. Bananas, for example, go black and mushy.

Formation of ice crystals during freezing
Pure water freezes as a solid mass of ice, but in food tissue, the water usually has substances like salts, sugars and acids dissolved in it, which gives it a lower freezing point. What actually happens when the temperature drops is that freezing draws the water out of cells to form ice crystals. This means that the liquid inside the cells gets more and more concentrated and so its freezing point gets lower and lower. Because this concentration goes on changing, the freezing point of a particular food is not one specific temperature but happens over a quite wide temperature range.

If freezing takes a long time, the cells lose almost all their liquid, and when the food is defrosted most of this liquid will not go back into the cells and will leak out as 'drip'. The pool of liquid that surrounds a joint of meat that has been frozen in an ordinary home freezer and then defrosted is, in fact, liquid that used to be contained within the cells of the meat. This means that only a little liquid is left in the cells, and when the meat is cooked it tends to be rather dry and stringy compared with a fast frozen joint. Very fast freezing makes ice crystals form inside the cells as well as between them, so the cells get much less dried out.

Three stages in the growth of ice crystals in food during slow freezing are shown in the diagrams below.

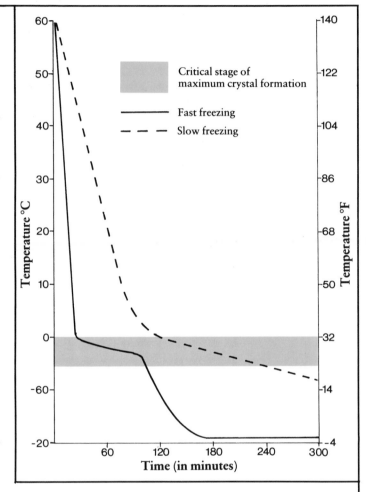

The temperature of the food drops steadily as it is cooled, until the freezing process begins. Once this happens and the liquid begins to turn to ice, most of the energy is being used to bring about this change (from liquid to ice) and so the temperature takes longer to drop from 0° to -5°C (32° to 23°F). At this point most of the water in the food will have turned to ice crystals. The temperature then drops faster again.

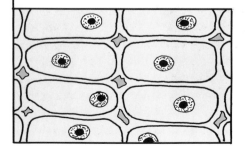
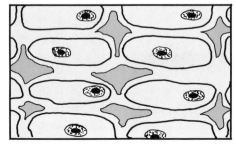
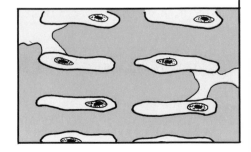

How freezing affects different foods

Fruit

When fruit or vegetables turn brown, it is because of the action of enzymes. Apart from causing discoloration, the processes they set off also gradually destroy the nutritional value of the fruit. Refrigeration usually slows them down a little, and freezing will slow them even further but not stop them completely. For best results the fruit should be either blanched or completely cooked (which will stop almost all the enzyme processes before freezing).

The freezing process also has a softening effect on the texture of the fruit. So it is fine for fruit which is enjoyed soft (and often cooked partly for this reason) like cooking apples, under-ripe pears and apricots. It is not suitable for fruit that should remain firm, for example grapes or strawberries that are to be used to decorate a frozen gâteau – they will just collapse in a mushy heap when defrosted.

For fruit that is at its best uncooked, like grapes, the enzyme action can be slowed down (before freezing) by adding ascorbic acid (a manufactured product) or by submerging the fruit in syrup so that air cannot get at it.

Meat, poultry and fish

Freezing does not stop the enzyme activity in meat, poultry or fish that makes the fat present in the flesh go rancid. When the fat contains a lot of unsaturated fatty acids, as it does in pork, poultry and fish, this effect is particularly bad. Excluding as much air as possible, for example by covering the food in a sauce or gravy, can help, but pork, poultry and fish should never be stored frozen for more than 2 or 3 months. Always trim off as much fat as possible and use only a minimum of fat in cooking when preparing food for freezing.

Cooked meat, poultry and fish which have already changed from their raw state during cooking, are not significantly affected by freezing. Raw meat, on the other hand, is easily damaged and may well, as a result, lose fluid when it is defrosted. When it is cooked it will tend to be drier and tougher than fresh meat would be.

▶▶▶ TO DO

Imagine yourself in the position of having to recommend cook freeze products to the catering manager of a North Sea oil rig. Write down the advantages you would claim for them and discuss these with your colleagues.

Vegetables

As with fruit, many vegetables that are deep frozen will gradually deteriorate in colour, flavour and nutritional value unless they are blanched (briefly steamed or boiled) first.

Again like fruit, the texture of vegetables suffers a certain amount in freezing, but as many vegetables are enjoyed soft (as when they are cooked) this is no great problem. The vegetables that are not suitable for freezing are the ones that are usually preferred raw – and crisp – like lettuce, cucumbers or radish.

Frozen storage and quality

Three conditions are important to maintain the quality of food during frozen storage:

1. Temperatures should be at least -18°C and preferably as low as -30°C (0°F to -22°F). The lower the temperature, the less chance food spoilage organisms have.

2. Storage temperature must be kept as constant as possible. Even a few degrees' increase in temperature may cause some of the ice crystals in the food to melt. As the temperature drops again this liquid will refreeze, usually with bigger, more damaging crystals.

3. Food must be properly covered to prevent it losing moisture. Serious moisture loss causes freezer burn, and the food surface discolours (dark spots form on fresh meat, grey areas appear on cooked meat).

A second reason for keeping food covered is to protect it from frost. If warm air containing moisture enters the freezer, for example, when the door is opened, once the door is shut again the air will quickly cool and no longer be able to hold so much moisture. The moisture will then form frost on exposed food and food packaging.

Freezing food demands as much care and understanding as any other method of preparation to ensure that the benefits of the process are not outweighed by the extensive damage that can be caused by poor practices. And even if the freezing process itself is carried out properly, inefficiency at the preparation and cooking stages, or when the food is reheated, can spoil the food or even make it dangerous, so destroying all the benefits of the cook freeze system.

Many foods are suitable for use in cook freeze systems but as there is often a slight loss of flavour or texture during freezing it is important to start off with the best quality ingredients. Correct preparation (including some special cooking techniques) and packing are also essential. Some foods should be avoided because they respond badly to freezing.

Meat

The tendency for fat in meat to oxidise and go rancid, even in frozen storage, means that lean meat is better than fatty meat for freezing. In any case, unnecessary fat should always be trimmed off before cooking.

Chicken fat contains a natural antioxidant so it is less likely to go rancid than other types of poultry.

Only good-quality pork, smoked or cured ham, sausages and bacon should be considered for cook freeze and storage life should be kept to a minimum (exactly how long depends both on the quality of the food and on the speed of freezing).

Meats change colour during frozen storage and will eventually turn a brownish grey.

Fresh meat must always be used for cook freeze dishes. Never use meat that has previously been frozen. This is because each time meat is thawed, even in cool conditions, there is a chance for food-poisoning bacteria to multiply.

Rice and pasta

Rice and pasta should be slightly undercooked before freezing, so that they do not overcook during reheating.

Fish

Some loss of the delicate flavour of fish is inevitable in freezing, and any surfaces left exposed can suffer from oxidisation which produces a rancid taste. So a good way to use fish as a cook freeze product is to coat it in some way, for example, with a covering of breadcrumbs or batter (in which it will have been deep fried or shallow fried) or in a sauce (after it has been poached). Batter recipes have to be modified so that the batter does not peel off as a result of freezing, and special sauce recipes need to be used, so that the sauce does not separate.

No fish dish should be stored for more than eight weeks, otherwise the fish itself or another ingredient, for example, the batter on a deep-fried item will deteriorate through oxidisation.

Some meat and fish suitable for cook freeze production:
1) Crab 2) King prawns 3) Délice of lemon sole 4) Paupiette of lemon sole 5) Suprêmes of cod 6) Lobster 7) Diced stewing beef 8) Thick flank of beef 9) Diced lamb's kidneys 10) Diced stewing veal 11) Carbonnades of beef 12) Trimmed noisettes of lamb 13) Strips of fillet of beef 14) Médaillons of fillet of beef 15) Diced fillet of pork 16) Diced venison 17) Chicken wings, drumstick, thigh and breast 18) Suprême of duck.

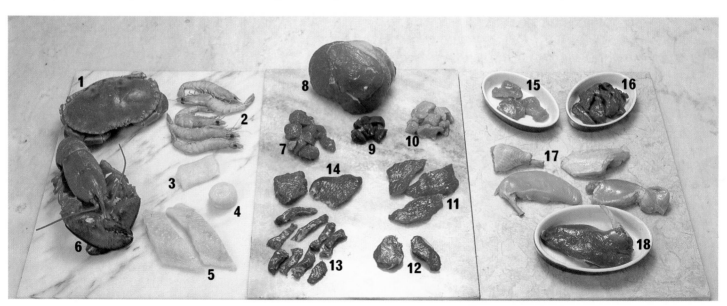

Vegetables

Unless a cook freeze unit is able to purchase vegetables direct from a farm and freeze them within a few hours of harvesting, the quality of produce cannot be relied on, and it is better to buy commercially frozen products.

If it is possible to purchase absolutely fresh vegetables for freezing at the cook freeze unit, the following points should be kept in mind:

- Any bruising which has occurred during harvesting or processing will cause a 'hay-like' taste to develop.

- Blanching time should be just long enough to stop the enzymes from creating acid flavours later, but not so long as to fully cook the vegetable. Blanching in a high-pressure steamer rather than in boiling water reduces Vitamin C loss. Also, with the large quantities likely to be processed in cook freeze systems, if water is used it will be in such volume that it will take a considerable time to return to the boil.

- If sprouts are not blanched sufficiently they will turn pink in the middle.

- The colour of peas, beans and spinach, whether frozen on the premises or bought in, will fade if they are stored for lengthy periods.

- Cauliflower will turn first yellow then brown.

- Not many salads can be frozen but those made with carrots or beetroot are satisfactory. Salad cream (using a modified starch), lemon or orange juice dressings can be used, but mayonnaise separates.

- All types of cooked potato can be frozen satisfactorily. Chipped, sauté and roast potatoes need to be partly cooked to a pale colour in fat before freezing, and will later be browned and reheated in deep fat or in an oven. Mashed potato also freezes well, particularly if it is prepared as croquettes or piped spirals which are later reheated by deep frying or baking. As creamed potato is very dense, it should not be packed with a level surface but should have a dip made in the middle.

Fruit

The texture of fruit softens as a result of freezing, so only fruits and dishes where this is not a disadvantage are appropriate. The cut surfaces of raw fruit such as apples and peaches, which might be used in salads or flans, tend to go brown but this can be prevented by freezing them in acidulated liquid or a syrup.

Eggs

Hard or soft boiled eggs are difficult to freeze successfully because the soft egg yolk changes into a stiff paste when frozen and the white ends up rubbery. Scrambled eggs can be frozen. Baked egg custards tend to separate, but if great care is taken they can be frozen satisfactorily.

Recipe modifications

Sauce, batters, thickened soups, stews and gravies will break down (or separate) unless the flour used in the recipe contains waxy starch. Wheat flour is not suitable, but waxy rice, waxy maize and tapioca starches are suitable. Wheat flour can sometimes be used if it is blended with a suitable starch.

Modified starches which do not separate, such as Col-flo and Purity 69, are produced commercially for use in cook-freeze recipes.

For thick sauces, eggs can be used as well as the thickening agent.

Jellies and other gelatin mixtures are unsuitable because they become granular in the cook freeze process, unless the mixture is stabilised. Reconstituted dried milk, condensed milk or stiffly beaten evaporated milk in fruit jellies and salad cream in savoury jellies can be used to stabilise the mixture, although they will also, of course, change the flavour and appearance.

Standard recipes and standard production procedures are usually worked out and followed in a cook freeze establishment to ensure consistent quality and portion size and to take account of the modifications needed for recipes used in the process.

The extent of 'drip' and texture loss depends on the water content of the food. Strawberries, like tomatoes, have a high water content and a fragile structure. They tend to get damaged easily during freezing and lose a great deal of liquid when defrosted.

9 COOK FREEZE

Terms

Cook freeze is a system of prolonging the life of prepared and cooked food by rapid freezing, storage at very low temperatures and regenerating (reheating) at the time of service.

Batch production or *batch cooking* is used when the quantities of a particular food to be cooked are larger than it is possible to cook in one go, or too large to be frozen at one time. The food is split into small amounts or batches which are then cooked and frozen one after another, each load matching the capacity of the freezer.

In *continuous cookers*, the food is fed through a cooking zone (often on a conveyor belt) at a controlled rate and pre-set temperature, and then travels on to the portioning and packaging equipment. Eventually it is transported (again, often on a conveyor belt) to be frozen. Continuous cookers are available for all the basic cooking processes: boiling, steaming, roasting, grilling, shallow and deep frying. This method of cooking is called *flow cooking* or *flow production*.

Blast freezing is often used to refer in general to fast freezing, but its name actually describes one particular method: the use of high speed cold air to reduce the temperature quickly.

Thawing or *defrosting* food involves raising the temperature, usually very slowly in a cool place, until the food has returned to its pre-frozen state.

Cooking equipment

In a cook freeze production system, the preparation and cooking methods, and to some extent the equipment, are adapted from the working methods and equipment used in conventional kitchens.

A cook freeze kitchen should be planned so that there is a clear flow from raw preparation, through cooking, to the packing and freezing areas. How and where the food is to be stored and then made ready for delivery are aspects that also need to be given consideration. A good system of quality control is also very important.

To ensure a top-quality result and to minimise the risk of harmful bacteria remaining in the frozen product, the time between cooking and freezing must be kept as short as possible. For these reasons, cooking is either by batch production or flow production.

Both systems allow small quantities to be cooked fast with rapid heat penetration and far less stirring than would be needed for a great mass of food.

Drip is the fluid that is drawn out of the food's cells during the freezing process. Because it cannot all be reabsorbed, some 'drips' out when the food is thawed.

Recrystallisation (or the reformation of crystals) occurs in thawing before the ice melts completely. The smaller ice crystals melt first. Some of the water that has been released from them attaches to the bigger crystals (which are still frozen) and re-freezes, making the crystals even larger. Recrystallisation, which happens especially easily during uneven thawing, will damage the food cells' ability to store fluids. Fluctuating storage temperatures can have the same effect.

Instability. If certain foods are referred to as 'unstable' this means that they have a tendency to break down or separate during the cook freeze process.

Regeneration is returning food to as near its pre-frozen state as possible by thawing and, if necessary, reheating. Many of the changes caused by freezing are reversed in the reheating, although some cannot be. Slow freezing or thawing, poor storage and the use of ingredients which break down irreversibly in freezing are among changes for the worse.

Reconstitution is another word for the regeneration of frozen food.

Continuous cookers

Roasting machines rotate the food inside the oven, ensuring that it browns all over. The meat baskets are located above each other, so drips from the top joint fall on to the one below, and so on.

Sauce-making machines use automatic stirrers and scrapers and can also be used for stewing.

Boiling pans also use automatic stirrers, which are available in various designs to stir soup, mash potatoes, etc.

Steamers are available in both atmospheric pressure and high-pressure versions with inlet and outlet chambers to seal off the main pressure chamber.

Automatic boilers move the food in wire mesh containers through a bath of boiling water.

Grills have layers of heating elements between which the food travels. The food is turned over automatically so that it cooks evenly on both sides.

Shallow fryers carry the food over the frying surface which is coated in a thin layer of oil.

Deep fat fryers work like automatic boilers but the bath contains hot oil instead of boiling water.

Packaging

The size of the containers used to store and regenerate the food, and possibly to serve it in, is a very important consideration because of the effect it can have on the rest of the operation.

Containers must protect food against oxidisation during storage and allow it to be both cooled and heated quickly. They must be watertight, non-tainting (not give off or react with the food to produce a bad taste) and easily disposable, or re-usable. Lids must fit tightly or be machine sealable, so that no moisture is lost and the risk of microbiological contamination is virtually eliminated.

Containers come in a variety of materials including plastic compounds, tin or aluminium and cardboard plastic laminates. They are usually available as:
– single portion packs
– complete meal packs
– bulk packs, when serving up takes place in a finishing kitchen near the point of service.

The choice of container will affect:
– *The quality of the food*. Freezing time is affected by the depth of the food, so bulk packs, where the food is relatively deep, may not survive the freezing process as well as single portion packs. Bulk packs are also liable to overheat during regeneration, with drying out, possibly burning and discoloration at the edges occurring. They also rely on the ability of serving staff to present the food attractively and to portion it accurately. Regeneration instructions can be complex if complete meal packs contain different food items that should in theory have different lengths of reheating time. If the food is grilled, baked or fried, and it needs crisping up during reheating, it is easier to do this with single portion packs.
– *Menu choice*. Single packs provide the greatest flexibility.
– *Food value*. The over-heating of some items in complete meal packs and the edges of bulk packs will, if it occurs, damage the nutritional value.
– *The handling time*. After cooking, bulk packs are the quickest and easiest to fill whereas complete packs are the most complex. On the other hand bulk packs have to be portioned at the service point and this stage can take more than twice as long as for single packs.
– *Storage space*. Bulk packs make the best use of space.

Advantages and disadvantages of cook freeze and cook chill systems
The running costs of a cook freeze system are higher than they are for a cook chill system. More energy is consumed in the freezing process, in the longer period of storage at lower temperatures, during transportation and in the regeneration through a greater temperature range.

These higher costs are one reason why cook freeze systems in Britain are no longer as popular as they used to be. Cook chill systems are seen as providing a wider choice of menu items, with far fewer problems regarding food stability (for example, the separation or breaking down of sauces).

Perhaps the most important factor in the financial success of either a cook freeze or a cook chill system is making full use of the capacity of the equipment. A conventional kitchen, which costs a few thousand pounds to equip, can run at half capacity, probably with fewer staff, and still keep going. But a cook freeze production system, which costs hundreds of thousands of pounds, has to operate at almost maximum capacity to be cost-effective.

▸▸▸ TO DO

Draw up a rough layout plan of a small cook freeze unit capable of producing around 300 meals a day. Show on your plan what equipment would be required. (You will need to refer to the Terms & Equipment sections in this module and in Cook Chill.) Use arrows to show the flow of goods from the delivery of raw food through all the stages to frozen storage.

Freezing equipment

Ordinary storage or domestic freezers cannot lower the temperature of food fast enough for the cook freeze process, so specialist equipment has to be used.

Air blast freezers or *blast freezers* take 75 to 90 minutes to freeze food depending on how it is packaged. Very cold air – between -32° and -40°C (-26° and -40°F) – is blown by powerful fans over and around the food. The warmed air is constantly drawn out and recirculated through the heat exchange unit to lower its temperature.

In the larger models of freezer the food is pushed in on a trolley at one end and the trolley is then wheeled out at the other. The largest models of all take the food automatically through a kind of freezing tunnel.

Cryogenic freezers are the fastest. Most models use liquid nitrogen and a typical freezing time is 25 minutes for uncovered food; food covered by lids takes a little longer. Liquid nitrogen at -196°C (-321°F) is sprayed through special nozzles into the freezing chamber. Fans circulate the cold nitrogen so that the food freezes evenly. The nitrogen absorbs heat from the food until the food freezes, and the warmed gas is pumped out of the cabinet as more cold nitrogen is fed in.

A few freezers use liquid carbon dioxide but this tends to be more expensive than nitrogen. Freezing time is longer, typically around 45 minutes.

The gas for these systems, whether nitrogen or carbon dioxide, has to be delivered by tanker to a special storage tank outside but as near as possible to the kitchen. The pipes that feed the gas into the tank and freezer and the tank itself are vacuum-insulated in much the same way as a thermos flask.

Unlike air-blast freezers, cryogenic equipment does not have to be defrosted.

Plate freezers and *tunnel freezers* are more likely to be used in commercial frozen food factories than in cook freeze catering centres. The plate system is used to freeze meat, fish and fragile vegetables such as spinach and asparagus. The food (usually wrapped) is held between hollow plates through which a special refrigerating liquid is circulated.

In tunnel systems, whole vegetables such as peas and sliced vegetables like carrots toss on a conveyor belt over jets of very cold air, which freezes them rapidly and keeps them moving so that they do not stick together.

Storage equipment

The main production unit and often the finishing kitchens or distribution units have deep freezers or freezer rooms where the food is stored once it has been frozen. These must be able to keep the temperature in a range from -20° to -30°C (-4° to -22°F). The DHSS Guidelines on freezing say that the highest the temperature should ever get is -18°C (0°F). It is also very important that the equipment is powerful enough to keep the temperature at this level, even if the doors are opened (when packages are removed or delivered, for example). To make doubly sure that the temperature stays constant, a machine is often used which forms a curtain of cold air in front of the door every time it is opened. If the temperature does vary at all, both the texture and taste of the food will be spoiled.

Most cold stores have stand-by refrigerating equipment for use when there is a breakdown or maintenance has to be carried out on the main equipment.

⚠ SAFETY

Doors in cold stores have escape handles which can be operated from inside in case they close accidentally. A warming element on the lock prevents it freezing shut.

Small, reach-in blast freezers are available with a 20-30 kg (44-66 lb) capacity. These are not suitable for continuous use, because they have to be regularly defrosted to ensure efficient rates of freezing.

Nitrogen makes up about 80% of the air we breathe. It is neutral, has no smell and is inert.

Transport

Frozen packaged food has to be delivered to finishing kitchens at the same temperature as it was held at in storage. For short distances insulated containers are sometimes used. These are cooled before being packed and the food will keep for a few hours with the temperature rising only very slightly. But most delivery systems use refrigerated vans. To maintain the low temperatures these vans must have one of the following:

– a special mechanical refrigeration system

– solid blocks of carbon dioxide (known as dry ice) which surround the food

– a special system that automatically sprays liquid nitrogen over the food during the journey

– a special pre-frozen panel which slides into the roof of the van.

Finishing kitchen equipment

The finishing kitchen is the last stage of a cook freeze operation in which the meals will be regenerated (reheated) and served. Some fresh goods such as salads may be prepared at this stage but there is no need for the usual range of kitchen equipment.

A *thawing cabinet* works like a forced-air convection oven, but uses temperatures of only about 10°C (50°F). It is sometimes used to speed up the thawing of cold sweet courses, or of containers of food for reheating in a microwave oven.

A *rapid thawing cabinet* can be used to defrost containers of frozen meals before they are placed in an oven, and will halve the reheating time. The temperature of the food is brought from -20°C to 3°C (-4°F to 37°F) in approximately four hours, under safe conditions, and warming is kept at a steady, controlled rate by a process of alternating low-volume heat with refrigeration.

Exactly what kind of equipment is used for regenerating (or reheating) the food depends on how much has to be dealt with – *see* Cook Chill/Terms & Equipment.

Microwave ovens are suitable for regenerating small quantities in a short space of time, but there are special procedures to follow, including using non-metallic containers, making sure that food is not more than 3.5 cm (1½ in.) deep in its container, and defrosting food in a rapid-thaw cabinet before reheating it.

Problems in thawing

In a refrigerator
When frozen food is placed in a refrigerator the temperature drops even lower than normal and because the compartment is insulated against any external heat source, thawing will take much longer than it would in a cool room.

By exposure to air
Thawing time will be unpredictable. If the food is uncovered, airborne micro-organisms will be attracted to the surface.

In warm water
The outer surface of the food will thaw quickly but the centre will remain frozen. If it is left in the water long enough for the centre to defrost, the outer surface will have been held at a dangerously warm temperature encouraging the growth of harmful bacteria.

The way to avoid all these problems is to use thawing cabinets whenever possible. They provide uniform, carefully controlled conditions with an alternating supply of heat and cool air. The food is kept covered and thawing times are predictable.

Dual-purpose ovens are microwave ovens which incorporate a second heat source such as an infra-red grill and a defrost control which switches the microwave power on and off. They can be used both to thaw and to regenerate the food, and are therefore very useful in a cook freeze system.

Forced air convection ovens were in fact originally designed to regenerate frozen meals, although they are now also frequently used for conventional cooking of fresh food. The fan blows hot air around the food in the oven ensuring fast and even heat penetration. For best results the oven should be full.

Special ovens using infra-red, radiated, convected and conducted heat are available which can regenerate large quantities of frozen meals. Some models also have a refrigeration unit so that they can act as a freezer for storing meals before they are used for reheating.

▸▸▸ TO DO

Make a list of at least five cook freeze products used at your place of work. For each item note how it should be thawed and regenerated and which equipment should be used.

9 COOK FREEZE

Essential points

The first stages in the cook freeze system – preparing and cooking the food – are in general very similar to these stages in a cook chill system. Here is a short checklist of points to remember for preparation and cooking. Please refer to the Method section of Cook Chill in this book for important, more detailed information.

Preparation

1. Make sure that the area where you are going to work is ready and that equipment is clean.

2. Collect together the various ingredients and foods before you begin preparing anything.

> Never use frozen or canned products. The only convenience foods that you should consider using are pre-prepared raw items such as portion-controlled lamb cutlets or chicken breasts.

3. If there is any delay between preparation and cooking, this should be as short as possible and the food should be stored at below 10°C (50°F) until required in the cooking area.

Cooking

1. Check that you have chosen the right cooking process for the food or dish being cooked, taking account of flavour, texture and nutritional value.

2. Use temperature probes to check that the centre of the food has reached a safe temperature before cooking is completed.

> Recipes should be standardised so that reheating times and temperatures can be as similar as possible. This is particularly important for complete meal packs.
> Limit the maximum weight of joints for roasting and braising to 3 kg (6½ lb) so as to speed up the rate of cooling and slicing, and avoid the risk of harmful bacteria multiplying. The centre of the food should reach a temperature of 70°-75°C (158°-167°F).

For the Caterbase *Cook Freezing* module you will be tested on portioning, labelling, blast freezing and storing (*see* below).

Portioning and packaging

1. Prepare your work area, ensure that it is absolutely clean and that you have the space you need to work in.

2. Ensure that the containers/packaging you require are ready to hand and the right size and that you have any equipment you will need.

> Re-usable containers should have been cleaned and sterilised.
> Do not touch the inside of the containers, and handle tin foil, paper or thin plastic containers carefully as they are not very rigid except when frozen.
> No glass objects should be allowed in the kitchen because of the risk of fragments of glass getting into food if there are breakages.
> You should wear gloves and make sure that any utensils you will be using have been sterilised. Also take care to have utensils that are the right size for portioning.

3. Accurately portion the food as requested.

> Joints of meat should be cooled as rapidly as possible before slicing. This should take no longer than two hours. Place the food in the freezer within 30 minutes of slicing.
>
> Handle and package fragile foods carefully so that they do not break up when they are thawed or regenerated.

4. Do not pack the food to a depth greater than 5 cm (2 in.). If a microwave oven is being used for regeneration the depth should be no more than 3.5 cm (1½ in.).

5. Keep the food free of the edges of the containers as far as possible.

6. Cover the food before freezing (sealing the container if necessary).

7. Check and record the temperature of the food.

8. Set aside a sample of each batch, labelling it and storing it as instructed.

Labelling

1. Check that you have a good supply of the labels you will need.

2. Make sure that the labels have all the right information on them and they can be easily read.

Information should include:
– production and eat-by date
– name of dish/description of contents
– storage life
– number of portions
– instructions for regenerating (type of oven to be used, temperature, timing, lid on or off, egg wash or similar special finishing instructions, stirring before service etc).

3. Attach the label firmly in a position where it can be read during subsequent storage and handling.

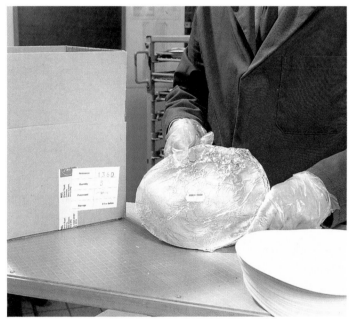

Freezing

1. Check that the fast freezer is ready for use.

2. Freezing should happen immediately after cooking.

> If there is any delay, 30 minutes is the maximum permitted.

3. In 90 minutes the foods should be frozen to below -5°C (23°F).

4. There should be at least 2 cm (¾ in.) air space between layers of containers in the freezer.

5. Immediately after freezing transfer the food to the deep-freeze storage. As you do this check that the labels are still clear and firmly attached.

9 COOK FREEZE

Storing

1. The food must be kept at the correct deep-freeze storage temperature between -20° and -30°C (-4° and -22°F), and at least below -18°C (0°F).

2. Keep up-to-date and accurate records of deep-freeze performance temperatures.

3. Store the food (in covered or sealed containers according to the dish and freezing method) on shelves or racks above floor level, away from the door, and with enough space around them to allow the cold air to circulate.

> Wear protective clothing and thick gloves when entering a deep freeze store. These have to meet the hygiene requirements so an anorak or gloves you wear outdoors will not do.
> Do not stay inside the freezer for more than two minutes.

4. Maintain stock rotation (on a first-in first-out basis) and keep stock record systems accurate.

5. Destroy any foods that have passed their eat-by date (and notify your supervisor of what has happened).

Distribution

This information will help you with the Caterbase module, *Distributing Cook Freeze Foods*

1. While the food is in the refrigerated vehicle or insulated containers (during transport) exactly the right temperature range must be maintained.

> DHSS guidelines state that if the food is going to be regenerated within 24 hours, the permissible temperature range is between 0° and -18°C (32° and 0°F). Otherwise the temperature must be kept below -18°C (0°F).

2. Loading and unloading should be quick and efficient so that these temperatures can be maintained.

3. Good organisation is important so that the right quantity of the right food is packed for each delivery point.

> Food to be delivered last should be loaded first, and so on so that the first delivery is the easiest to get out.

4. Take care during handling and transport that the containers and the labels are not damaged.

5. Documentation and control systems for checking on delivery should be followed carefully.

6. On delivery the food should be taken straight away to deep-freeze storage or to fast-thawing cabinets, or reheated at once.

▶▶▶ TO DO

Wash and trim three portions of fresh Brussels sprouts (or French beans or 3 pieces of broccoli). Put portion 1 raw into an airtight plastic bag, remove as much air as possible, seal the bag and place it in a blast freezer. (If you only have access to a home freezer, that will do for this particular exercise.) Blanch portions 2 and 3 in boiling water for 3 minutes, wash under cold water, drain. Place portion 2 in an airtight bag and freeze as before. Place portion 3 in a tin-foil or plastic container without a cover and freeze.

After 3 weeks, remove the three portions from the freezer. Note any difference in appearance between them. Place each sample separately in boiling water and simmer until cooked. Note the texture and colour after cooking, then taste each sample to compare the flavours. What conclusions can you reach about the effect of blanching and covering on deep-frozen vegetables?

△ SAFETY

Food should be thawed before being put in a microwave oven. If it is still frozen, microwaving will cause over-cooking in some parts of the food while leaving cold spots in other parts because ice does not absorb microwave energy as rapidly as water. (Some microwave ovens have a defrost control to overcome this difficulty.)

Regenerating cook freeze foods for service

This information will help you with the Caterbase module, *Regenerating Cook Freeze or Cook Chill Foods.*

1. Check that your work area is ready for operation and that all the equipment you will need is to hand.

2. Remove from the deep freeze or delivery container the food you wish to regenerate, checking the labels to see that you have the correct items and that none have passed their use-by date.

> If the food is to be used in a cafeteria, it will be reheated on a staggered system (in batches). This is because it is hard to estimate what will be used at once, and holding it in a hot cupboard would spoil the taste and texture of the food, so losing all the benefits of the cook freeze system.

3. Check that the thawing cabinet (if you are using one) and the regenerating oven are ready for use. Check the packaging instructions (to see if lids or covers should be removed).

> Food to be served cold, such as fruit flans and baked custards, should be thawed for as short a time as possible, and the next two stages (4 and 5) are unnecessary.
>   Never refreeze food that has been even partially thawed.

4. Have the equipment at the correct temperature for the food you are regenerating and follow either your workplace instructions or what it says on the label. You should also follow the timing instructions carefully.

5. The food should be reheated to at least 70°C (158°F) but preferably to 75°C (167°F) immediately before service. Check that this temperature has been reached by using a sterilised temperature probe.

6. Serve the food as soon as possible after regeneration.

> Food that has not been eaten within two hours should not be served, but thrown away. Food which has been allowed to cool must never be reheated.

Personal hygiene

Some bacteria spores will survive very long periods in frozen storage. During the thawing, regeneration and service stages these spores have a chance to become active again and multiply to levels which cause food poisoning. All this means that the strictest standards of hygiene are necessary in cook freeze systems. Equipment and working areas must be thoroughly cleaned and disinfected regularly.

There are special procedures that all staff should follow before entering a work area:

- forearms, hands and finger nails should be scrubbed with a disinfected brush

- a shower should be taken before the person changes into clean uniform

- clean, disinfected rubber boots should be worn

- after changing, forearms and hands should be washed again in disinfectant and the person should walk through a footbath

- no jewellery should be worn

- no-one who seems ill, has a cold or has any uncovered cut or graze should go into the work area

- there should be regular medical check ups for staff (so that no-one suffering from an infectious condition handles food).

In many establishments the last three precautions are checked up on by someone questioning staff at a control point near the entrance to the work area.

▶▶ TO DO

Obtain two single-portion prepared dishes of your choice, preferably with similar ingredients, one frozen, one chilled. Regenerate them according to the package instructions then sample both of them, jotting down your reactions under the following headings:
- portion size
- colour, taste and texture
- ease of reheating
- comparison with equivalent fresh product
- value for money.

201

What went wrong

Food has separated or broken up after regeneration.

> 1. The recipe has not been modified correctly, for example, the wrong flour has been used.
>
> 2. Finely chopped vegetables (which might be used in a soup or garnish) are likely to break down during regeneration, so should be avoided where possible.

Meat or fish tastes rancid.

> Food has been badly prepared or stored for too long and the fat has gone rancid.

Coated food, pastry or bread is soggy.

> Cover of the container has been left on when it should have been removed before regeneration.

The food did not get into the freezer within the 30 minutes allowed after cooking.

> 1. Too much food was cooked to fit into the freezer.
>
> 2. The production system has been badly timed, for example, a previous batch of food is still in freezer.

Freezer burn.

> The package has been damaged or was not sealed properly or the food has been stored for too long.

The sauce covering the chicken in the picture above was thickened with a roux made of ordinary flour and butter. It has separated and lost its smooth, creamy texture because of the effect very low temperatures have on products containing certain types of starch.

A special thickening agent which can stand the effects of freezing was used in the sauce shown in the picture below. Very waxy starches like tapioca do not separate as badly after freezing as wheat starch. On the other hand, they tend to form a slimy paste and so have to be chemically treated to produce a satisfactory result for cook freeze production.

Freezer burn – note how this chicken liver has discoloured.

Tips

Slices of meat should be separated by waxed portion papers as they are packaged, to make them easier to serve later.

Soups should be frozen in a concentrated form and the main amount of stock or water added when the soup is regenerated.

For a fruit pie, the pastry lid covering the fruit filling can be raw or part-baked, and the pie then frozen. The pastry will cook through during regeneration and in fact will probably both look and taste better than if it had been completely cooked before freezing.

But beware: uncooked pastry or sponge that has been made with baking powder will not rise properly on regeneration. Use an alternative recipe.

Avoid using meat or poultry drippings in gravies because they easily develop a rancid taste. Always thicken gravies and sauces with a modified starch, because ordinary starches may well cause separation during freezing.

Some hospitals still use a type of large-scale food service called the Ganymede system, which was very popular some time ago. In this system, food is portioned in a central kitchen onto extra-strong plates. These can withstand the heat from a metal disc preheated to about 150°C (302°F) that is put under the plate to keep the food hot for up to 45 minutes until it has finished its journey to the wards.

The Helithermic system is used in similar situations. In this system the plates are made of a special material that can hold the heat and are placed in shallow insulated boxes, which serve as trays.

TEST YOURSELF

1. Give one reason why it is important to freeze food at a particular rate.

2. Give one reason why it is necessary to blanch green vegetables before freezing them.

3. For each of the following, name one step which should be taken to prevent deterioration as a result of freezing:
a) flour-thickened sauce
b) pork chops.

4. Name three types of food that are not suitable for cook freeze.

5. Describe briefly two methods of fast freezing food.

6. Name two pieces of equipment which can be used for regenerating small quantities of frozen foods.

7. In a cook freeze system, what temperatures should the food reach or be held at:
a) after preparation and before cooking
b) during freezing
d) during storage
e) during delivery?

8. List three advantages of using a cook freeze system for feeding a large number of students at a time.

City and Guilds

Packaging cook freeze food – note distribution board in background.

GLOSSARY

à la carte
Menu offering individually priced dishes.

accompaniments
Items served with particular dishes, e.g. horseradish sauce and Yorkshire pudding with roast beef.

aerate
Incorporate air or gas into a mixture.

al dente
This Italian expression (which translates literally as 'to the tooth') is used to describe pasta or vegetables that remain firm after being lightly cooked.

aspic
Savoury jelly usually based on meat or fish stock.

au gratin
Sprinkled with cheese or breadcrumbs and browned.

bacteria
Microscopic living organisms. The harmful varieties are called pathogenic.

bain-marie
A utensil for gently cooking food while keeping it away from direct heat. One example is a double saucepan with hot water in the bottom section and the food in the top.

   A bain-marie is also sometimes used to describe a type of counter used in self-service restaurants which keeps food warm. Below the trays of food is a space heated from beneath by gas or electricity.

barding
Covering food with a layer of fat to protect and moisten its surface during roasting or braising.

basting
Spooning oil or liquid over food during cooking to prevent the surface drying out.

batch cooking
The technique of cooking small quantities of food as required, rather than a large quantity in one go.

battening
Tenderising food, usually meat, by a beating it with a heavy implement such as a cutlet bat.

beating
Combining ingredients thoroughly, often so that air is incorporated into the mixture.

béchamel
White sauce made with a roux and milk.

bed of roots
Roughly cut vegetables used to protect the base of food in braising and roasting and to add flavour to the dish. Also sometimes called matignon or mirepoix.

beurre manié
A paste made from blended butter and flour which is used to thicken liquids.

blanc
Cooking liquid consisting of water, lemon juice and flour which is used to protect the colour and texture of white vegetables and meats during poaching or boiling.

blanching
A method of pre-cooking or part-cooking food. Vegetables are blanched by being plunged briefly into boiling water before being refreshed under cold water.

   Also a method of removing impurities from poor quality meats, by bringing them to the boil in cold water, discarding the water, using fresh water to complete cooking.

blanquette
Type of stew. Meat is blanched to remove impurities, and then cooked in unthickened liquid, from which a sauce is made before service.

blast chilling or blast freezing
Rapid lowering of the temperature of food by using powerful chillers or freezers.

blending
Thoroughly mixing two or more ingredients.

bouquet garni
Collection of herbs used for flavouring in soups or stews. Traditionally fresh herbs including a bay leaf, parsley stalks, thyme and rosemary are tied in a bunch. If dried herbs are used, they are placed in a small muslin bag or even wrapped in a stick of celery or leaf of leek which has been previously softened by blanching.

bratt pan
Large item of floor-mounted cooking equipment that acts as a huge shallow saucepan, used for large-scale catering, such as stewing in bulk.

breaded
Coated in breadcrumbs before cooking.

brine
Solution of salt and water. Used for curing meat.

broiling
American term for grilling.

browning
Colouring food by heating it (usually quite fiercely).

brunoise
Very fine dice.

caramelise
Cooking sugar until it turns brown.

carbohydrate
One of the main classes of nutrient found in food. They include starches and sugars and most of them are converted by the body into energy.

carry-over cooking
The cooking in roasting and microwaving which continues for a few minutes after the food has been removed from the oven.

cartouche
A piece of greased paper used to protect the surface of food (usually from drying out), which is shaped to fit inside the pot, tray or bowl.

cellulose
A carbohydrate which is the main substance in the cell walls of plants and therefore in vegetables. It cannot be digested by the body.

cereal
Grasses such as wheat and rice that produce edible grains. Also used to describe the grain itself, and food made from it, as in breakfast cereals.

chinoise
Conical strainer.

cholesterol
Substance produced in the body (by the liver) from fats, particularly saturated fats. Too much cholesterol causes heart disease.

clarifying
The stage in making consommés and aspics when the flavouring ingredients are separated out to leave a clear liquid.

   Also refers to making fat (especially butter) clear by gentle heating.

clouté
Studded, for example, an onion pierced with a clove (usually holding a bay leaf in place) is called an onion clouté.

collagen
The protein of connective tissue in meat which turns to gelatin when heated.

combi ovens
Ovens that can provide more than one form of heating, e.g. convection and microwaving.

concassé
Roughly chopped, usually tomato flesh.

conduction
The transfer of heat through a material, e.g. the base of a saucepan.

connective tissue
The membranes and tendons in meat. They contain tough proteins called collagen (which can be broken down during cooking) and elastin (which stays quite tough even after cooking).

convection
The circulation of heat through air or liquid.

cooked out
Describes flour that has been cooked to the stage when it loses its starchy taste, as in a roux.

court-bouillon
Cooking liquid made of water and other ingredients such as stock, wine or vinegar and vegetables, used to improve a food's flavour and sometimes to tenderise. An important use is in poaching fish.

covers
Cover means a place setting, and covers is used as shorthand for the number of customers expected for or served at a meal, e.g. 12 covers.

creaming
Beating to a light consistency, especially butter and sugar.

cross contamination
Transfer of food-poisoning bacteria from an infected source (usually raw food) to previously uninfected food, for example, food that has been cooked.

croûton
Shaped piece of fried bread.

darne
Steak cut across the bone of a round fish.

decant
Pour off liquid after sediment in it has settled, for example, fat from a roasting tray once the meat juices and food particles have settled to the bottom.

déglacer
Swilling out cooking pan with water after shallow frying or roasting to collect juices and food particles left from the cooking. The liquid can then be used as the basis for sauce or gravy.

dehydration
Removing of water content from food – a method of preservation.

délice
Fillet from a small fish with both ends folded under for neatness.

demi-glace
A basic brown sauce.

dice
Cut into cubes, as in diced vegetables.

dress
Arrange food in a dish or on a plate ready for service.

egg wash
Beaten egg (sometimes mixed with a little water) used in baking to seal joins in pastry or give a shiny golden appearance to the food (when cooked) and used in shallow or deep frying to hold coatings on food.

elastin
A protein in connective tissue which remains fairly tough even after cooking.

emulsion
A mixture of two liquids, such as oil and water. It may stay mixed for some time, e.g. mayonnaise, or may separate very quickly, e.g. some forms of vinaigrette.

enzymes
Chemicals produced by living cells (plant or animal) which speed up chemical reactions between other substances, for example, in digestion and fermentation.

fibre
Parts of edible plants or seeds which cannot be digested by the body, but which are important in digestion because they provide bulk which helps food travel through the digestive system.

filleting
Cutting and preparing fish by removing the bones to produce fillets (whole sides or lengths of flesh). Filleting is also used occasionally to describe certain methods of preparing meat.

flambé
Describes food that has had alcohol, such as brandy, poured on it and set alight so that it flames briefly and produces a distinctive flavour. This is often done in the presence of the customer for dramatic effect.

flash point
Temperature at which oil bursts into flames.

flash roasting
Placing food in a very hot oven to brown or sear its surface.

floured
Coated in flour.

flow cooking/production
Continuous preparation and cooking of food, normally in large quantities, using special continuous cookers.

folding in
Carefully blending ingredients with a mixture (often already whisked) by gently turning or folding one part over the other with a spatula or spoon so that the mixture's lightness is retained.

frappé
Served on a bed of crushed ice.

fricassée
Type of stew, in which the meat is cooked in a thickened liquid.

fumet
Very concentrated fish stock.

garnish
Decoration, usually edible, made to make a dish look attractive, for example a slice of lemon with a veal escalope or a tomato basket filled with shrimps accompanying a cold poached fish dish.

glazing
Giving food an attractive, shiny appearance, for example, by repeated basting with the cooking liquid, or reducing with butter and sugar, or coating with a thickened fruit juice or thin jam.

goujon
Strip cut diagonally from a fish fillet.

gratinate
Brown the surface of a cooked dish, usually under the grill or in a very hot oven.

griddling
Shallow frying on a solid surface.

gutting
Removing the internal organs from fish or fowl.

hors d'oeuvre
Preliminary dish in a meal, designed to stimulate the appetite.

jointing
Cutting up meat, poultry, etc., into joints or at a joint.

juliennes
Thin strips of food, as in juliennes of carrot.

jus lié
Strong brown stock thickened with arrowroot.

kneading
Working dough into a properly blended mixture.

knocking back
Kneading dough after a period of fermentation to reduce its size and increase the effectiveness of the yeast.

larding
Inserting strips of fat (or occasionally vegetables) into lean meat or fish to ensure that it remains moist during cooking.

leaching
Leaking out of substances from food into cooking liquid. This is what happens to some water-soluble vitamins in vegetables, when the vegetables are boiled, for example.

liaison
Mixture of egg yolks and cream beaten together and then added to a cooking liquid (in a stew, for example) to thicken.

macedoine
Mixture of fruit or vegetables cut into small dice.

marinading or marinating
Soaking food in a flavouring (and sometimes tenderising) liquid.

matignon *see* bed of roots

minerals
A group of essential nutrients that occur naturally in many foods and help control the body's functions and maintain health.

mirepoix *see* bed of roots

mise en place
Collecting together all the ingredients and equipment necessary for a particular dish or range of dishes.

nappé
Coated with sauce or aspic.

nutrients
Chemicals in food which provide essential substances for the health and proper functioning of the body. They include carbohydrates, fats, minerals, and vitamins.

offal
Edible internal organs of animals such as the heart, tongue and liver and also the parts of the animal that are left after the meat has been removed, such as the feet and tail.

oven-proof
Description of utensils that are able to withstand the high cooking temperatures reached in an oven.

oxidisation
The effect that oxygen (and therefore air, which contains oxygen) has on certain substances. Many foods are affected, e.g. fats turn rancid.

pané
Coated in breadcrumbs.

parboiling
Boiling food until it is partly cooked, usually for a very short time.

pass
Strain food such as a soup or sauce through a sieve.

pathogenic
Harmful, as in pathogenic bacteria.

paupiette
Thin slice or fillet of meat or fish stuffed and rolled into a cylindrical shape.

pectin
A form of carbohydrate that occurs naturally in plant cell walls, and is used for setting jams and jellies. It cannot be digested by the body.

plat à sauter
Shallow frying pan with vertical sides.

poêler *see* pot roasting

polyunsaturated fat
Type of fat. Better for healthy eating than saturated fat.

pot roasting or poêler
Cooking food in the oven in a sealed pot on a bed of vegetables with butter.

protein
One of the groups of nutrients that are essential for the body to function properly and remain healthy. Proteins are especially important for the body's growth and are present in a wide range of animal and vegetable foods, especially meat and dairy products.

proving
Final stage of expansion for a dough made with yeast.

pulses
Edible seeds from plants of the pea and bean family, e.g. lentils and beans.

purée
Smooth mixture obtained by forcing food through a sieve or blending it in a liquidiser.

quenelles
Food formed into small cigar shapes, e.g. finely minced meat, fish or vegetables.

radiation
Transfer of heat through the air directly from the heat source.

rancid
Fats or fatty foods which have gone bad and taste or smell unpleasant because of oxidisation.

reconstituting
Another word for regenerating.

recrystallisation
This is a second stage of freezing that happens if temperature variation has occurred during freezing and should be avoided if possible. Ice crystals that have already formed start to melt and then refreeze, forming fewer but larger new crystals (which will damage the food's structure).

reducing
Boiling a liquid such as stock so that it is greatly reduced in volume, becoming thick and strong-flavoured.

refreshing
Plunging food into cold water to lower the temperature rapidly and so stop the cooking process.

rendering
Melting suet or other hard fat to become dripping or lard.

regenerating
Reheating cook chilled or cook frozen food so that it is ready for service.

roux
Paste of flour and fat that is cooked for a short time before being used to thicken liquid, e.g. in sauce or soup making.

sabayon
Egg yolks mixed with a liquid and then heated until the mixture thickens.

salamandering
Browning the surface of food under an overhead grill.

saturated fats
Type of fat found most commonly in dairy products and meat. A less healthy alternative than polyunsaturated fats.

sautéing
A shallow frying process: cooking food quickly in very hot oil or fat so that it browns.

sauteuse
Shallow cooking vessel with sloping sides.

scoring
Cutting just through the surface of food. This might be done to stop the skin bursting in grilled fish or to allow food to take in the flavour of a marinade, or simply for decorative effect.

sealing
An old-fashioned term for searing.

searing
Using high temperatures to brown the surface of food.

seasoning
Adding salt, pepper and other savoury flavourings to food to improve its flavour.

shortening
Term for fats used especially in baking.

shredded
Very finely sliced.

simmering
Gentle boiling when the surface of the liquid is only just broken by small bubbles.

skimming
Removing surface fat, scum and impurities that rise to the top of a liquid, especially during boiling.

smoke point
Temperature at which oil gives off a visible blue smoke.

soft flour
Flour which does not form much gluten.

sous-vide
Alternative term for vacuum cooking.

standing time
The short period of time when meat is deliberately allowed to rest between cooking and carving or serving in roasting and microwave cooking. This is both to allow carry-over cooking to finish and to allow meat to set.

starch
A type of carbohydrate, and therefore an important nutrient. It occurs naturally in many vegetables and grains, e.g. potatoes and rice, and is converted by the body into energy.

sterilisation
Use of heat or sometimes chemical disinfectant to kill any bacteria, for example, on jars being prepared for preserves.

stir frying
Shallow frying very fast at a high temperature while constantly stirring the food.

stock
A liquid made from water in which bones and vegetables have been simmered for long enough to extract the flavour. A vegetarian stock can be made without bones. Used as a flavouring in many cooking processes involving a liquid, e.g. stewing, braising, boiling.

straining
Passing liquid through a sieve or cloth to separate off any solids.

strong flour
Flour that is capable of forming a lot of gluten.

suprêmes
Cut of poultry which includes one side of the breast and sometimes the first part of the wing bone. A fish suprême is a piece cut on the slant from a large fillet of fish.

sweating
Shallow frying food gently without allowing it to brown.

sweetbreads
A variety of offal: the pancreas or parts of the thymus gland found in the throat and chest of an animal.

table d'hôte
Fixed price menu offering a meal of two or more courses.

temperature probe
Instrument which is inserted into food and measures its temperature.

tenderising
Making food tender and therefore easy to chew.

thermostat
Instrument usually incorporated into equipment like an oven, which adjusts the temperature to keep it constant.

topping and tailing
Trimming off the tough extremities of foods such as French beans or gooseberries.

tronçons
Steak cut across the bone of a medium to large flat fish.

trussing
Securing food (usually a joint of meat) with string so that it keeps a neat shape during cooking.

turning
Shaping pieces of food, e.g. potatoes, often in an oval or barrel form.

velouté
A sauce made with a roux and white stock.

vitamins
Group of essential nutrients that help the body to function properly and remain healthy. Different vitamins occur naturally in different foods, e.g. Vitamin A in carrots and egg yolk.

white fats
Fats produced specifically for baking.

INDEX